DEVELOPMENTAL ART THERAPY

Other books in this series:
Developmental Therapy,
    Mary M. Wood, editor (University Park Press, 1975)
Music in Developmental Therapy,
    Jennie Purvis and Shelley Samet, editors (University Park Press, 1976)

DEVELOPMENTAL ART THERAPY

by
Geraldine H. Williams
Instructor, University of Georgia and
Art Therapist, the Rutland Center
and
Mary M. Wood
Professor of Special Education
University of Georgia and
Director of Training, the Rutland Center
Athens, Georgia

University Park Press
Baltimore • London • Tokyo

UNIVERSITY PARK PRESS
International Publishers in Science and Medicine
Chamber of Commerce Building
Baltimore, Maryland 21202

Typeset by The Composing Room of Michigan, Inc.
Manufactured in the United States of America by Bay Printing, Inc.

Library of Congress Cataloging in Publication Data

Williams, Geraldine H
Developmental art therapy.

Bibliography: p.
Includes index.
1. Art therapy.   2. Mentally ill children.   I. Wood,
Mary M., joint author.   II. Title.
RJ505.A7W54   618.9'28'9165   77-8121
ISBN 0-8391-1140-1

Contents

Acknowledgments

Without the constructive, critical help of Dr. Henry Dupont, Dr. Faye Swindle, Dr. William Swan, Jacqueline Tucker, Carolyn Combs, and Diane Weller, and the typing skills of Eileen Patrick, Nora Mitchell, Daisy Fleming, Sara Richardson, and Cathy Felton, this text could not have been completed. The photographs that illustrate the text were taken by a very creative and patient Art Blum. Finally, the staff and the children at Rutland Center were the raison d'etre for *Developmental Art Therapy*.

Introduction

This book is intended as a resource and guide to teachers and therapists who seek to promote sequences of development that foster emotional growth in children. A basic assumption of the book is that all children, including those handicapped by mental or emotional problems, can develop certain manipulative, conceptual, social, and communicative skills in a sequential manner. When functioning in an interactive way, these skills enable children to cope effectively with the demands of childhood. The aim of *Developmental Art Therapy* is to facilitate a child's ability to make the most constructive use of these developmental skills through art.

We selected the title with considerable care, hoping that it conveys our intent. *Developmental* refers to the way the therapy is organized. It is critical for a practitioner to know the developmental sequences all children go through, so that art experiences can be properly sequenced and structured to gain the continuous, successful growth each child can achieve.

Art refers to the treatment medium. Art provides an expressive form for communication, socialization, creativity, self-expression, self-exploration, and manipulation of the environment. It adapts easily to every stage of development. It documents segments of the past, present, and future; it reflects a child's ability to recall and to convey the past; it documents aspects of the present condition; and it lends itself to expressions of things to come. Perhaps the greatest usefulness of art comes in its potential as a motivating, gratifying activity for nearly every child.

Therapy clearly states the purpose for which the book was prepared. Art, as therapy, is a healing experience. It mends where developmental processes have broken down. It is an opportunity for new learning where a gap has existed. It is a means for venturing into the next, new steps among the challenges of childhood.

Developmental Art Therapy therefore uses the knowledge of a child's developmental stages to plan and to conduct the therapeutic art experience. It involves whatever skills a child may have, however limited, in these areas: behavior, nonverbal and verbal communication, socialization, and cognition. This form of art therapy does not use art for clinical or symbolic interpretation nor does it rely on art for catharsis or insight. Instead, *Developmental Art Therapy* provides growth oriented experiences so carefully tuned to a child's precise developmental needs that it becomes the medium for emotional growth.

Training in art is not a necessary prerequisite for including it in clinical or educational therapy, nor is artistic skill required. It simply requires adherence to developmental principles and the creative use of simple art lessons designed to meet specific objectives and goals for each stage of development. Beyond this, the teacher or therapist needs to become familiar with an array of general art materials. There also are art resources available in most communities and libraries. Find them and incorporate them in your therapy. They can open new doors for children, bringing universal human experiences to children in ways we can never put into words.

This text has been designed primarily as an extension of the procedures described in 1975 in *Developmental Therapy*. However, it is not necessary for the reader to be trained in that method in order to use these art activities with special children. Because *Developmental Therapy* is based upon developmental sequences of social and emotional growth that all children experience, there seems to be numerous opportunities for its adaptation.

In this text the first chapter summarizes key aspects of art education and art therapy as they relate to Developmental Art Therapy. There is a chapter for each stage of therapy describing the characteristic way children respond to art materials and activities according to stage of development. There are examples of the way successful art activities change across the four developmental stages. At the end of each chapter there are sample lessons for each stage of therapy, using a variety of materials. Particular emphasis is put on motivation, because it is characteristically different at each stage. The final two chapters contain a review of techniques for using clay and an illustrated discussion of the contribution of an art exhibit to each stage of therapy.

Each activity described in this text is planned first to focus on particular Developmental Therapy objectives; equally important, the activity should allow children to *enjoy* the art experience. Finally, these activities should be considered a beginning point, a challenge to create other activities. We hope that through such creative experiences teachers and therapists can help unhappy, handicapped, and alienated children experience the joy of creative moments, growing not only in artistic skill but also in understanding and appreciation of themselves and the world around them.

This book is dedicated with deepest appreciation to Zada Williams, an inspiring and creative person, and a giving mother, and to Lillie Ehemann, whose artistry and spirit endure.

chapter 1

WHY A DEVELOPMENTAL APPROACH TO ART THERAPY?

This beautifully lined design was created by a child who had been in Developmental Therapy for 30 weeks. Over a sustained period, he worked on this with ruler and magic markers. Each day he was able to give the partially completed work to the teacher. He stopped coloring when he thought it was done and offered it for the art exhibit. What a large decision for a child who had never approved or accepted anything of his own in the past!

The process of drawing, painting, or constructing is a complex one in which the child brings together diverse elements of his experience to make a new and meaningful whole. In the process . . . he has given us more than a picture or a sculpture; he has given us a part of himself: how he thinks, how he feels, and how he sees. . . . Creative activities become meaningful only when the dynamic interdependence among growth, development, and creation is understood.

Lowenfeld and Brittain, 1970, p. 1

Using art with handicapped children can be a most effective way to reach them, to bring awareness, and to build bridges of communication and motivation in place of isolation. Where there is isolation, a child can begin to express feelings. A child consumed by anger can find expression without retaliation. A self-destructive child can find something of himself that is of value. A child delayed in development can gradually explore a complex world at a pace suitable to his own learning rate. Experiences in art are beneficial also to a child with physical handicaps, to a child who is blind or deaf, or to a child with neurological damage which distorts sensory perceptions, producing bizarre responses or fragmentation and disorganization of cognitive processes. For a child with specific learning disabilities, art may help correct a problem that can produce serious maladjustments through continual failure. Carl Fenichel points out that problems in socialization, experienced by most seriously disturbed children, have roots within the interactive development of cognition, language, and perception. He describes the resulting impact on further maturation clearly:

> . . . their deep isolation and withdrawal from life, their problems in using and understanding language, their bizarre behavior and strange rituals, their anxieties often bordering on panic, are all closely related to serious disorders of perception, learning,

and language. Their disorders not only interfere with formal learning but inevitably reduce or impair their ability to receive and interpret accurate impressions of social situations and to respond appropriately. . . . The demands and complexities of these social processes, when they are beyond a child's capacities or comprehension, will usually result in continuous failure that leads to avoidance and withdrawal from people, preoccupation with self, and rigid, repetitive behavior (Fenichel, 1976, p. 220).[1]

Perhaps there is no more potentially effective way to understand and to cross the chasm between these alienated children and "the others" than through creative art experiences. For such children, as with nonhandicapped children, art experiences can be a vehicle for development. Pine has succinctly summarized this potential in art:

> It is a universally pleasurable experience and therefore expansive of the self. It affords this most important and appropriate gratification while at the same time it may be used to serve other functions. Creative experience allows for the loosening of rigid defenses, fosters integration, and so pro-

---

[1] Numerous researchers have drawn similar conclusions concerning the development of autistic children. Studies of these severely impaired children by Hermelin and Frith (1971), Ruttenberg and Wolf (1967), Rutter (1970), Treffert (1970), and others have concluded that cognitive and linguistic development may hold the key to understanding the mechanisms of this particular form of childhood psychopathology.

vides the opportunity for a restoration of the wholeness of the individual (Pine, 1975, p. 94).

Perhaps the trends of the seventies in the fields of education and behavior management have led us inadvertently to underestimate critical elements in human emotional growth. While pursuing such contemporary activities as goal directedness, on-task behaviors, reinforcers, shaping, extinctions, and other such externally directed concepts, we may do well to reconsider carefully the inner life forces at work in every child and to prepare experiences designed to tap into feelings, creative needs, and cognitive structures that are changing at each phase of a child's development.

It is essential that all children be afforded creative opportunities. Play, art, story telling, and child drama have been the natural tools by which every child, handicapped or not, expands his own capacities. Through such creative experiences, a child experiments with new ideas, expresses feelings, experiences fantasies, and resolves fears.[2]

Children's art is a means of experiencing and expressing the process of integrating present reality into past experience. For example, somewhere near age two, a child experiences rapid acquisition of hand movements, and art activity serves as a medium for experimentation, practice, and sensory feedback about his preliminary place in the world of things. Soon, this phase is expanded into a new phase in which each art activity acquires a special meaning for the child, providing symbols of experience that have inner significance. This phase is often accom-

panied by verbal commentary. Eventually, as the young child becomes facile in producing these visual symbols he can begin to express what he knows and fears about his enlarging reality.

Miriam Lindstrom describes the role of art in this process as a vehicle for the child to ". . . triumph over chaos" beginning near age two and concluding at a point sometime after age seven. She has eloquently described the emotional and existential intensity of this stage of development:

> Adults, who seldom give themselves so completely to any experience as little children do, could not stand the emotional wear and tear of living as they do, so intensely, so passionately, so without perspective or philosophy to sustain them beyond moments regarded not as transitory but as all of life (Lindstrom, 1957, p. 11).

Many handicapped children have significant delays of development in this early period. Art and other creative experiences can be especially effective for them. From her extensive work with a number of types of handicapped children, Rubin (1975) describes the benefits art experiences can hold for such children. Summarized, an art experience can be:

A means to explore and find pleasure in the environment

A way to control and have mastery over something

A means to experience success and achieve skill

A means to ventilate and express feelings

A way to organize and obtain order from confusion

A means to experience

A means to self-awareness and self-esteem

A way to create

A way to elaborate on the real world

---

[2] For fully developed writing on this subject, see Bobroff (1960), Crane (1951), Castillo (1974), Crosscup (1966), DiLeo (1970), Ekstein and Caruth (1976), Kramer (1971), Lindsay (1972), Lowenfeld and Brittain (1970), Moore (1976), Piaget (1951), Pine (1975), and Robbins (1973).

ART AS A THERAPEUTIC PROCESS

Creative elements apparently exist to some degree in almost everyone. Even more evident is the daily ebb and flow of emotional drives. Explanations about the relationship of these two forces to each other have taken several forms. In some instances emotional drives have been viewed as the central force behind creative expression. For others, it is the creative drive itself which is the basic source for accomplishing eventual integrity of the self. For example, Champernowne (1971) attributes unconscious exchanges with ego functions as the fountainhead for creative energy. It is this drive for a manifest expression of an individual's own identity which undergirds the creative experience. Recognizing that the ability to mediate inner drives and external experience is indicative of emotional health, Kramer (1972, p. 232) suggests that art provides the "symbolic equivalents" for achieving this integration.[3]

E. Paul Torrance offers us another way of looking at this same process of adjustment. He views creative needs as providing the drive for constructive adaptations and adjustments to new situations. He describes these creative needs in children as having curiosity; meeting challenges; attempting difficult tasks; becoming completely immersed in a task; being independent in judgment and convictions; having sensitivity, intuition, and openness to experience. In many respects he could be describing attributes of mental health. These characteristics, he writes, are summated in the basic need, "to be oneself" (Tor-rance, 1970, p. 21). It is this need, whatever explanations are given for its origin, which gives creative art expression its great value as a vehicle for the emergence of the self and concomitantly as a tool for therapy.

There are several significant interpretations of the ways art may be used in the therapeutic process. Ulman (1975, p. 3) points out that in the broadest interpretations art therapy is the use of any visual materials "in some attempt to assist integration or reintegration of the personality." The various forms art therapy seems to take may in large part emerge from the setting in which it is practiced. For example, art in clinical settings has produced psychoanalytic and psychodynamic applications, while art in educational settings has produced an emphasis on the integration of cognitive and emotional processes to enhance development, motivation, behavior, and learning.[4]

Naumberg (1973) has developed the widely accepted practice of using spontaneous art productions as symbolic speech between therapist and client. Such symbolic imagery bypasses the restrictions of conscious, verbal communication and taps unconscious emotion. According to Naumberg and others, the cathartic aspect of this process has major significance in the therapeutic process. Release of unconscious conflict and un-

---

[3]Kramer further cautions against inordinate reliance upon the subject matter or emotional content. She writes, "Art always reveals truth, but not necessarily the whole truth. Different pictures may show different, sometimes contradictory facets of personality" (Kramer, 1971, p. 32).

---

[4]In clinical settings, Kramer (1958; 1971), Naumberg (1973), and Ulman (1975) have provided major formulations for the practice of psychodynamic art therapy. In contrast to the approach of psychodynamically oriented therapists who elaborate on the symbolic, unconscious, and cathartic aspects of the art process, Rhyne (1973) provides support for the Gestalt approach, emphasizing the use of art as a deliberate, conscious feedback system through which a person expands self-awareness through viewing his own productions. This process provides the bridge between inner life and outer reality. When assimilation and accommodation between inner and outer forces occur, ego integrity can be maintained.

expressed drives reduces these forces as a source of psychic pain.[5]

Kramer emphasizes the importance of art in the process of ego integration. "Art," she writes, "serves as a model of ego functioning. It becomes a sanctuary where new attitudes and feelings can be expressed and tried out, even before such changes can take place in daily life" (Kramer, 1971, p. 219).

Denny (1972) has encompassed an eclectic position into his art therapy techniques. With an emphasis on the client's needs, he suggests that art may be effective in a wide range of behavioral processes, including ". . . catharsis, increase or decrease in effective communication, self-disclosure, and changes in attitude and behavior" (p. 118). He further elaborates on art therapy techniques under six headings: exploration, building rapport, expression of inner feelings, self-perception, interpersonal relations, and the individual's place in his world. These categories, each describing a different focus, suggest one approach to guiding the art therapy process.

In describing art education practices used with three successful Japanese artists, who were also mentally handicapped, Morishima (1975) observes that the intrinsic pleasure in doing the art task was more important to the young artists than external reinforcers.[6] This point emphasizes the need to begin motivation within the context of a child's private world. This same idea has been reiterated in another art form by the famous dance therapist Janet Adler (1973), who suggests that at the beginning of an adult-child relationship when working with schizophrenic or autistic children, the adult must reach into the child's world, however bizarre, distorted, or limited it may be. The child's point of reference represents the beginning point.[7] Kaufman (1975, 1976) also found this "tuning in" procedure to be critical in his successful work to reach his own autistic son in his private world.

Rubin (1975) emphasizes the need for a psychological climate in the art experience where a handicapped child finds acceptance, openness, and empathy from the adult. She points out that there are many challenges in working with handicapped children, for example: their need for extended exploration; regression as the child's way to communication; slow progress; the unexpected and unusual; intense feelings and violence; the need to destroy art work; and dependency.

Concern with breakdown in interpersonal communication has been expressed by numerous specialists who have worked extensively with handicapped children (Alkema, 1971; Gonick-Barris, 1976; Schwartz, 1974). From her work with learning disabled and emotionally disturbed youngsters, Gonick-Barris (1976, p. 74) concludes that:

Children with learning disabilities and problems in social or emotional adjustment are in even greater need of creative art experiences than are children who do not have such disabilities. Precisely because they are so often unable to make themselves understood in more usual ways, these handicapped children need alternative modes for expressing the same emotional impulses and attitudes they share with all children.

---

[5] Jung (1964), Maslow (1971), and Rogers (1961) provide theoretical support for art therapists with this orientation.

[6] A number of art educators and art therapists also caution against too much emphasis upon a child's product or upon the materials used (Cane, 1951; Kawasaki, 1971; Lowenfeld and Brittain, 1970; McKay, 1975).

---

[7] Moustakas (1959) describes this principle clearly in his play therapy procedures.

Many of these same concerns are reflected by Carter and Miller (1975, p. 245) in their creative art program for minimally brain-injured children. Their experimental program for eight children between the ages of seven and ten years was designed with two basic guidelines. "Art activities," Carter and Miller state, "provide the incentive or motivation to learn." They also theorize that "art activities encourage the development of perceptual awareness and manipulative skills . . ." Therefore, art activities should be an effective procedure for achievement of perceptual and motor skills by children with learning disabilities. The results of their six-week experimental program showed significant gains made by each child on the Frostig Developmental Test of Visual Perception. Perhaps one of the most interesting observations made in this study was that lessons designed for each perceptual modality had to be further adapted to various developmental levels for individuals within the class.

Attention to these sequential, developmental aspects of art therapy is beginning to emerge. An elaboration of Frank Hewett's original Educational Model for special education with emotionally disturbed children (Hewett, 1968) was among the first to recognize the importance of developmental sequencing in art for exceptional children (Taylor, Artuso, and Hewett, 1970).

DEVELOPMENT FOUNDATION FOR ART THERAPY

In the previous review of art as a therapeutic process, several important theoretical points were brought out. One, the therapeutic value of art lies in the experiential process. It is the child's involvement and the implementation of the act itself which makes the art experience of value. Second, the relative value of a particular art experience is directly related to particular developmental themes already at work within a child.

How can art experiences contribute to a child's development? First, we must recognize that each stage of development has a new goal, a different focus, and new interests. Art can be a responsive medium to experience and express these changes. It can stimulate different mental processes and utilize different skills. By doing so, art becomes an ever adaptable means to try out new skills and express new feelings while building on prior accomplishments.

Henry Dupont has elaborated on this idea with five specific contributions of art to development at every stage: [8]

1. Art adds form to feelings
2. Art helps a child develop skill in communicating feelings and ideas to others
3. Art provides a child opportunity to see himself through his own products
4. Art challenges a child to express and create
5. Because there is no right or wrong in an art production, a child's art becomes a source for success

It seems evident that organization of thought (or its lack) plays a significant role in the emotional development of children at all stages. And if organized, rational thought is the tool by which each child mediates his own process of development in the world, then symbols are the units of rational thought through which a child develops his operational schema. Art and dramatic play are natural forms for experimentation with

---

[8] These points were provided through a personal communication in 1976.

symbolic representation. Piaget (1951, p. 155) states that "the symbol is essentially the expression of the child's present reality." He describes developmental sequences as emerging from concomitant interaction of biological maturation, the child's responses to stimuli, and an integrative operation which he calls "equilibration" achieved through assimilation and accommodation. Wolff (1975, p. 3) describes this process as "a creative transformation of experience rather than a direct copy of reality." Elaborating on this same point, Langer (1967, p. 75) states:

> ...we call the symbol...a projection of the artist's idea into some perceptible form; the expressive object he creates is called a projection of the life, mood, emotion or whatever he makes it express.[9]

The clear implication is a dynamic bond between intellectual and emotional development. Loevinger (1976) substantiates this view in her theoretical and empirical research into the commonalities and characteristics of various stages of ego development. Citing *impulse control, character, interpersonal relations, conscious preoccupations*, and *cognitive style* as important dimensions of ego, Loevinger and her group present evidence of a general sequence of stages that can be identified as distinct yet with subtle overlaps as transitions. Loevinger's research lends significant credence to viewing each individual within a developmental context. It also suggests that development can be viewed in sequences and that these sequences have certain commonalities which lend themselves to clustering by phase, stage, or level. In a

discussion of issues in defining stages, these researchers offer a number of important cautions. First, no single behavior can be unequivocally associated with one particular stage of development. Second, a child can display behaviors at more than one stage of development. Third, the continuum of a developing behavior permits a particular behavior to appear at more than one stage of development. Fourth, there are many aspects of a child which are evolving simultaneously. Finally, one behavior can contain many, varied aspects of development. Each of these points needs to be considered when translating theory into practice. These ideas, stressing the significance of the interactive, sequential nature of development, can be a guide for constructing a developmental art curriculum.

Using a construct validation procedure rather than empirical research, Peter Wolff provides further support for a developmental approach to understanding and planning for children's programs. Wolff's detailed comparisons of psychoanalytic theory with Piaget's theory of sensorimotor development concludes a basic compatability between the two approaches, both formulating certain similar developmental trends. Motivation is one major point of difference between the theories according to Wolff. However, careful scrutiny of both concepts of motivation endorses the idea of the interactive dependency of intellect and instinct. "No actual developmental progress would ever correspond exactly to either reality-adaptive [Piagetian concept of motivation] or instinctual-drive-controlling tendencies [psychoanalytic concept of motivation]; no cognitive structure would develop independent of the mental representation of instinctual needs (organic needs); and no instinctual-drive control structure would stabi-

---

[9] It is interesting that such an interpretation parallels many of the ideas of ego psychologists and other developmental psychologists including Anthony (1956), Bobroff (1960), Elkind (1976), Flavell (1963), Henry (1956), Kohlberg (1970), Rappaport (1960), Wolff (1960; 1975).

lize, integrate, and generalize without the participation of cognitive schemata." (Wolff, 1960, p. 122). This interaction can be seen clearly in a very young child's development. His hands and eyes are the means by which he reaches out to obtain knowledge.[10]

Lowenfeld and Brittain (1970) have made a monumental contribution to the understanding of art as a preeminent means by which we can witness the development of this interaction of sensori-motor and cognitive skills. By examination and analysis of normal children's art work within a developmental framework, these authors have formulated a way to describe stages of mental growth and artistic skills. As they point out, stages and sequences of conceptual development and skill can be seen in all children's art work. These sequences are identified in a child's art work by characteristics that serve as signposts indicating the emergence of specific cognitive and affective processes in the maturing child. To consider interpreting a child's creative product as "symbolic speech," to select effective motivators, or to plan a significantly therapeutic art experience, one must first consider the developmental context. These developmental sequences are summarized below.

Random Marks—Evident in the infant's experimentation with waving hands in air, holding objects (crayon, carrot, rattle), or using fingers in finger paint or strained food.

Uncontrolled Scribbling—The continued experimentation and elaboration of kinesthetic experience. A child's attempts at a form of self-exploration is occurring. Babbling often accompanies the child's efforts.

Controlled Scribbling—The child conceptually recognizes a connection between a mark on paper and himself. Lines are often repeated and readily varied. Lines take on meaning to the child as do colors. This stage parallels the preschooler's interest in all forms of exploration. A milestone in this stage is naming of scribbling. The sharing of this new world will be verbalized to all who will listen and respond! This stage culminates with the emerging of recognizable shapes.

Preschematic Drawing—The child makes representational attempts and is aware of himself as the center of his world. First attempts produce human figures, houses, and trees. Color is less significant. Form is the focus now. No spatial relationships are established yet. The child is not yet ready to read or to socialize. The experience itself is the teacher. With increasing awareness, more details are evident in a picture. Individual creativity will begin to emerge now.

Schematic Drawing—A child's art work is highly individualized and signifies his "ordered" world. When he deviates from his normal schema, an important conceptual change has occurred and he is artistically demonstrating it to others. Space relationships are important with the use of a base and sky line. Colors realistically approximate the object. With the emergence of a schema, the child moves from egocentric behavior to social interaction.

Dawning Realism—Peer influences are evident now with more attention to details, realistic interpretation, greater use of shades and hues of colors, use of decoration for art projects and disappearance of sky line. Sky now meets earth! What a child's friends think of his work is more important than what the authority figures in his life think of it.

---

[10] In the following chapters, specific developmental formulations are expanded as they apply to each stage of therapy.

Pseudo-naturalistic Drawing—There is heightened concern for natural surroundings. Greater interest is shown in proportion, perspective, color variation, detail, and sexual characteristics.

A dramatic example of the Lowenfeld-Brittain schema can be seen in the five illustrations, Figures 1 to 4, on pp. 136—137 in Chapter 6. These drawings were done during a period of eight months by a four-year-old girl with a diagnosis of childhood schizophrenia. Her drawings demonstrate the normal growth possible during the course of therapy.

When first enrolled in a therapeutic preschool, this severely disturbed young child spoke only to imaginary friends, had violent temper tantrums, and screamed incessantly. She had refused, day after day, to participate in any activities (Williams, 1975). After six weeks of therapy, her first major attempt to communicate constructively with her teachers came through art work. She used her crayon defiantly to "shout her anger" through uncontrolled scribbling (Figure 1). She did not respond further that day. During the next few weeks she continued her defiant scribbling but became interested in the process and began to control her scribblings (Figure 2). Within a month came the emergence of the preschematic phase with the drawing of one of her favorite animal "friends" (Figure 3). The verbal monologue she had with her teacher about this drawing was recorded on the picture.

> "This is Wylie Coyote.
> He's sad.
> He has black britches.
> He has a tail.
> He has a sore throat.
> T—is for tear.
> It's a stethescope.
> H—is for heartbeat."

This communication was significant in that she was willing to share her private world for the first time with her teacher. Note that this sharing was done both verbally and visually and reflects a significantly higher level of cognitive and ego integration than she had ever reached before. In fact, she moved developmentally from a toddler level to an age-appropriate level in six months. Figure 4 shows the emergence of herself and the beginning structuring of her real world. Two years later, Figure 5 shows how this seven-year-old now sees herself. She is enrolled in the third grade of a public school and is a successfully functioning member of her family.

During the eight months' period reflected in the first four pictures, the child participated in a Developmental Therapy class. The aim of the program is to make the most constructive use of normal developmental sequences in order to help disturbed children cope effectively with the demands of childhood.

There are five assumptions basic to Developmental Therapy with severely disturbed children (Wood, 1975, pp. 3—4). These are presented below with applications for a developmentally based art therapist.

Assumption 1: *Emotional and behavioral disturbances in a young child are interwoven with normal functioning and often are difficult to differentiate.* Symbolic representation of normal and disturbed functioning are extremely difficult to differentiate in a child's art work. The art therapist can avoid making errors in interpretation by emphasizing art activities which assist a child in acquiring developmental skills.

Assumption 2: *Normal processes of physical and psychological development follow in a hierarchy of stages and sequences well documented in the literature.* To assist a child in mastering normal skills, the art therapist must be well informed about the sequences of developmental milestones all children go through in behavior, socialization, communication, cognition, and perceptual motor areas.

Assumption 3: *The normal process of change is uniquely individual, yet predictable, and occurs in relation to environmental conditions, experiences, biological constituents, and the foundation laid in prior experience.* In addition to knowledge about normal developmental milestones for all children, the art therapist must be able to assess accurately the development of each child. Through such individual assessment, the child's art program can be carefully planned to target precisely on his unique pattern of strengths, deficits, feelings, interests, and experiences.

Assumption 4: *The young child's knowledge of himself, his confidence in himself, his willingness to risk himself in new situations, grows out of significant pleasurable experiences.* The art therapist must recognize which developmental skills are needed to be successful with each step in an art activity. Then, by planning art activities that are developmentally motivating, utilizing presently developed skills, and avoiding demands for performance above developmental capabilities, the art therapist can assure success and pleasure for each child as well as for the group.

Assumption 5: *The young child learns and grows by experience.* Every art experience should afford the child opportunity to explore freely his own potential within the art medium. This mandates that the art therapist stimulate exploration and encourage process rather than product.

A child of any age can be developmentally delayed. It is the responsibility of the therapist to identify the pattern and stage of each child's development and to plan developmentally appropriate experiences. As a child begins Developmental Therapy and the process of achieving normal developmental milestones, art can provide experiences and practice for each new skill. As a child's repertoire of appropriate and pleasure-producing responses increases, the child experiences the joy of being able to DO, SAY, CARE, and THINK through art. Surely this is a goal of therapy with young children, whatever the handicap may be!

STAGES OF DEVELOPMENTAL THERAPY

The general goal of social and emotional growth (by doing, saying, caring, and thinking) has been conceptualized within Developmental Therapy into five stages. Table 1 is an overview of the stages, with goals for each stage and a summary of appropriate teacher techniques, experiences, and activities generally needed by children at a particular stage.

For art to be used successfully in this developmental approach, the art experience and the teacher's or therapist's techniques must be carefully selected to achieve specific objectives at each of

Table 1. Summary of Developmental Therapy Stages[a]

STAGE I: Responding to the environment with pleasure

General Description:	*Responding and trusting*
Therapist's Role:	Arouser and satisfier of basic needs
Techniques:	Body contact and touch; physical intervention; classroom structure and consistent routine; control of materials by teacher; controlled vocabulary
Intervention:	Constant physical contact; caring, arousing
Environment and Experiences:	Routine constant, luring rather than demanding; stimulating, arousing sensory activities

STAGE II: Responding to the environment with success

General Description:	*Learning individual skills*
Therapist's Role:	Motivator; redirector of old coping behavior to successful outcomes; reflector of success; predictable point of reference
Techniques:	Classroom structure; consistent routine; verbal interaction between lead and support teachers; physical and verbal redirection; holding limits; reflection of action, feelings, and success
Intervention:	Frequent, both physical and verbal; supportive
Environment and Experiences:	Structured, successful exploration; activities leading to self-confidence and organization; communication activities; beginning cooperative activities; simple group experiences

STAGE III: Learning skills for successful group participation

General Description:	*Applying individual skills to group procedures*
Therapist's Role:	Model for group participation; stimulator and encourager of appropriate group interaction; upholder of limits and group expectations; reflector and interpreter of behavior, feelings, and progress
Techniques:	Redirection; reflection; verbal interaction between lead and support teachers; individual Life Space Interviews; predictable structure and expectations reflector of feelings; predictability; frequent verbal intervention, consistency
Intervention:	Frequent, primarily verbal, group focus
Environment and Experiences:	Group activities that stimulate cooperation, sharing, and beginning friendships; focus on group procedures and expectations; approximate real-life situations and conditions as much as group can tolerate

STAGE IV: Investing in group processes

General Description:	*Valuing one's group*
Therapist's Role:	Group leader; counselor; reflector of reality
Techniques:	Interpretation of feelings and behavior; individual and group Life Space Interview; reality reflection
Intervention:	Intermittent, approximating real life
Environment and Experiences:	Reality-oriented environment; activities, procedures, and expectations determined by the group; emphasis on group academic learning experiences; role play, field trips, elements of normal competition

STAGE V: Applying individual and group skills in new situations

General Description:	*Generalizing and valuing*
Therapist's Role:	Counselor, teacher, friend
Techniques:	Normal expectations; relationships between feelings, behaviors, and consequences; nonclinical
Intervention:	Infrequent
Environment and Experiences:	Normal childhood settings; conversations about real-life experiences; support in solving problem situations; independent skill building

---

[a]Modified from Wood (1975, pp. 7–8).

References to chronological age have been deliberately omitted in order to emphasize that the *sequence* of development is important rather than a comparison to a norm.

these developmental stages. Certain art projects and media are of genuine use to children at the various stages of development; others are of little value. Through experience with severely disturbed children ages two through fourteen and multihandicapped preschool children in the Developmental Therapy program begun in 1970 at the Rutland Center in Athens, Georgia, art activities and techniques were developed and field tested to provide successful art experiences for children in each developmental stage.

CURRICULUM AREAS

The elements of social, intellectual, perceptual-motor, and emotional growth have been woven into four Developmental Therapy curriculum areas. Every art experience should involve all of these areas to promote maximum development.

Behavior (Doing)

Behavior has reference to the physical, adaptive responses a child makes toward his environment. At its most basic point, behavior refers to a child being aware of his surroundings. With awareness, other processes can begin to grow: attending to a stimulus, simple motor responses, body control, recognizing essentials and nonessentials, and participating in routine activities. More advanced behavior processes include impulse control, organizing responses according to expectations of others, and involvement with rules as one basis for functioning in a group.

Communication (Saying)

Communication implies interpersonal processes. For this reason the area of communication includes all forms of verbal and nonverbal efforts to interact with another child or adult. Included in this area are gestures, watching and imitating others, producing speech sounds and verbal approximations, and using sequences of words. As communication skills increase, a child learns to listen, describe feelings and characteristics of himself and others, convey information, and express his feelings through words.

Socialization (Caring)

Socialization involves processes that lead a child into relationships and group experiences. These processes begin with awareness of adults and peers and soon develop into parallel and cooperative play. Socialization takes on a definitive form when a child has the interpersonal skills for successful interactions with a number of different people. To do this he must have a sense of self, self-confidence, and an interest in others. Processes include taking turns, suggesting activities, sharing, participating in what others suggest, recognizing characteristics of others, developing preferences for friends, supporting others, and eventually participating as an invested member of a group.

(Pre)academics (Thinking)

(Pre)academics includes processes used for cognitive functions which will contribute to mastery of symbolic content for the purpose of personal enrichment and creative problem solving. Such processes include eye-hand and perceptual skills, body coordination, memory, discriminating similarities and differences in all sensory modalities, classifying, concept building, receptive language, use of objects, recognizing details in pictures, concepts of number, and conservation.

These basic processes lead to more complex ones such as expressive language and recognizing signs and symbols (Wood, 1975, pp. 5–6).

DEVELOPMENTAL THERAPY OBJECTIVES

On first glance, anyone observing art time in any of the groups would see a simple art lesson where children are enjoying themselves. In reality, carefully sequenced, multiobjective therapy is taking place. Focusing on individually selected developmental objectives in each of the four curriculum areas (behavior, communication, socialization, and (pre)-academics), the art lessons are constructed to help children master developmental objectives as pleasurably and quickly as possible. Sequences of objectives lead to the accomplishment of general goals at each stage of development and in each curriculum area. These goals are summarized in Table 2.

The particular focus for each art experience is provided by the 144 Developmental Therapy objectives (Wood, 1975, p. 263 ff).[11] Each experience is planned to achieve a combination of specific individual objectives for every child and for the group. From the first introduction of materials emphasizing the day's lesson,

to the distribution of materials, through actual work time, to clean up, the art activity is designed to facilitate mastery of these developmental objectives. As a child achieves objective after objective, social and emotional growth will occur. This growth will enable him to be increasingly more effective in his home and school. Along with increased emotional maturity the child will reflect other noticeable changes—verbally, conceptually, and artistically.

Activities described in the following chapters have been field tested with more than 1,000 children between the ages of three and fourteen years. In each chapter, the activities are designed to help teachers and therapists use art for particular Developmental Therapy objectives at specific stages of development. At all stages, the joy of art experiences should lead a child to the use of art as a means to express himself. Perhaps no statement can more eloquently summarize the potential in art for youngsters than this one from Edith Kramer:

> . . . art fulfills for the disturbed child the function which it has for all men: to create a realm of symbolic living, which allows experimentation with ideas and feelings; to make apparent the complexities and contradictions of human life; to demonstrate man's capacity to transcend conflict and create order out of chaos; and finally to give pleasure (Kramer, 1971, p. 219).

Such benefits can be realized for all handicapped children if the art experiences are planned and conducted within a developmental context.

---

[11] See the Appendix of this text for the revised objectives. These objectives can be used as a means to assess the developmental status of an individual child and are designed to guide the day to day planning of therapeutic experiences. See Combs (1975) for the actual procedure for rating children.

Table 2. Developmental Therapy goals for each curriculum area at each stage of therapy[a]

Stage	Behavior	Communication	Socialization	Academic skills
I	To trust own body and skills	To use words to gain needs	To trust an adult sufficiently to respond to him	To respond to the environment with processes of classification, discrimination, basic receptive language concepts, and body coordination
II	To successfully participate in routines	To use words to affect others in constructive ways	To participate in activities with others	To participate in classroom routines with language concepts of similarities and differences, labels, use, color; numerical processes of ordering and classifying; and body coordination
III	To apply individual skills in group processes	To use words to express oneself in the group	To find satisfaction in group activities	To participate in the group with basic expressive language concepts; symbolic representation of experiences and concepts; functional semiconcrete concepts of conservation; and body coordination
IV	To contribute individual effort to group sucess	To use words to express awareness of relationship between feelings and behavior in self and others	To participate spontaneously and successfully as a group member	To successfully use signs and symbols in formalized school work and in group experiences
V	To respond to critical life experiences with adaptive, constructive behavior	To use words to establish and enrich relationships	To initiate and maintain effective peer group relationships independently	To successfully use signs and symbols for formalized school experiences and personal enrichment

[a] From Wood (1975, p. 9).

Here are some mini-guidelines for using Developmental Art Therapy.

Art is perhaps the MOST personal form of expression a child will attempt and, therefore, art time can be highly therapeutic—or very disruptive.

Children who have little self-confidence or inadequate developmental skills will exhibit hostility, resistance, or anxiety at art time.

Different art materials motivate different responses from children at different stages of development.

Ensuring success for each child in a group at art time will require careful preparation, sequencing of each step, clarity and structure in each procedure, and individually motivating materials.

Flexibility and creativeness of the teacher will need to be matched by a bond of trust between the teacher and each child.

Recognizing the developmental implication in a child's art work is necessary to plan future lessons successfully and to use art successfully to meet each child's specific developmental needs.

chapter 2
STAGE ONE: RESPONDING TO THE ENVIRONMENT WITH PLEASURE

Many children at Stage One must be moved through their first art experiences. The cool, wet paper and gooey finger paints are highly stimulating and encourage spontaneous involvement.

For weeks, Billy, a severely impaired, autistic child in our Stage One class, has been physically helped through each art lesson. He shows no awareness of the materials and seldom responds to my verbal statements. Then one day, as I am placing a brush in his hand, guiding it into the paint and moving hand and brush to make a line, I leave him momentarily to help another child. His hand stops as soon as I let go. As I turn to help the other child, out of the corner of my eye I see Billy's hand still clutching the brush. Then slowly but surely his hand seeks out a clean piece of paper on the table near him. I move away to let him have more room. Pulling the paper toward himself carefully, he begins making paint strokes on the paper. I help him get more paint on the brush and then let his hand go. *Again* he goes back to this new sheet of paper. Then, to further explore this newly discovered object in his hand, he carefully places the paint brush in his mouth to taste and feel the bristles. Billy has made an assertive move to explore his world for the first time!

THE CHILD AT STAGE ONE

Stage One includes the normal developmental milestones usually associated with the first fifteen months of life. The overall emotional goal is to learn to respond to the environment with pleasure (Wood, 1975). Trust in oneself and others is the key to accomplishment of this goal, and sensory processes provide the major vehicle for motivation.

There is a significant preamble to social and emotional growth at Stage One which involves sensory motor learning. The very first sensations felt by a new-born infant probably are proprioceptive, kinesthetic, thermal, and visual. Often, severely handicapped, Stage One children must be reached with these same fundamental sensory experiences, each with the potential for either comfort or discomfort. For Stage One children, most experiences can be considered in these polarized terms: comfort-discomfort; pleasure-pain.[1] Rapidly such sensory experiences become the foundation for the development of a child's emotion and affect, providing the groundwork for feelings and attitudes. Such fundamental emotions are the direct outgrowth of sensory motor experiences with pleasure and pain, and they permeate the child's perception of people and the world as pleasurable or painful. These perceptions probably can be interrupted and reconstructed, but the foundations are clearly laid at the earliest developmental levels.

It is important to remember that the normal infant not only tries to avoid painful experiences but also actively seeks comforts and pleasures. Similarly, the developmentally delayed child also is actively, dynamically seeking comfort and pleasure. By utilizing a child's quest for pleasant results, a teacher can assist the child in building up a series of responses that assist him in obtaining gratifying comforts. This process is the foundation for positive motivation. To meet a Stage One child's needs, then, one must not only compensate for deficits or delays but, more important, stimulate skills that can bring pleasures.

At this stage of development, a child's pleasure comes primarily from two sources: people and the child's own body. Such basic pleasures for a Stage One child include interactions with people, eating, touching, and muscle move-

---

[1] In this discussion "pain" is used in the broadest possible sense, including psychological discomfort, disorganization, confusion, and anxiety.

ments including movements of arms, legs, and mouth (sucking, chewing, mouthing, random vocalizing, blowing, etc.). In an infant these behaviors are appropriate, but when evident in a severely delayed twelve-year-old the same behaviors evoke feelings of frustration or dismay from adults. However, if viewed as indicators of comfort-seeking in a developmental context, the same behaviors can provide important keys for motivating a child to begin gradual developmental expansion.

From the basic pleasure-pain response system, the child develops feelings and attitudes about himself (his own body) and about others. The major emotional growth for this stage of development has to do with these two points. They present a very simple guideline for the Stage One child's teacher, therapist, and parents: provide experiences in which the child associates his own actions and people with comfort and pleasure.

Socialization and Trust

Associating one significant person as the comforting provider is the first step in the normal development of socialization. A major milestone is accomplished when an infant looks at the person who is providing pleasure. Looking leads to recognition and association of the provider with the pleasure. Every child, whatever the handicap, must have these same nurturing experiences in order to develop emotionally. The result is a primary form of relationship. With normal infants this accomplishment has been called the first attachment.

Trust is the basis for this first relationship. It also is the essential ingredient for continuing emotional development. Erikson refers to the emergence of a "basic trust" during this first stage of life.

... trust furthermore, implies not only that one has learned to rely on the sameness and continuity of the outer providers but also that one may trust oneself (Erikson, 1973, p. 46).

Trust must be established preparatory to the emergence of two major dynamic themes of childhood: *dependence* and *independence*. This is the beginning of a dynamic interplay that starts with the infant's complete emotional and physical dependence and permeates the successful accomplishment of each subsequent stage of development. These first attachments also are the foundation for later capability to develop interpersonal relationships, which finally culminate in the ability to form mature love relationships.

The origin of the first relationship can be traced to an autistic-like presocial phase of development (Loevinger, 1976). Biological dependency is characteristic of this phase, and the infant (or delayed child) does not differentiate self, objects, and others. Physical and psychological nurturance is the primary ingredient for continued development. Usually this is provided by the person who satisfies day-to-day biological needs while providing stimulation through social contact.

Loevinger (1976, p. 177) provides a description of the change that occurs as a result: "The progress out of the Autistic Stage appears to require confidence in the stability of the world of objects. Even symbiotic interpersonal relations imply the existence of another person." She cites Piaget's work (1954) in the "construction of reality" as particularly relevant to this phase of development. In order to recognize the existence of another person as separate from self, the child must develop a concept of object constancy; that is, maintain a stable mental image of object or person. This ability clearly separates the autistic phase from the subsequent phase of intense interpersonal dependency that develops as a result of consistent physical care and emotional nurturance. When a teacher or therapist works with a child at this stage of development, it is necessary that these elements of physical and psychological nurturance be major components of the program. These must be carefully planned for inclusion in each activity, material, and management technique.

As the relationship bond is established between a normal infant and mother, a second phase begins in which the bond becomes intense and excludes others. Mahler (1952), Freud (1973), and Loevinger (1976) identify this phase as "symbiotic." Mahler also describes the phase as an egocentric progression from total dependency to eventual independence. This progress is seen in several universal processes: *feeding* (from nursing to weaning and self-feeding), *wetting* and *soiling* (to bladder and bowel control), and *play* (from biological unity with the mother to play with mother and objects). Teachers of Stage One children must become involved in all of these processes because each is a critical milestone for development. Considerable priority must be given also to establishing a relationship bond that conveys both physical care and a stimulating interpersonal relationship.

Sensory Motor Learning

Piaget (1954) has conceptualized this first phase of development as the sensory motor period. The process he describes is one of "equilibration." Think of it as a process of balancing inner needs and outer stimuli so that the infant assimilates, accommodates, internalizes, and adapts into his own response system aspects of his experience that bring comfort. Similarly,

he rejects discomfort. Although Piaget prepared this model to describe the sensory motor phase of cognitive development, it is a useful way to think about all forms of early psychological development. Loevinger (1976) suggests that at this first phase of life the sensory motor foundations are as relevant to ego development as to intellectual development. From a psychodynamic viewpoint the same process might be described as the process of mediating the integration of inner drives and external forces through ego functions.

At the most primitive level, the process can be viewed as a stimulus-response paradigm. This explanation serves as the basic unit for the developmental hierarchy, but rapidly this explanation becomes too simplistic. Piaget (1936) conceptualizes the process as one of reproductive assimilation and accommodation, which produces a phase of response stabilization. In simple terms, his theory suggests that a potentially useful random response should be followed with repetitions of a stimulus that can evoke the response. These repetitions should be continued until the response becomes a part of the existing sensory motor response network. At that point, the response can be freely generalized into new situations. There is an important guideline in this paradigm for conducting art therapy with Stage One children. Initially the art material may have to follow or be paired with random responses. For example, a flailing arm movement can be physically directed to touch a large sheet of paper and finger paint as the teacher says, *"Paper"* . . . *"Paint."* Through repetitions of this movement, the child eventually can produce the arm movement to the paper and paint either from the visual or verbal stimulus.

The subsequent phase of this sensory motor learning process is one of elaboration, i.e., magnification of a basic response into new ones. This phase also suggests a much more complex level of development, an indication that the basic stimulus-response has expanded to new utilizations and adaptations.

Expansion of a child's skills requires taking his responses, however limited, and building new, more complex skills. Through new stimuli the child can now develop new responses and greater adaptation pretty much on his own. The essential ingredient for doing this is developmentally appropriate *experience*. A teacher must provide not only a variety of materials and activities that stimulate adaptations of basic responses but also provide experiences that use the child's current responses while encouraging expansion of new skills.

DEVELOPMENTAL ART
THERAPY FOR STAGE ONE

A Stage One child's artistic and conceptual abilities can be estimated by observing the manner in which he responds to the basic art tools in the first few days with art materials. Typically, a child's art work in a Stage One classroom will take one of three forms. A child unable to hold any tool (brush, pencil, crayon) or make any mark on any material (paper, wood, cloth) could be identified as in a *prescribling, nonproductive phase*. A child able to use these same tools and to make marks or lines could be classified as in the *random mark, uncontrolled scribbling phase*.[2] However, with the achievement of most Stage One objectives, a higher form of artistic and devel-

opmental functioning becomes evident. Such children control their scribbling and make simple, one-word verbalizations or approximations while involved in an art experience.

Each Stage One child can be motivated to develop higher level art productions. Careful observation of the child should be the first step. Is the child attracted to a particular color, sound, object, or person in the room day after day? Are there certain motor movements he seems to prefer? Is there an activity when the child seems more alert than at other times? Careful observation generally will produce some important information about what attracts the child, what causes negative responses, or what evokes no response. Lesson after lesson can go by with the teacher having to "motor" the children through the activity.[3] Unexpectedly, because of a new material, a new sensory exploration in art, or the repetition of familiar responses, a new developmental milestone is reached. A child reveals a new ability that the teacher has never observed in him before. Or, the child may finally demonstrate mastery of a long-practiced skill. Choices are beginning to emerge from each child, and feelings (positive or negative) are being expressed outwardly, perhaps for the first time.

Using Sensory
Modalities to Obtain Responses

The key to successful growth through art in Stage One is the use of sensory-arousing art media and experiences so that

---

[2] The Lowenfeld-Brittain schema (1970) described in Chapter 1 is used here to estimate the child's creative and mental development in planning developmentally suitable art experiences.

[3] This expression, "motoring through an activity," was coined by teachers of the autistic in the Los Angeles Unified School District, Vera Newman, Advisor, and Eugene Greenfield, Coordinator. It is used to describe the technique of supportively moving a child through the physical motions needed to participate in an activity or task.

each child can find the most satisfying means to express this arousal. Some children find great satisfaction in working with a particular material while others are only confused and frustrated by it. Why does one person love spinach and another detest it? It is up to the teacher to get the child's attention and then to keep it by a wide variety of sensory art experiences!

All of the child's senses should be used for art lessons (e.g., smell: let each child smell an orange, then draw with orange chalk. Hearing: play rhythmic music; clap to music; then, on paper, clap hand on blob of finger paint to music. Feeling: "feeling" boxes are covered shoe boxes with a hole in one end; inside is a variety of materials with different textures. Taste: lick gold stars, then stick them on black paper). A great many Stage One children are able to relate consciously to these various stimuli with the expected responses, but it is important to stimulate all sensory channels and to observe those children who might be responsive to the experiences.

The developmental objectives for Stage One children cluster around obtaining spontaneous responses to the materials, to the teacher, and to the other children. These responses are sought in behavior, communication, socialization, and (pre)academics, and each response should result in a pleasurable, satisfying feeling. Because the typical Stage One group is made up of three to five children, each experience should include individual developmental objectives. The experience can then be of value to the most delayed, primitive child as well as to the most responsive child in the group.

Stage One experiences must require responses from each child. The critical matter of motivating and individualizing the expectation requires timing, accurately reading a child's behavior, and deciding when a child is "hooked" on the experience. When the child really wants a material, the teacher can demonstrate an appropriate way to seek. The first weeks should involve simple expectations. When responses are *not* given, then motoring the child through the activity is necessary. This procedure is always accompanied by soothing or pleasing vocalizations and touch from the teacher. As the daily routine and the art time become more and more exciting for each child and certain materials have proven highly response-evoking, the decision can be made as to whether or not the child is progressing enough to refuse him the supplies until he gives a desired requesting behavior. This can be the right moment to help the child reach out. However, if withdrawal occurs, the child needs to be enticed back into succeeding art lessons to begin the process of responding all over again.

Conducting a Stage One Art Lesson

Lessons that produce exciting sensory feelings are most effective. Each art lesson should be so rewarding that a child is eager for more. Then each art experience will become a step in a sequence motivated by the child's own volition. Most Stage One art lessons should be of extremely short length, ending when each child has participated pleasurably to some degree, either on his own or with help. Art lessons can begin with short, one-step experiences that have instant results (see hand print lesson listed under "Tempera Paint" in Activities section). As progress is shown by the children in their attention, responses, and interest, they rapidly begin to achieve basic developmental objectives.

As a day-to-day routine is established, art should be included in the same sequence of activities and at the same location each day. The work area for art time should be large and easy to clean, preferably one table large enough to allow room for 18″ X 24″ paper for each child, with chairs appropriate to table and children. All necessary art supplies for a particular art experience should be within arm's reach of the teacher yet stored out of reach and sight of children. Also, always have a second art activity planned for the occasion when the planned activity fails to arouse!

Simple, brief instructions of the day's art lesson with concise visual demonstrations, paired with a controlled vocabulary, are necessary as the children demonstrate increased awareness and interest. Then lessons can evolve to greater complexity, for example: the use of three different materials in a collage; exchanging colors with another child upon request of the teacher; or making a verbal approximation for a desired art material.

The teacher should use a simple key phrase to begin each art lesson, *"Now it's art time. Go to the table."* Equally simple, controlled vocabulary is used during the activity. A profundity of words will not help focus the children's attention to the specific task at hand; simple, key words will. The teacher pairs key words with the art experience in order to begin teaching the child that vocal sounds can be cues to experiences. This process builds the foundation for communication skills that will develop subsequently. For children with more advanced receptive language skills, the teacher can verbalize simple statements that will reinforce what they are doing, seeing, feeling, and experiencing with the materials: *"The water feels cool." "It's beautiful the way the colors red and blue make purple." "Joey is making a nice circle."* In any case, arousing, pleasing qualities of the teacher's sounds, rather than what is said, is the most powerful tool for motivation.

It is often disheartening to place materials in front of a Stage One child, move his hand throughout the activity, and see no response at all. Sometimes offering a "surprise" at the end of art time, such as blowing bubbles or introducing a portable radio or a kaleidoscope for each child to experience, *can* provide a pleasurable response and increase the probability of greater interest in the next art lesson. It may take many weeks to stimulate positive responses with art materials. Here is the sequence needed for one Stage One group.

Weeks 1 and 2

Materials were placed in front of each child. The children were physically moved through each activity with positive verbal reflection and controlled vocabulary.

Weeks 3 and 4

Materials were shown to each child with a request for a verbal approximation or word in order to obtain materials. (With a few children, eye contact or gesture was considered sufficient.) As interest and attention waned, the teacher praised work with touch and a praise.

Weeks 5 and 6

Materials were shown and demonstrated with accompanying verbal model: *"Paper . . . Brush . . . Paint."* (#2 brush dipped in paint to demonstrate one sweeping circle.) Then each child was encouraged to produce some assertive single word or approximation to ask for each material.

While the children used the materials, the teacher reflected what each child was doing.

"Tommy is painting."

"Mary has a brush."

"Do you want more paint?"

"Who wants paper?"
"Tommy, what do you want?"
"Good talking!"
"Sue, what do you want?"
As long as children were invested in the activity, the art activity was kept going, but it was always ended while attention was high and on a positive note.

Weeks 7 through 9

Art activities were continued as above with stress placed on making use of each child's individual expressive capabilities. If one child used figures, then the teacher reflected the details. *"Tommy is drawing a face. It looks like a happy boy. He has two eyes. Are they blue like yours, Tommy?"* If a child responded to the routine but was able only to hold tools and make random marks, then his "designs" were complimented, his hands moved through the motion of making shapes (circles, triangles, squares). The most productive procedure followed was to give a child sheet after sheet of paper to scribble on, vary the materials, and verbally and physically reward each positive attempt to vocalize along with the art activity. (Any sounds, grunts, or word attempts got an immediate warm response from the teacher.)

Verbal Communication through Art

Especially significant for Stage One children is the use of art as a means of communication, especially for those who do not yet have the verbal skills to express themselves. With increased awareness, hopefully, comes the beginnings of *spontaneous* verbalizations, as with normal children. But for Stage One children this often is not the case. As a child begins to achieve developmental objectives, he may begin to make systematic vocalizations of sounds or words, but usually only on command. Spontaneous speech seldom occurs during art. It is possible that the process of being stimulated by the various art materials and the manipulation of them is an arousing end in itself. It may take so much psychic energy for a child to mobilize his thought processes throughout an art activity that little or no energy is left to attempt verbal communication. Or, the execution of the art work is pleasurable, a vehicle for nonverbal interaction with the teacher; therefore, the child has no need to extend himself to communicate. Repetition of favored art activities, coupled with restricted, controlled verbal patterns, may be the way to break through this barrier.

In one particular Stage One group, stereotyped verbal responses were predominant, yet developmentally these children were ready to extend their verbalization skills. How to bring more spontaneous verbalizations out of the children was the question. It was decided first to stop changing art materials each day. Use of unwrapped, broken blunt crayons (kindergarten and regular size were mixed up in one box for each child to choose his crayon) and 12 X 18 white paper was used each day; the only variables were different instructions and drawn models for each art time. Weeks went by with drawings of simple flowers, trees, stick figures, houses, and forms being demonstrated each day but with the children producing only uncontrolled and controlled scribbling and still no spontaneous verbalizations. The children enjoyed the art time and did not appear turned off by using the same tools each day. Perhaps showing tangible objects to draw would help make the connection between art and verbal expression.

One day, the art teacher brought out a green, fuzzy ball. She let each child touch the ball while she repeated, *"Ball, green ball."* Then she quickly drew a green circle and colored it. Holding up the drawing to the children, she again repeated, "Ball, green ball." The children watched with interest and responded appropriately by grasping for the ball as it was offered to each child. However, when the crayons were chosen there were no spontaneous verbalizations, only echolalic verbal responses when requested. During the drawing time, some attempts were made by the children to produce a circle form. But the only real change occurring after repeated sessions was that each child had a "favorite" crayon and would not participate until he could find it! Obviously this approach lacked relevance to motivate these children for involvement further than the pleasurable art expression.

The art therapist was aware that the art activity was holding each child's attention without her varying the materials, but it seemed to be going nowhere. So, she changed the presentation format and the motivation with dramatic results. The first change in the presentation was in drawing a large circle first and saying, *"Circle!"* Keeping eye contact with each child, she changed the circle into a face (☺) saying, "BOY." Then she reflected that the boy was hungry and asked, *"What does he want to eat?"* No response. She suggested a hamburger and colored in an area *over* the boy's mouth (☻) exclaiming, *"Mmmm, good!"* Then one child spontaneously said, *"French fries!"* She quickly took a brown crayon and made a mass of short lines (➷). *"Coke"* said another child, and she drew a bottle (🍶) with a black crayon. Then she stopped and handed each child a sheet of paper with a circle already drawn on it.

Some of the children contained their scribbling within the predrawn shape. Others abandoned it and made the same shape on their own! As the children worked, she stroked their backs and re-

flected imaginary goodies they were producing.

This same lesson was used with slight variation in shapes every day. Key words were repeated often (*"hamburger," "French fries," "coke," "boy," "face," "ears," "eyes," "hair,"* etc.). These verbalizations came spontaneously in words or approximations from the children. They also began spontaneous attempts at making specific shapes! In an eight-week period a breakthrough in the spontaneous association of words, ideas, and symbols had occurred!

Combining Art and Music

When Stage One children are overloaded with stimuli they often withdraw, perseverate, or become highly agitated and fearful. For this reason there was considerable reservation about trying to combine art activities with music. (Purvis and Samet (1976) have elaborated on the use of music at each stage of Developmental Therapy.) Yet the possibility existed for the children to be aware, organized, and responsive through such a multisensory approach. Initially, two activities were used, with a high degree of success: 1) pounding and rolling clay to a strong melodic tune, and 2) making marks with magic markers while cheerful, familiar music played. This particular Stage One group had previously responded to daily separate art and music activities. In music, specific songs and tunes had been used regularly with body rhythm and music sticks.

The combined lessons were attempted with no demonstration. Clay was placed directly in the child's hands. The music had been taped ahead and when each child had his clay, the music was started. The art therapist served as the model for the action. All of the children responded spontaneously to the music with rhythmic hand motions. It was clearly evident that they found the activity to be great fun! It was as if the music reinforced each hand motion pounding with the clay. The first week's success was followed the next week by magic markers and the music of "Jimmy Cracked Corn."

During the clay lesson, pounding was the first motion. Before interest was lost, rolling the clay back and forth was demonstrated as the music continued to play. The last motion was holding the clay in one hand and slapping it with another, attempting to keep in rhythm for some children, others being oblivious to this action. Whatever each child could manage was warmly praised and rewarded with a stroke or hug.

Some days after the music was turned off, more time was spent working with the clay. The children were encouraged to manipulate the clay, using a pencil to make polka dots or to draw designs on the clay. It was equally enjoyable to put the music back on so the children could "march" to the bathroom to clean up! The actual time of these art-music lessons averaged four to six minutes each day.

Much the same was true for the magic marker lessons. Markers were chosen because they have bright colors, are easily held and manipulated, and produce a pleasant tactile effect as they make lines on a sheet of paper. One thing was noticed quickly at the beginning of this lesson. As the papers filled with marks, two of the children lost interest. As soon as new sheets of paper were placed in front of the children, the art work began again. In subsequent lessons, as the children became confident in drawing to music, more emphasis was placed on requiring a response from each child to obtain additional paper. The music was lowered in volume, and, to end the les-

son, it was turned off. Quick, productive, and pleasant, this activity produced some quite beautiful designs.

Whenever these special art-music times were scheduled, other standby art or music activities were planned in case the children were not successful, but they were never needed.

Stage One children have also experienced success with making instruments. The results are not as spectacular as at higher stages but are equally productive in mastering development objectives. To fill any closeable container or coffee can with dried beans requires minimum response and manipulative abilities. Yet it gives each child a productive activity and results in a dramatic use of a musical instrument he has just experienced putting together.

Here is a narrative by the art therapist of a typical Stage One art experience designed to foster the accomplishment of the overall goal for this first stage: responding to the environment with pleasure. Specific Developmental Therapy objectives are noted in the margin.

A TYPICAL STAGE ONE ART EXPERIENCE

The children are coming to the end of their play time. It is now time for art, and the lead teacher, Miss Anne, knows that I am outside the door waiting for her cue. She announces, *"Play time is over. Now it's ART TIME,"* and begins moving the children back to the work table and their chairs. The same words are used each day. I enter the room on this cue and move to the children's work table, waiting for her second cue.

Miss Anne verbally motivates the children to move to the table on their own, but those who can't respond will be assisted through physical contact to move to their seats. Sometimes only part of the group will actually be at the table when we begin. The materials serve as a great motivator for the others. While I begin,

B-7
to indicate recall of classroom routine by moving spontaneously to next activity area without physical stimulus; verbal cues or touch may be used.

B-4
to respond with motor and body responses to complex environmental and verbal stimuli (through imitation, "Do this"; through completion of verbal direction; minimal participation in the routine; given physical intervention and verbal cues).

B-2
to respond to stimulus by sustained attending to source of stimulus (continued looking at object or person after initial stimulus-response has occurred).

C-3
to respond to verbal stimulus and single object with a recognizable approximation of the appropriate verbal response (child gives verbal approximation to indicate use or correct answer to question, "What is this?" (object present; function or name acceptable).

C-3
to respond to verbal stimulus and single object with a recognizable approximation of the appropriate verbal response.

S-2
to attend to other's behavior (child looks at another when attention is not on child directly).

C-2
to respond to verbal stimulus with a motor behavior (object present; teacher does not use gestures).

B-1
to react to sensory stimulus by attending toward source of stimulus by body response or by looking.

Miss Anne rounds up any child who has not made it to the table.

The art materials are hidden in a colorfully decorated box. A rattle and shake of the box increases the attention of several children. I reach in and hold up a clear plastic container of wooden beads in assorted colors and sizes.

Looking from child to child, touching the children or calling each by name, I ask, *"What is this?"* This procedure helps to introduce each child to the materials and to bring the children's attention to the beads. Each child's response is warmly received, and I use verbal reflection and a controlled vocabulary to help them connect the arousing material to spoken language.

"Tony sees beads."

As Tony reaches for the beads, he is encouraged to touch the container to help him connect the teacher's words with his response.

"Tony wants beads."

Patty moves her hands eagerly toward the container. She makes a verbal approximation spontaneously. Repeating the child's /B/ sound reinforces her verbal attempt. Then I give her the complete word to model, *"/B/ . . . Beads."* Her response is rewarded with a hug.

Now, I hold up a 12-inch length of wire. *"Wire!"* I slowly thread the plastic coated wire through one bead while conveying immense pleasure at doing this activity. Then, moving the supplies closer to the children, I pick up another bead. Now the children are with me, attending and eager. I sense that one more demonstration is needed.

"A blue bead." I show this bead to each child quickly and then thread it. Again I convey my pleasure in doing the task.

"Who wants beads?" I thrust the container of beads forward as I repeat the phrase to each child. My interaction with each child will be individualized at this point. But the goal is the same: connect words to a tangible, desirable item in front of them.

Tony is grabbing for the beads and is rewarded with a bead and a wire. No verbal response is required from Tony in the beginning. Miss Anne moves closer to help Tony successfully thread the first bead. She then takes a supply of beads in her lap, and, as Tony

threads each one, she asks him, *"Tony, what do you want?"* After asking the question, she gives him the single verbal model, *"Bead,"* with an emphasis on the /B/ sound. In time, this procedure during art will help him achieve the first step in communication. If he completes one wire, he can then begin another. Each bead is obtained by the same verbal process. His attention is sustained in the activity because of Miss Anne's touch, close proximity, and pleasure in his activity. If she notices sustained attention without her contact, she carefully pulls back to allow Tony the freedom to string the bead and seek another on his own. However, her expectation for a verbal approximation from Tony for a bead will be continued. If his responses begin to diminish, Miss Anne notices immediately and remotivates him if possible. She will not push him beyond his interest level. Art time will end when the majority of the children have had a happy and rewarding experience.

While Tony is being helped by Miss Anne, I am helping Terry, who is the most advanced child in the group. Since she is using a few words, she is asked to request both the bead and the wire at the beginning of the activity. *"Terry, what do you want? Say, 'I want bead.'"* When she does this, I give her a hug and say, *"Terry wants bead. . . . What is this?"* Whether I hand her several beads at once and let her work by herself or hand them to her one at a time after she requests each will depend on her investment in the activity and her ability to handle the more complex procedure. She seeks out teachers spontaneously, and so I know she will ask for more beads after she uses up a small supply. Because she shows progress in mastering the communication objectives, I can begin to work on moving her up academically by letting her choose between certain colors. *"Terry, this bead is red; this bead is blue. Which do you want?"*

I turn my attention to Jim. He is unable to verbalize at all and is working on the first developmental objectives, attending to any stimuli, being aware. To achieve any looking or holding of the beads will be a victory for him. I take his hands in mine and stroke them softly. He responds to this. I begin, very softly, to say, *"Bead,"* in a singsong pattern. I think he hears me, so I slip the bead in his hand, close his fingers around it, and rub again. I feel his fingers tighten around the bead, then he releases the grasp. This procedure is repeated several times until we connect the bead and hand in his field of vision. When he shows some indication that eye and bead have met, I repeat the wire-and bead-stringing demonstration just for him. I show "bead" each time in front of him. No response. I continue to hold and to stroke his hands. Then I take his hand to thread the bead! *"Good, Jim. See the bead."* The action is repeated. Each time, I pull back slightly to encourage Jim in sustaining the act on his own.

Such children may lose interest at any point, and it is up to Miss Anne and me to continually redirect each child back into the activity. Moving close to a child might be just enough to help him continue. Offering another bead directly in front of him, at eye level, or placing my hands over the child's to help thread the bead may keep him in touch with the experience. As the child becomes involved again, a word of praise may be all that is needed to let him know we are here. Pulling back, allowing the child to respond on his own is therapeutically effective and certainly encourages sustained attending.

Because four minutes have now elapsed and each child has had some satisfying contact with the teachers and materials, it is up to me to end the lesson. *"Art time is nearly over. Terry, put beads in the box. Tony, give beads to Miss Anne. Jim, give me beads."* As each child follows the request as best he can, I gather all the supplies back into the box. As a part of doing this, I praise and touch each child. *"Miss Anne, art time is over."* Miss Anne responds, *"Goodbye, goodbye,"* and waves. Terry has learned this ending and spontaneously joins in. The others wave. Miss Anne guides the children into the next activity as I leave the room. The lesson took eight minutes.

For simple beadwork the children need a lot of individual attention at this stage. It also requires a high degree of effervescence and interest on the part of the teachers to beguile the children into staying interested in each step.

Paint can be used in the same way. The teacher offers a small container of paint to each child with the spoken word, *"Paint."* Then a brush and paper, described with a single word, are given out. Each child gives the necessary response to obtain the supplies. The teacher demonstrates dipping the brush in color and making a line on the paper. The teacher would offer the brush to a child with the question, *"What do you want?"* Or she may ask a child to identify the brush or water or paper only with eye contact or a verbal approximation. As each child participates to the degree he is capable, the teacher encourages continued exploration of the brush across the paper. Intermittently the teacher may have to redemonstrate dipping the brush in the color. Each time the teacher restructures the activity, she pulls back to allow the child opportunity to continue on his own.

Painting does not always motivate children at Stage One, but there is value in holding a brush, directing it into a limited area (the container of color), and watching the color appear on the paper. These processes can be useful in determining his manipulative abilities, eye-hand coordination, and awareness of his surroundings. It also stimulates awareness of himself as a person who makes something occur in his environment.

These general procedures result in developmental progress, and before long the teacher will be working on new, more advanced developmental objectives. When this occurs the teacher's techniques and procedures also change.

The following pages contain suggestions for using many standard art materials successfully with Stage One children. The activities are listed alphabetically. Specific development objectives for individual children can be accom-

B-1
to react to sensory stimulus by attending toward source of stimulus by body response or by looking.

A-16
to perform fine motor coordination activities at the three-four-year level. Child must master at least two skills in order to master objective.

B-4
to respond with motor and body responses to complex environmental and verbal stimuli (through imitation, "Do this"; through completion of verbal direction; minimal participation in the routine; given physical intervention and verbal cues).

S-1
to be aware of others.

plished in each of these activities. However, each teacher or therapist must be cognizant of which developmental objectives are needed for each child and make necessary adaptations to those individual differences. The Developmental Therapy Objectives and Rating Form (DTORF) contained in the Appendix is a method for obtaining such information. The DTORF, used at five-week intervals, also permits you to adjust your lessons to new developmental objectives as a child increases in skills. Perhaps most important, you have a record of the child's developmental progress (or regression) in behavior, communication, socialization, and preacademics druing the time you work with him.

All of the techniques, materials, and activities used by teachers of Stage One children should be envisioned in this context. The principle is: take a child's basic (or random) response and, through sensory-arousing materials and intervention techniques, help the child to utilize his existing response and extend it into new applications and elaborations. This implies a variety of sequential experiences that are elaborations on the child's basic responses. It is at this point that the developmental hierarchy comes into major significance. Each step of this experience should be a bit more elaborate, exciting, and complex than the one before.

ART ACTIVITIES FOR STAGE ONE

Medium	Special Preparation	Suggested Content	Step-by-Step Motivation
Acrylics *Art Appreciation*	Not applicable at this stage Select several dynamic prints showing simple figures, flowers, landscapes, or abstractions that can be used to stimulate looking (e.g., a Miro print). *Note:* This lesson should be used late in Stage One when some degree of responsiveness has been developed.	Simple, stimulating	1. Show a picture; then cover it up! What did they see? Was there an animal? A person? What colors do they remember in the picture? 2. Show picture again and point out answers to your questions. 3. Praise good verbalization or eye contact. Reward attentiveness and responses with touch and positive verbal reinforcements.
Batik	Not applicable at this stage		
Beadwork	You will need: 1. Plastic-coated telephone wire, with a knot at one end. 2. Large beads easily pierced by the wire.	Necklaces; wall decorations; or wind chimes	1. Hand out plastic-coated wires after verbal or eye response from each child. 2. Supply of beads to each child. For more responses, hand out each bead after appropriate verbal or eye contact. 3. Reflect each effort, e.g., *"George has yellow bead."* 4. When child fills wire, teacher ties ends together to make necklace. Help child put it on and take child to mirror to admire it and beautiful self, e.g., *"Joe has a lovely necklace! He looks happy!"*
Candlemaking	Not applicable at this stage		
Cast Stone	Not applicable at this stage		
Charcoal	Not applicable at this stage		
Clay *Lesson 1:* *Exploring*	You will need: 1. Palm-size amounts of clay in damp cloths or in plastic container ready for each student. 2. Pencils. 3. Wet towels ready to clean up. 4. Bucket of water and paper towels to clean table.	Discover feel of clay: roll, mash, pull, create logs or balls	1. Depending on degree of children's response, they can just "finger" it or manipulate it without further directions. Help can be given to roll logs or balls of different sizes. 2. Teacher demonstrates how to tear clay apart (dramatically) in two pieces; then smash them together in the air. 3. Use music in class to set up rhythm to pound by!

(continued)

ART ACTIVITIES FOR STAGE ONE (continued)

Medium	Special Preparation	Suggested Content	Step-by-Step Motivation
Clay *Lesson 1* *(cont.)*	5. Record player and records with a definite simple rhythm pattern (marches or pop tunes).		*Note:* If any products come out of class, these can be fired and brought into class for a later lesson and painted with water-color paint! However, this is usually more successful at Stage Two.
Clay *Lesson 2:* *Slab work*	You will need: 1. A different cookie cutter for each child. 2. $\frac{1}{2}''$ to $\frac{3}{4}''$ individual slabs of clay for each child. (Can be made on bread boards and carried into class for art time.) 3. Pencil for each child. *Note:* If class is highly responsive, each child can be given clay and rolling pin to make *own* slab. Have wet towels to clean up.	Cookie-cut shapes for pendants or three-dimensional pictures	1. Teacher can demonstrate procedure, then motivate each child to cut his designs. 2. Use pencil to make designs on slab. Hold child's hand, if necessary, to begin contact of pencil with clay.
Collage	You will need: 1. Color poster board or white tag board for each child (minimum size 9″ × 12″). 2. Rug scraps, cotton puffs, macaroni, etc. 3. A plastic bottle of glue for each child (2-oz. size, opened). 4. Scissors, if child can use them (left or righthand needed). 5. Crayons. (Children who work fast can be given crayons to draw on, around, or in between the glued objects to make an even more exciting design!)	Free design	1. Hand out poster board or tag board as child requests through eye contact, sound, or word, according to development. 2. Have a large box of many rug scraps, cotton, fabrics, etc. 3. Children make their own selection from box. This can be repeated many times. 4. Hand out glue to children after obtaining requested responses. 5. Praise first child who makes a move to put glue on paper or objects. Again respond when objects are glued down. 6. Hand out additional materials (scissors or crayons) upon request or to motivate further participation.
Copper Enameling	Not applicable at this stage		
Crayon	You will need: 1. Broken, unwrapped pieces of crayon (use all colors). 2. White drawing paper, any size. *Note:* Some children find regular-size crayons very satisfactory, while others do best with large primary crayons.	Scribbling, free choice or specific subjects	1. In early lessons, children can be given only one crayon and have additional crayons given either to remotivate, increase interest in art work, or to ask for different colors. 2. After child is "hooked" on this art experience, present child with two colors and ask child to make a choice.

(continued)

Medium	Special Preparation	Suggested Content	Step-by-Step Motivation
Crayon *(cont.)*			*"Joe, what color do you want?"* If child does not respond, offer verbal model by saying each color and extending crayon toward child as you name it. *"Do you want red* [extend red crayon] *or yellow* [extend yellow crayon]*?"* If child motions to one, names it, or attempts to make choice, acknowledge attempt warmly and place crayon in hand. In time, child needs to take crayon from you or say, *"Color."* 3. For higher Stage One children, give child a box of crayons to remove colors himself as he works alone.
Crayon Resist	You will need: 1. A *dark* color tempera (watery consistency). 2. #10 water color brush for each child. 3. Unwrapped crayons. (Remove crayon of same color as paint, e.g., when using black paint remove all black crayons!) 4. Smaller than usual size art paper to make the painting go quickly ($8\frac{1}{2}'' \times 11''$). *Note:* This lesson is most effective if children are showing some responses and attempting controlled scribbling.	Free design; controlled scribbling	1. Teacher demonstrates how to press hard with crayon. Do a dramatic quick drawing (white outline of ghost; yellow striped fish). 2. Verbalize action while dipping brush in paint, spreading over crayon work to make "resist." (*"I dip brush, I paint paper! Wow! See fish."*) 3. Each child is given paper and asked what crayon he wants. 4. If a child makes a single mark and stops, redirect quickly, *"Joe wants paint."* Provide brush and begin painting motion. Leave brush in his hand to see if he continues on his own. If not, give him another sheet of paper and try again. Continue procedure until end of art time.
Craypas	Use the same procedures as those for using crayons, but craypas are smoother to work with, provide different tactile experiences, and give brighter colors.		
Craypas Resist	Same procedures as with crayon resist		
Découpage	Not applicable at this stage		
Diorama	Not applicable at this stage		
Etching	Not applicable at this stage		

(continued)

ART ACTIVITIES FOR STAGE ONE (continued)

Medium	Special Preparation	Suggested Content	Step-by-Step Motivation

Finger Painting	You will need on different days:
	1. One color for class in early weeks; later, two colors.
	2. Newspaper spread on work area.
	3. Finger paint paper for each child.
	4. One container of water for your use.
	5. Wet towels to clean up.
	6. Smocks or coverups for children.
		Free experiment with finger paint	1. Teacher demonstrates with one sheet of paper. Show water to each child. *"What is this?" "Wa-wa,"* offers child. *"Right! Water! Put water on paper."* (Pour it from a foot high to *ensure* it splashing on the children and you!) *"That feels good!"* as you spread it.
			    Show paint to each child. *"What is this?" "Wa-wa, paint." "Good talking, Joe." "What color is this?"* No response. *"It's blue."*
			    Reach in jar and spread it on paper.
			2. Then help children to participate in activity.
			3. Place blob of color on wet sheets for each child. As children become "hooked" on lesson, let child reach into jar to get his own paint. Finally give each child a closed jar to allow *him* to open jar, get paint, close jar to end art time.
			Note: The amount of response necessary for each child is based on his *developmental* level. Extended verbal explanation would not be effective in early lessons with extremely delayed children. The higher the developmental level, the longer the activity.

Leathercraft	Not applicable at this stage		
Lettering	Not applicable at this stage		
Macramé	Not applicable at this stage		
Magic Markers	You will need: 1. Large sheets of white paper (18″ × 24″). 2. Magic markers with caps removed. 3. Record player and sprightly music.	Random marks, scribbling, line drawing, or specific shapes; with or without music	1. Magic markers are especially easy to use. Usually just placing it in the child's hand will motivate action. 2. Teacher can physically move a child to use markers or verbally suggest shapes, figures, or lines (wiggly, straight, skinny). 3. After repeated lessons, give child the marker with top on to allow him to get it off and place on end with or without help. Require child to make color choices, exchange colors, replace tops, etc.

(continued)

Medium	Special Preparation	Suggested Content	Step-by-Step Motivation
Magic Markers (cont.)			4. Music can increase responses and designs.
Metal Work	Not applicable at this stage		
Mixed Media	You will need: 1. Several types of art media for each child (e.g., one child has a crayon and a blue magic marker; second child has black tempera with brush and a red crayon, etc.). 2. Different sizes of papers for each child (e.g., give a large 18″ × 24″ sheet first, then an 8½″ × 11″ sheet, etc.).	Free design or specific subject	1. Teacher must carefully prepare each child *verbally* for lesson because two media can be overwhelming. Set up structure so they can use both or only one. (It's an experiment!!!!) 2. Help children begin lesson with one medium and verbally attempt to motivate them into using the second. *Note:* It is imperative that the children will have used all the art materials at some previous time so they are familiar with each. This activity is suitable for children at advanced Stage One.
Mobiles	You will need: 1. A collection of various materials for each child to choose from (e.g., styrofoam balls, ribbons, costume jewelry, cotton balls, Christmas ornaments, leaves). 2. A large multi-branched branch or hangers put together in X shape with tape for "mobile" base. 3. String with ornament hook at end for each child to hang his chosen objects on mobile.	Free choice	1. Have supplies ready and give string with hooks to each child. 2. Child selects and requests object and attaches hook to it (with help when necessary). 3. Child comes to *mobile* (hanging so each child can reach it) and selects place for his object. 4. Repeat as often as time and motivation allow 5. All touch and move finished mobile!
Model Building	Not applicable at this stage		
Mosaics (precut)	You will need: 1. Assorted color paper squares, precut 1″ × 1″ in open box. 2. Glue (individual 2-oz. bottles). 3. Sheets of colored construction paper for base. 4. Record player and records with good rhythm can be added for repeated lesson.	Free design (with or without music)	1. Teacher demonstrates how to put one drop of glue on one mosaic. Place down on paper. Repeat. *"Who wants paper? Glue?"* 2. Hand out construction paper or glue as each child requests it. 3. Let each child reach in box and take his supply of mosaics. If more response is required, hand out one at a time, upon request from each child. 4. Any design is acceptable. 5. If music is used, "slap" mosaic down in tune to music.

(continued)

ART ACTIVITIES FOR STAGE ONE (continued)

Medium	Special Preparation	Suggested Content	Step-by-Step Motivation
Natural Materials (pebbles, shells, leaves, flowers)	You will need: 1. A collection of natural materials. Children may gather them over a period of time outside. 2. Sheets of tag board or poster board, any size. 3. A dark color enamel or flat spray paint (black is most dramatic on white paper). 4. Newspaper for spray paint area.	Print a free design	1. Gathering process can be during outside recess periods. Children may gather materials, or you can bring a variety of materials for the children to choose from. 2. Glue several pieces down for demonstration or teacher can arrange a selection and spray it ahead of time. 3. Help each child request supplies and arrange their designs. 4. Children help to spray their work. 5. After spraying, help child to dump off materials to "see the print."
Oil Paints	Not applicable at this stage		
Papier Mâché	Not applicable at this stage		
Pastels (color chalk) Lesson 1 Dry method	You will need: 1. Large sheets of color construction paper for each child (18″ × 24″). 2. Box of pastels. 3. Smocks or large button-up front shirts to cover children's clothes. 4. Wet towels to clean up. *Note:* This is an excellent activity for very delayed Stage One children.	Free design, specific shapes, or lines	1. Show chalk to children demonstrating how to draw with it: flat on its side or held like a pencil. 2. Help children to request chalk. 3. Early in program, place chalk in child's hand and help child to make marks. As progress is shown, let child take chalk from you. Later, place box of chalk in front of each child and see if he will remove his choice and draw by himself. 4. Praise positive action and physically move nonresponding children through the experience with nurturing verbalizations.
Pastels (color chalk) Lesson 2 Wet method	You will need: Same as in Lesson 1, but with a container of water for teacher to use as described in finger painting lesson.	Same as Lesson 1	1. Same as Lesson 1, but add water to paper before chalk work begins. 2. Show children how to spread water with hand. This added tactile experience is very motivating to Stage One children.
Pen and Ink	Not applicable at this stage		
Pencil	You will need: 1. Various sizes of papers available for each child (2″ × 3″, 8½″ × 11″, 12″ × 20″, 18″ × 24″).	Scribbling, making wavy lines, straight lines, round lines, etc.	1. Teacher can talk about being a good "Scribbler." 2. Demonstrate scribbling slowly, rapidly, and with eyes closed!

(continued)

ART ACTIVITIES FOR STAGE ONE (continued)

Medium	Special Preparation	Suggested Content	Step-by-Step Motivation
Pencil *(cont.)*	2. Soft lead pencils for each child (extra in case lead breaks). *Note:* Use size pencil most easily handled by each child. Some children do best with a regular #2, while the large primary pencils might suit others.		3. Help children to request paper and pencil. 4. Praise and touch children who begin scribbling. As soon as individual child fills one page, give a second sheet and allow child to begin again and again and again. 5. Children unable to respond can have their hand moved through the activity with pencil in place. Then leave pencil in child's hand. Can he do one by himself? Give a new sheet to each child as any response is given on the paper. If child still does not respond, praise him for *looking* at the sheet—and the way he can hold the pencil by himself! 6. When children do respond, direct the activity, *"Can you scribble fast? Good! Slowly? Good! I like your design. Did you know you made that while you were scribbling?"* etc.
Plaster	Not applicable at this stage		
Play-plax *(crystal climbers)*	You will need: Enough cylinders, squares, and circles for each child to have a good supply of each shape. *Note:* This activity is for very high Stage One children who can manipulate objects well. It is more appropriate to Stage Two.	Three-dimensional free experimentation	1. Teacher demonstrates "connecting" process. 2. Explain how difficult this process is and say that you will help anyone who needs help. 3. Help children request plastic. After response, give "plastics" and start child on building. If child finishes, then give more to keep working or give one at a time so that child has opportunity for frequent requests. 4. To end this activity or for a child not responding, show him how to hold it up in front of his eye and look at the world through red or blue or yellow plastic!
Pliable Plastics or Plexiglass	Not applicable at this stage		
Printing Lesson 1 Sponge print	You will need: 1. Simple tag board stencils previously made by teachers of any interesting simple shapes.	Any pattern	1. Show materials to children and hand out stencils and paper to each child as he requests. 2. Demonstrate and verbally direct

(continued)

Medium	Special Preparation	Suggested Content	Step-by-Step Motivation
Printing Lesson 1 (cont.)	(Christmas tree, animals, flowers, geometrics.) 2. White drawing paper for each child, any size. 3. One container of tempera paint (thick consistency). Later, each child has an individual container. 4. Moist sponge (natural, palm-size is best) for each child. 5. Wet paper towels to clean up. *Note:* Very delayed Stage One children will have difficulty with this lesson.		children to place stencil over white paper (help those who cannot do this). 3. Help children to request sponge. 4. Demonstrate and verbally direct children to dip sponge into paint and then dab it through stencil with one hand while holding stencil down with other. 5. When no white paper is showing through stencil, ask child to put down sponge on table, lift up his stencil, and see his print! 6. This activity can be repeated on new paper or stencils exchanged if children's interest is held.
Printing Lesson 2 String print	You will need: 1. Several lengths of wrapping string for each child. 2. One bowl of thick tempera. (More than one color for higher objectives.) 3. White paper, 18″ X 24″.	Free design or specific shape	1. Dip one string in paint and name the supplies as you go through the demonstration. 2. Lay string on one part of paper in any manner. Fold paper in half, pressing the string in between. Show the print! 3. Help each child to ask for supplies. 4. Provide assistance as needed to each child as they go through the process. 5. Repeat with new string and different colors if class is responsive.
Printing Lesson 3 Vegetable prints	You will need: 1. Different vegetables (potato, turnip, carrot, bell pepper, etc.). 2. A paring knife. 3. One container of tempera (thick consistency). 4. #10 brush for each child. 5. Heavy-duty paper for each child (construction or water color quality). 6. Paper towels.	Repetitive design	1. Demonstrate by slicing vegetable sideways. Dry vegetable with paper towel. Paint cut surface with brush and print by pressing design on paper. 2. Distribute brush to each child. 3. Cut vegetables and give one to each child. 4. Help them to start painting their vegetable surface. 5. When their vegetable is ready, give sheet of paper and remove brush. Hold child's hand (which holds painted vegetable) and gently press design. React. Let child do it by himself. React to his doing it by himself! Hopefully, child will repeat action.

(continued)

ART ACTIVITIES FOR STAGE ONE (continued)

Medium	Special Preparation	Suggested Content	Step-by-Step Motivation
Printing *Lesson 3* *(cont.)*			6. Encourage repeated movement until paper is filled. *Note:* Advanced Stage One children should make choice of vegetable and exchange paints and vegetables for more exciting prints after first attempt.
Rubbings	Not applicable at this stage		
Sand Castings	Not applicable at this stage		
Sand Designing	You will need: 1. Sand or gravel. (Different colors may be used. If different colors of sand are not available, fish bowl gravel may be used.) 2. Sheet of tag board for each child. 3. Bowl of watery glue for each child. 4. A #12 brush for each child. 5. Empty shoe boxes for each color of gravel or sand.	Free design	1. Demonstrate how to paint "design" with brush dipped in glue and brushed on tag board. Reach into box containing gravel and sprinkle on entire sheet. Pick up paper gently with both hands; let excess sand spill off into empty shoe box. 2. Help children to ask for supplies. 3. React to each child's beautiful design. 4. Repeat procedure with children as often as time allows and interest remains.
Sensory Lessons	You will need materials for each sense: *Taste*—candy, spices, fruit, instant pudding, etc. *Hearing*—records, sounds outside, water dripping, lights clicking on, etc. *Smell*—familiar foods, soaps, toothpaste, etc. *Touch*—fabrics, cotton balls, sponges, etc. *Note:* These lessons are particularly successful with severely delayed Stage One children.	Focus on the sensory aspects of the material	These lessons are limited only by the imagination and resources of the teacher; e.g., *taste*—finger paint with instant pudding; *smell*—sprinkle oregano over a glue covered sheet to make a design; *hearing*—crumple aluminum foil, fold styrofoam plates or tear newspaper; *touch*—make a "feelie" collage with steel wool, velvet scraps, balsa wood shavings, or sponge pieces.
Shell Jewelry	Not applicable at this stage		
Soap Carving	Not applicable at this stage		

(continued)

ART ACTIVITIES FOR STAGE ONE (continued)

Medium	Special Preparation	Suggested Content	Step-by-Step Motivation
Stitchery	Not applicable at this stage		
Styrofoam *(and toothpicks)*	You will need: 1. Assorted styrofoam shapes ($\frac{1}{2}''$ to 5" size). 2. Multi-colored toothpicks. 3. One large block of styrofoam as a base for each child's work (2" × 2" × 6" approximately). *Note:* This lesson has considerable flexibility for adapting to a wide range of skills within a group.	Free shapes and design	1. Show how to put one toothpick into a piece of styrofoam. Connect it to a second piece. Then take a second toothpick, and stick it into a base so that the two smaller pieces can be attached. 2. Give each child a base. Then help each child request "foam" and "picks." Give out one or two items at a time. 3. As a child uses materials, motivate him to request additional supplies by holding them within reach. You may have to redemonstrate the basic motor movements for individual children. 4. End the lesson when all children have had some success with process and have connected at least two pieces to the base.
Tempera Paint *Lesson 1* *Hand prints or foot prints*	You will need: 1. Large sheets of white paper on floor for each child. 2. One container of a primary color (red, yellow, or blue) mixed with some liquid soap. Liquid soap will allow the paint to be easily washed off skin! Use approximately $\frac{1}{4}$ cup of soap to one pint of paint. 3. One large, flat bristle brush #12 or #18 for teacher's use. 4. Wet paper towels, or cloth and basin ready to clean up. 5. Record player and march records. *Note:* This is a very arousing activity!	Paint hands or soles of feet of each child to make "prints" (with or without music)	1. As dramatically as possible, remove your own shoe, paint the sole of your own foot surface. Describe what you are doing and feeling. (Hand prints can be used in a previous lesson if the group needs to ease into this activity.) 2. Make as many prints as one coat of paint allows as you march to music on paper! 3. Wipe off your own foot; replace shoe. 4. Ask children to take off their shoes. In turn, as the shoes come off, paint each child's feet and encourage each child to walk on his paper. 5. A child finishes when the paper is filled with prints. 6. Each child is helped through process of making prints while another teacher washes off each child's foot or hands.
Tempera Paint *Lesson 2* *Brush painting*	You will need: 1. One open container of color (if children are working on high Stage One objectives, have a different color paint for each child in a	Free painting	1. Hold up each material, name it, and demonstrate how paint is used. If using more than one color, name each color as you hand it to a child; or if any child can request a specific color, grant

(continued)

Medium	Special Preparation	Suggested Content	Step-by-Step Motivation
Tempera Paint *Lesson 2 (cont.)*	sturdy container). A cut-off milk carton or coffee can is ideal. 2. A #12 brush for each child. 3. White drawing paper (18″ × 24″) for each child. *Note:* This activity is particularly successful with severely delayed Stage One children and may be among the first activities to reveal developmental progress		request with additional praise and touch. 2. Help each child to request supplies and assist in beginning use of the three materials. 3. If a child does not respond, physically move the child's fist through random marks, scribbles, circle face, or any design you can verbalize with special meaning for the child (e.g., *"You have a yellow shirt. You are painting with yellow paint!"*) Also reflect the painting process as you help a child to paint (e.g., *"Dip your brush into the purple paint. Wipe it off. Now, paint lines."*). Help the child to feel the movement as the brush glides along the paper. 4. As the children's responses increase and indicate more awareness, change colors of paints at one-minute intervals. This stimulates more exciting designs and mixing of colors. If children can request different colors, encourage this skill. Always supervise change. Recognize and praise new designs, and if a new color is mixed, praise the child's discovery!
Tempera Paint *Lesson 3* *Body painting*	You will need: 1. One container of tempera paint mixed with liquid soap (see Tempera paint lesson 1). (Finger paint can be substituted because it washes off best.) 2. A mirror. 3. One #6 water color brush for teacher's use. 4. Wet paper towels or basin and water ready to clean up. *Note:* This activity should be used with considerable caution. Children can be traumatized by such an experience. A good lesson to precede this would be hand or foot prints.	Hand or face painting, Indian war paint, or African mask designs	1. Show children pictures of painted Indian faces or African masks. 2. Demonstrate by first painting your own face or the most responsive child's. (Painting hands is less frightening than the face for some children.) 3. Describe how paint feels on skin, how different designs can be made: lines, triangles, circles, spots. 4. Wash paint off to show that all will be O.K. 5. Paint design on each child or motivate him to do it himself. 6. Help each child to see his own results in mirror. 7. Assist children in clean up.
Tempera Paint *Lesson 4* *Music painting*	You will need: 1. Various styles of music pretaped or	Paint to music	1. Begin with music that has strong beat (march or rock and roll).

(continued)

ART ACTIVITIES FOR STAGE ONE (continued)

Medium	Special Preparation	Suggested Content	Step-by-Step Motivation
Tempera Paint *Lesson 4 (cont.)*	records (jazz, rock and roll, classical, gospel, etc.). 2. One sturdy container of paint for teacher. 3. One #6 brush for each child. 4. Several sheets of paper for each child (18″ × 24″ or smaller).		2. Demonstrate dabbing paint to the music as dramatically as possible. Stop music. 3. Help children to request paint and paper. 4. Repeat some music and lead group through lesson with dabbing process again. 5. As paper fills up, give child a new sheet. 6. If children can stand, move to music and paint at the same time for a multi-coordinated activity.
Tie-dyeing	Not applicable at this stage		
Tissue Paper Design	You will need: 1. Tag board (or any heavy-weight paper) precut for each child (approximately 9″ × 12″; in unusual shapes). 2. Bowl of watery glue for each child. 3. #10 brush for each child. 4. Assorted colored sheets of tissue. *Note:* This lesson can be adapted to a wide range of individual skill levels at all stages.	Tear and glue	1. Give glue, tag board, and brush to each child. 2. Encourage children in painting glue on tag board in any manner as long as it covers the paper. 3. Collect brushes and glue. 4. Show colored tissue sheets. Help each child to request paper or color according to his ability. 5. Demonstrate tearing sheet and encourage them to tear any way they want. 6. When sheets are torn, lead children in placing each torn piece on glue surface to make design. *Note:* If response level is high enough, children could change colors by exchanging with others or asking teacher for new colors. If children are working on low objective, do tearing together first, then glue pieces down.
Vocational Art Studies	Not applicable at this stage		
Water Colors	Not applicable at this stage		
Wire or Pipe Cleaners and Spray Paint	You will need: 1. 8″ to 12″ lengths of wire or pipe cleaners. (Have many extra pieces	Twisting shapes and designs	1. Hand out wire. As soon as each child has a piece, demonstrate how to wrap it around fingers (corkscrew effect), bend

(continued)

Medium	Special Preparation	Suggested Content	Step-by-Step Motivation
Wire or Pipe Cleaners and Spray Paint (cont.)	available in different colors if possible.) 2. One can of gold or silver spray paint. 3. Newspaper to cover floor for spraying.		it, tie it. (This may be enough for the first lesson.) 2. After each child responds to wire with some degree of manipulation, help them place it on the newspaper and step back. 3. Either the teacher or the child with teacher's help sprays it gold. 4. Activity can be repeated if children express interest. 5. If a child does not respond, wrap wire around child's hand or finger in a playful manner (*"Joe, we are using wire today."*) Then ask everyone to hand you their left-over wire! Joe should respond in just getting it off his finger.
Wood Structures	Not applicable at this stage		
Woodwork	Not applicable at this stage		
Yarn Design	Not applicable at this stage		

chapter 3
STAGE TWO: LEARNING SKILLS THAT BRING SUCCESS

Each child was given a precut mask shape and any scraps of colored paper he selected to make a monster face. The mask shape was used upside down in this creative work because the child felt it was "better that way."

The one thing Joey wants to do is color so it will look smooth and pretty. When he enrolled in our Stage Two class, this severely deprived six-year-old boy was preoccupied with the idea that no one would be pleased with him until he could color like other children. So simple and mundane an exercise for most children, coloring came slowly and painfully for Joey. Considerable learning disability and neurological dysfunction made coloring nearly impossible at first. With each uneven line there were frustration and anger. The strokes did not look smooth and pretty to him. He could not control them inside the line!

I plan every art lesson to provide manipulation of various art materials in ways to bring success. But no matter what lesson he did, successfully or not, Joey wanted to end his art time with coloring.

So often in planning art lessons for Stage Two children, ditto coloring sheets and predrawn shapes are the least beneficial to a child's exploration of his world. Yet with Joey, coloring well on predrawn designs was important to him, and so his continued "practice" was encouraged each day. I kept a supply of dittos for him. Gradually, as mastery of developmental objectives occurred, his coloring improved. He was the first to point it out, even though he used negative approaches, *"You don't want to put this up do you?"; "I bet no one here saw my dog I colored?"; "I'm just going to throw this away, O.K.?"*

Before he left our center to return to school full-time, he brought a folded-up paper for me to see . . . a carefully colored pink puppy. Joey asked if I could put it up for all the kids to see. "It's the best I did."

The Child at Stage Two

Stage Two spans the developmental period associated with the toddler and preschool years, approximately ages two to five. The overall theme of this phase of development is one of learning individual skills for responding to the environment with success. During Stage Two, a child is moving from the safety and protection of dependency to *autonomy* and increasing independence. Erikson (1963) describes autonomy as the phase of personality development when the individual has developed a sense of himself as an individual with some basic capacity to accomplish and master simple situations. The culmination of the Stage Two experience is the development of *initiative*. At this phase, the child's newly acquired skills in language and locomotion equip him for new demands to be "more himself." Mussen, Conger, and Kagan (1969) describe this phase of development as one in which the child learns to master his impulses and fears, sees fantasy and reality as different, and learns about himself in relation to parents and peers. As a part of these accomplishments, a child must struggle with his own impulsivity and unpolished, aggressive characteristics. Loevinger (1976) describes this struggle as one in which the child's demands are for immediate gratifications and people are seen as needs providers. Emotional responses are usually physically expressed and most experiences are seen as "good" or "bad."

The Toddler

There are two predominant themes during the development of the toddler[1]: 1) changes from dependence to inde-

---

[1] The term "toddler" is used as a label for the developmental activities normally occurring around ages two to three years.

pendence in relation to other people, and 2) exploring and manipulating the environment around them. These two themes are closely related. It is easy to see how exploration and manipulation of objects lead to increased skill, greater independence, and decreased dependence. At the same time, however, the toddler's need for adult approval and attention is a clear indication that his dependent needs are far from met. It is from the safety of his dependence upon adults that the toddler learns successful exploration and pleasurable results. When these two processes combine in a balance between protection and independence, the toddler develops autonomy. While the toddler is developing a sense of self, he is learning that he needs and enjoys adults. He also is learning that he is able to explore on his own.

The developmental milestones the toddler masters can be grouped under four major headings: 1) communication, 2) socialization, 3) large-muscle skills, and 4) fine-muscle skills.

Communication Activities for the toddler in the area of communication have to do with those processes which help him to express himself: "me" and "mine." His communication efforts go into the process of remembering, of learning words and meaning, in order to facilitate his explorations. Before the toddler reaches three years, he has mastered approximately 500 to 700 words. He is using pronouns, adverbs, adjectives, prepositions, possessive form, and plurals. He delights particularly in stories that describe himself or use his name. Keep in mind that all of this focus on self is an attempt to validate himself. The child is trying to find out exactly who and what he is. He uses three to four phrases at a time to elaborate and express. He is able to follow several directions at a time, particularly those involved with moving objects from one

place to another. He knows the uses of objects; he knows body parts; he is able to look at pictures and associate certain words with the pictures. All of these activities are facilitated and enjoyed when they are done with significant adults. These are usually the adults in his family and those upon whom he has depended.

Socialization Socialization for the toddler is focused around doing things with adults. The toddler learns to express affection: to kiss, to smile, and to express other basic feelings such as anger, frustration, and uncertainty.

With other children, he engages in solitary or parallel play and as he emerges from the toddler stage he begins interactive play. Primarily, however, his attention is directed toward adults. Perhaps most significant of all, socialization during the toddler phase is through imitation. The toddler learns a great deal from imitating adult actions, from the smallest response to more complex patterns of responding.

Large-muscle Skills Exploring and manipulating the world around him is done through large and fine muscles. Large muscles generally focus upon concepts about "how I work." Again, the child is trying to learn more about himself; in this case, expressing himself through motion. Movement is perhaps the most significant part of large-muscle experiences. Here, body-in-space movements are refined and become tools for success. Rhythmic motions are particularly pleasant for the toddler. During exploratory and rhythmic experiences he is learning to organize sensory inputs. He is learning to connect what he feels to things he sees, hears, and tastes. Other significant muscle milestones include throwing a ball, kicking a ball, going down stairs, and assisting in the dressing process. In short, the large muscles all provide him with a more effective means for exploring and manipulating the world around him with success.

Fine-muscle Skills The fine muscles show him "how things work." Among the most significant processes occurring early in this stage of development is the toddler's learning about object permanence, that is, objects exist even if they disappear from view. This process begins during the first year of life but develops in finer detail during the toddler phase. Like the infant, the toddler is interested in pursuing disappearing objects. But now the toddler will seek them out in a hiding place.

There are many manipulative activities that the toddler is able to master, such as stringing beads, turning pages of books, stacking six to eight blocks, imitating horizontal and vertical lines in pencil with simple strokes, using a spoon and cup successfully, filling containers and emptying them out again, and assisting in dressing, toileting, and washing hands.

Summary Keep in mind the major effort of the toddler: learning to use himself, his body, and his feelings. His explorations and assertions are attempts to validate himself. The more confident he becomes in himself, the more he will tend to explore and to assert himself. This healthy assertion of will is often misinterpreted by adults as a "negative period." Actually, this is an important step forward, verifying himself and his own individuality. With the toddler, this assertion is directed toward his family . . . those people he has learned to trust and to depend upon.

The Preschooler

There are two predominant themes in the preschooler's[2] development: 1) the fears and fantasy of his inner life, and

---

[2] The term "preschooler" is used to label the developmental activities normally occurring between three and five years of age.

2) a drive for increasing social contacts among peers and other adults in his outer life. The predominant reason for fears among children at this stage is the expectations placed on them by adults to suppress and redirect instincts. As the child is exposed to increasing expectations and rules in the world around him, he must continually put brakes on his own drives and learn new, more complex responses. As this is done it increases intrapsychic anxiety, perhaps for two reasons: 1) concern about how he will express the drive, and 2) concern about acceptance by significant adults if he fails to produce at the expected standard.

Fantasy is the preschooler's solution to this problem. Through fantasy, the child can express all of his uneasy feelings about growing up. He can direct the responsibility for situations onto something, some object outside of himself. There, in fantasy, all of the terrible possibilities that might occur can be safely considered. Imaginary friends, whether they be people or animals, provide a private means for a preschool child to blame, love, or experience his fears and needs vicariously.

If you look back to the toddler phase, you can readily understand why the preschooler is so caught up in these scary new horizons. The toddler has developed minimal skill and has learned to explore and to master the basics in the immediate world around him. The next obvious step for the preschooler is to move out and to conquer new realities, learn about new people, and learn about himself in new situations. Because his body is also more skilled and proficient, he is able to give more time to conditions outside of himself and less time to mastering and moving his own body. For this reason one often thinks of the preschooler phase as being one of aggression, but the aggression usually is indicative of unrefined initiative.

Communication Remember the toddler was learning the basic communication skills, trying to express himself. Now the preschooler is learning to use his basic verbal skills for verbal assertion, questioning "why." He is able to define words, knows opposites, and can tell "why." He uses his verbal statements aggressively and often is involved in name calling of peers. It is easy to see how his verbal skills and communication are used to cope with the fears and fantasies of this period of development.

Socialization Where the toddler was concerned with imitating significant adults in his family, the preschool child is experimenting with competitive interaction among peers and family. His interactions are an attempt to resolve his own anxieties and fears about himself and to see the limitations in his own ability. Play for the four-year-old is interactive; that is, children will share and respond occasionally, but basically they are interested in their own projects. By age five, play is cooperative; that is, children are playing together for a common purpose. Around this time the best-friend concept emerges. However, best friends change rather rapidly. Another important part of the aggressive drive of the preschooler is manifest through peer and sibling jealousies. Again this is an attempt of the child to protect himself from all sorts of imaginary fears related to finding his place among family and peers.

Accepting regulations and rules is another very difficult part of socialization for the preschool child. The expectations of others have increased, and again his acceptance and commitment to accepting game rules signals maturation of socialization for this stage. Dramatic play and make-believe are characteristic ways preschoolers resolve these many, complex relations.

Large-muscle Skills In the area of large muscles, social aggression is mani-fest through physical aggression. At this stage the child has learned many complex skills such as balancing on one foot, hopping on one foot, tricycling, catching a bouncing ball, running, running-broad jump, skipping, overhand throw, and taking turns. He uses these skills to assert, aggress, and, in short, tries to be "King of the Mountain."

Fine-muscle Skills He has success also in the fine-muscle area. He can dress himself and button. Handedness is beginning to develop. Many new expectations for coloring, copying, drawing, and fine eye-hand coordination are established by adults. While not particularly important to success with peers, these skills are significant in obtaining adult approval.

Cognitive Capabilities A new area has emerged—related to cognition. Although the foundations for this development have been occurring in the previous years, it is in the preschool phase that cognitive capacities emerge into specific processes. Here we see the child's thinking processes taking shape: associating new ideas with old ideas, perceiving, thinking, problem-solving. These skills are evident through activities such as categorizing, connecting cause and effect, having one-to-one correspondence, being skilled in block design and spatial relationships, drawing at least a three-part man, copying a cross, and understanding concepts of the past and the future and concepts of truth and fantasy. Perhaps these last points reflect most fully the status of the preschool child. All of his developing skills are becoming organized into efficient systems of functioning which help him find a place in the world that looks both exciting and fearful.

Summary A child of any chronological age can be delayed in development and functioning as a Stage Two child. When such a child is identified, it is essential that the therapeutic experiences planned for him be developmentally appropriate. By using the significant social-emotional milestones of Stage Two, therapy can be directed on a sequential, developmental course and the therapist can provide the type of adult-child relationship necessary to accomplish the goals of autonomy and initiative through learning individual skills that bring success.

DEVELOPMENTAL ART THERAPY FOR STAGE TWO

Developmental art therapy for Stage Two is concerned with enhancing each child's individual skills and self-expression. Emphasis is placed on a child's successful participation in each lesson with minimal physical and verbal assistance. Each child begins to use art as a constructive outlet for expressing his emerging self. During art, children begin to offer ideas and information spontaneously and are able to request specific supplies. In general, children at Stage Two are beginning to show interest in the world around them and are able to use basic art tools and supplies. Using Lowenfeld and Brittain's (1970) terms, Stage Two children are basically *controlled scribblers,* although children accomplishing developmental milestones toward the end of Stage Two begin to produce *preschematic* drawings. Characteristically, shapes are beginning to emerge in their art work and intermittent verbalizations are typical. They can usually explain what they are drawing or what is of interest to them at the moment. They experiment with repetitive designs and hopefully begin to attempt changing circular shapes into objects or people.

The Stage Two child's environment is reflected visually and verbally in his art work. It is this need to communicate that makes art experiences so invaluable for a Stage Two child. The more flexibility in ideas and variety of materials, the greater the opportunity for the child to express himself and his natural creativity. There are two general guidelines for ensuring that art experiences are constructive for Stage Two children. First, provide materials that all children in the group can make positive use of to some degree. Second, demonstrate the art process very simply and briefly.

The gift of spontaneity and creativity is so precious at this early stage that all possible care should be taken within the limits of the structured classroom to nourish and protect it. Art should always be FUN! When it becomes work to the children it has lost its value!

INTRODUCING THE ACTIVITY

With Stage Two children, complicated lessons should be attempted only after they progress in their expressive skill and self-control. Initially, all children should be given individual art supplies. They will gradually be able to move from working by themselves to sharing with a partner. Eventually, a class of six children making flowers (individually) can be directed to successfully put the flowers together for a garden mural (as a group).

In contrast to the extremely short art lessons in Stage One, a Stage Two child can sustain attention for art lessons up to fifteen minutes. Where the Stage One teacher has most items precut or premixed and predips brushes with one color of paint, the Stage Two teacher can expect the children to cut, color, draw, and create their own art work. This provides manipulative experience, allows a child to gain experience in following directions, and motivates his self-expression by using his own conceptual abilities, no matter how the product looks to adults! If the child has been creating his art, the end result is secondary to the experience.

As in Stage One, the need for a spacious and easily cleanable art area is imperative to the success of art lessons at Stage Two. Maintaining a structured art time is equally important.

By actually demonstrating an activity in front of children, a teacher provides the structure visually and verbally necessary to give reassurance that the activity is within each child's ability. Because most Stage Two children are acquiring new skills by imitating adults, they can be taught organizational and cognitive processes this way. Accept any positive attempt a child makes to participate in art. Each additional lesson should elaborate and expand upon earlier lessons until each child has the skill to use familiar materials to attempt new forms of self-expression. An important part of art structure is the teacher's careful use of key phrases, a standard vocabulary of art terms, and simple sentence structure in describing a demonstration (e.g., *"Watch the brush," "Do this . . . ,"* *"Shall we put it here?"*). Continued maintenance of expectations for participation along with carefully structured demonstrations to introduce each new activity provides the psychological security necessary for the children to venture into new art experiences.

At first, set up each lesson with clear, firm structure for behavioral expectations as well as artistic participation. A basic lesson might begin as follows.

On the table in front of each child is a small sheet of white paper. As you pass out each box of crayons, you might say, *"Now we are going to find out who can handle their crayons well today. Choose one crayon to work with and let me see the one you choose."*

"Now, everyone, take your crayon and draw lines from the top of the paper to the bottom of the paper. Fill up your paper."

You might first have to point out line designs on someone's clothes or on a zebra in a picture held up for the class to see and even take a similar size piece of paper and fill it with lines to demonstrate exactly what they are asked to do. Each child will attempt this with varying results. Some children might fill the paper with three lines; others might make lines going every which way. Accept all attempts with praise.

Pass out new sheets of paper as you collect the first products and as the children put the first crayon away and choose a second color. Compliment those who put the crayon back in the box on their own and then praise all who are ready again.

With their second color, ask them to fill the page with all the circles they want. If the children are able to accept this new direction, change a one-step procedure to two steps by telling them to choose one circle they like and to color it in with any color they like. At this point you either determine to go on with the lesson or end it. Then you could collect these pictures, pass out new paper, and ask the children to make any drawing they want.

At this early stage, pictures and art forms are probably unreadable. Acceptance of the work without explanation may be necessary in the beginning. As the children begin to respond to the teacher and the environment, interpretation can become part of the art lesson. Each child should be encouraged to talk about his art work. *"Willie, that looks like a person! It is a boy! What does he like to do best? Does he have any favorite foods?"* As you lead the child from simple answers, and he continues to draw, slowly you can draw out more therapeutic dialogue through hopefully spontaneous interchanges.

Always end art lessons when most of the children have had some degree of success (usually within eight to twelve minutes). Ending on a note of success is crucial to continued positive growth for subsequent art times. Stating final expectations from each child to end art time allows the children to know what next to do to get their final praise from their teachers. *"Johnny, if you will pass down your drawing and crayons I'll know you're done. Mary and Billy, too. Tony, you will need to put all your crayons in your box. Now everyone is finished with art and did super well. What a class of artists! Now who remembers what comes up next?"*

Selecting the Content

Children begin volunteering information about their work and themselves during Stage Two. The teacher's responsibility is to ensure that this continues and expands. When a child begins drawing a human figure, further elaboration can be obtained from the child through expression with his artistic or verbal skills. The teacher can ask questions about the original drawing, *"Tell me about your picture. It's a girl! Does she like her long hair? Does she have any friends?"* Through such exchanges the teacher is helping the child to conceptualize his random scribbles and shapes into organized visual memories and thought patterns. Then his verbal abilities can be expanded, practiced, and enriched throughout each art time. Favorite experiences, colors, flowers, foods, all can be used to stimulate this process. By taking each child's individual likes and dislikes and turning them into class art projects, the teacher can be assured that the chil-

dren will be motivated in art time. Such content also provides the children with an opportunity to express themselves and to see their ideas put to work in a structured and success-assured environment.

Art lessons must be geared to the children's individual developmental skills. Avoid magnifying deficits. For example, when children have manipulative problems, plan clay work, tearing projects, construction games like Play-Plax, or having Tinker Toy sets for creating *free* designs. Use words natural to the children and seek content from their everyday settings. Unusual and exciting adventures can be tried now. A treasure hunt in a public park can lead to textural discoveries. *"Who can find something soft? Something rough? A green leaf? A brown rock? Some red dirt? Something that smells? Two things that when rubbed together make a gritting noise?"*

For a Stage Two group, one hot summer day a muslin sheet was spread on the ground and held down by pegs at each corner. The sheet was sprayed with water and a basin filled with finger paint. Then each child, in his bathing suit, dipped his feet in the basin and made a design with his feet by walking on the sheet. Clean up was with the hose and then into the kiddie wading pool.

Acceptance of children and their artistic attempts is crucial to their continued growth. The end-product of all art lessons is secondary to the processes encouraging socializing with other children, interaction between teacher and children, and the expression of the child's world and sense of self in his art work. As a child's skill increases, his self-confidence increases, and conceptual abilities continue to expand. This process is reflected in the mastery of developmental milestones and can be seen in art work. Circular shapes become recognizable figures. Lines appear for arms, and faces emerge. Houses and lollipop trees appear. There may be sky, a sun in the corner of a picture, or a line for the ground. This is an important time for positive acceptance by the teacher and recognition for each effort. Preschematic forms have arrived and with them greater capacity for creativity, self-expression, and organization of abilities for coping with the demands of childhood.

Art with Child Drama

Stage Two children never seem to tire of acting out make-believe stories. Art can be an important aspect to many of these experiences. In child drama, the spontaneous efforts of the children are the creative, productive moments. Therefore, a minimum of props are needed to prod imagination into being. Creating a crown of colored paper and sequins and a magician's robe from burlap painted with stars might be all it takes to send the curtain up! Why not make some ears for the mean wolf or scary masks to hide behind to frighten off a monster? If everyone hides in a forest to escape the wicked witch, let each child make his own tree out of paper and paint. Once a story line is accepted by the children, it is up to the teacher to determine how far to stretch the children's skill and interest. A princess might need a crown (foil wrapped around wire and molded for her head), or a witch might require a hat (paper precut to make a cone and stapled together with the teacher's help). Perhaps pirates need a treasure (money made from green paper rectangles cut by the children or sequins glued to irregular shapes to become jewels), or a horse needs a tail (brown crepe paper cut in strips and tied to the waist by string). Painting decorations on the faces of each child to become Indians (with headbands

and armbands made earlier) could set the mood for a western story. Kites decorated with designs could become natives' shields to set the stage for an adventure in the jungles of South America or a hunting safari in Africa. Now is the time to put the child's magical world to work in a healthy and beneficial way.

Art with Music

It is easy to help Stage Two children get into the "musical mood" by simply asking them to make instruments from household items! A wide selection of everything from nails and bolts to crayons and egg cartons can be used to make instruments. The teacher encourages each child to combine any two materials so they will make a pleasant sound. Stage Two children can produce an amazing variety of sounds with handmade instruments. Sand paper rubbed against half an egg carton makes a delightful sound! Different pieces of hardware, nails, and bolts tied to string make a wind chime of delicate tones when struck with a huge nail. The limitations in making instruments as part of art and music time is hindered only by a teacher's imagination and ability to save all manner of cartons, odds and ends, and junk!

Another special art-music time can begin with, *"Have you ever played a music game?"* The game uses music tapes and pictures, and the children match music to one picture from a selection of several. One tape was "Twinkle, Twinkle Little Star" with a blue poster board displaying a picture of an elephant, a Kleé abstract print, and a picture of hand-drawn yellow stars on a black background. The children loved it! The stars matched the music! They listened to the next selection and each chose a picture from a new set that suited what they heard in the music. The discussion about the choices was productive and creative. Another song was played. One child chose a picture of a car because he had seen a movie about a car that flew; the music sounded like flying! Another child doubted that cars could fly, but everyone thought that flying would be fun! Other children preferred to match the music with a Rembrandt print and told family stories. Each tale was unique. The teacher listened to each, carefully assuring all that she liked each story. The developmental milestones that occurred in the five minutes of this lesson were tremendous! As the game ended, the children asked, *"Why don't we do our game to music now?"* Crayons and paper were handed out as the children continued their conversations. Stars, elephants, and cars emerged in their drawings as they exchanged more experiences of visiting circuses, seeing shooting stars, and on and on.

The opportunities for successful art-music activities at this stage are endless: using music to set the mood to draw by; creating lines to different rhythms; listening to storybook records and drawing what is heard; showing sad and happy pictures and then listening to music and matching the pictures to the music, etc.

Managing Stage Two Behavior

The major emphasis at this stage should be for the children to learn to respond to the teacher as a significant and trusted adult and to the demands of each art lesson with the confidence of success. There should be opportunity in each lesson for the fullest artistic and verbal self-expression possible for each child. When we talk about "art lessons" at this point, we are referring to limited experiences for children with very limited skills. Simple but motivating lessons tend to reduce behavior problems while allowing for achievement of developmental objectives in each art therapy session.

To begin working with children at this stage, your first expectations could be as simple as asking them to sit down for art time, or to clear their table areas so you may give them a sheet of paper. Each expectation the child is able to meet will allow you to do more at the next art time. If you run into difficulty having the children get ready for art, then perhaps you need to use some inventive ways to interest them. For example, if there is a child unable to respond to your simple direction to sit down, as you physically place the child in his seat hold up a beautiful box of new crayons and talk to the group about how neat it is for each to have his own box of crayons for art. Because you are now focusing on the group and not on your problem child, regardless of the problem child's resulting behavior throughout the lesson, you have put the emphasis where it should be—on the art lesson, not on the disturbing behavior.

Another variation is to set the table with the "tool" of the day. You can start verbalizing what is about to happen in art time. *"Play time is nearly over, and art time is next. Each child will get his own paint set for art today. While you put the toys away, I will put paint sets on the table for those who come to the table and will be ready for art!"* As the first child moves to his seat, verbally and physically reward him. *"Here is your paint set! Oh, what lovely colors it has!"* Every other child in the group is stimulated to come to the art table.

Stage Two children can be kept interested in demonstrations by focusing on each child with questions about what is being drawn, what each child is wearing that day, who in the room is wearing blue, etc. The group should be given art activities that will motivate the expression of a child's feelings (painting, not chain-making; clay work, not cutting out predrawn shapes). To begin to teach a child to use his art to "tell stories" and to express himself, the teacher needs to act as interpreter and to describe what she is "seeing" in his work. *"Mary, that could be a little girl playing. She is pretty—probably likes to help her Mom."* Or, *"Joe, can you tell me about your picture."*

The acceptance by the teacher of each child's interests and desires can be crucial to a child's continued development. Jeff was a child who refused to work with chalk because he claimed that it "grit" on his nerves. Was he expressing a genuine feeling to the art therapist, or was he testing the expectation to participate? Was this a child asking for sensitive understanding from others or for simple attention? Jeff was allowed to use crayons, and succeeding lessons showed that the chalk, not the art, was a genuine problem for him! Acceptance by the teacher, conveyed nonverbally and through voice quality when children are "testing," is difficult but necessary.

The expectation to participate must be maintained, but the establishment of trust between child and adult can be secured by a sensitive adaptation of the expected task to the child's individual interests. For example, if a child uses enormous globs of glue, the teacher can give a supportive direction for the child to dip the remaining pieces of paper into this glue supply. The teacher conveys a positive attitude not critical of the child's action. Or, if the project that day is to design animal mosaic shapes from pieces of colored paper and one child makes a flower instead, the teacher needs to evaluate the situation. Is this the first time the child has done anything to

be proud of in art? Did he make something other than the mosaic to test the situation? Is the child capable of carrying out the lesson and is he attempting to manipulate the situation? The teacher can compliment the effort and then ask for an animal shape to be made so it can "smell the flower." Or the teacher can tell the entire class that everyone gets additional pieces of paper so they too can make a flower or free design! However, first each person needs to *try* an animal shape. In one case, it was decided the child could not make the instructed shape and did what he was best at—making flowers! When help was offered to begin his animal, it was readily accepted and the child gleefully took over then.

Self-expression for the Stage Two child is often primitive. For example, the aggressive child can be redirected to use his anger constructively to make dramatic "swipes" at a painting project or to "smash" clay to make the air bubbles disappear before making a bowl. Art is a time to promote beginning socialization skills, too. *"You want to make friends with Joey. Call his name and show him your art work."* Or, *"You're sorry to see art end, but you don't have to stand on the table to tell me. You will have art again tomorrow"* (as you place him back in his seat and refocus on his success of the day). Redirecting negative behavior into positive outcomes while keeping the focus on the art experience is a constant test of a teacher's creativity and adaptability at Stage Two.

Often behavior that seems to be disruptive may actually be a request for assistance or instruction. A severely disturbed seven-year-old Stage Two girl named Aggie was willing to try each art activity, but her attempts were never satisfying to her. She was always unhappy with her productions. Each day, frustration led her to anger and destruction of her art work. Removing the art work before she destroyed it saved the work but not her self-confidence. Reassurance from the art therapist that she could help her do the day's lesson only made her more angry. Each day the art therapist presented the demonstration in simplified, brief steps. One day they used water color paints. The art therapist demonstrated how to use the water color brush and then painted a large, simple flower. As the art therapist finished, she said, *"Well, how about helping me make more flowers on my paper?"* The teacher started a second flower, stopping to allow Aggie to imitate each step in the process. That day, Aggie did her first recognizable picture and one that she liked too! She worked on a second sheet alone, and as her flowers blossomed forth on the paper, so did Aggie. She showed everyone her work, complimented another child over his, and then a third child asked Aggie to make her a flower like the teacher's. Everyone was happy—especially Aggie!

Socialization through Art

Art experiences provide an effective way to begin developmentally suitable social interactions. Theo was a child of few words and regrettably few skills with people or art. As his trust in his Stage Two teacher grew, art became his favorite activity. Theo usually drew mechanical-type designs or stylized cars. He found it hard to work with anyone and resented anyone commenting on his work. One day his teacher planned a free construction lesson using egg cartons, toothpicks, and styrofoam. This was scary to Theo, but the child next to Theo was even more alarmed. New activities seemed to heighten anxiety for most of the children in Theo's Stage Two group. The teacher verbally labeled

each material and described how each was used. As the rest of the class worked on a "car," a "house," and a "robot," Theo looked restless and angry. The child next to him continued to sit and stare. The teacher suggested that they might work together because some people are better with mechanical things than others. The "cue" took hold in Theo's head! He asked the immobile child next to him if he wanted to make a car. The child nodded his head and slowly Theo took command of the situation. He and his new friend completed a fine "car."

There are instances when the group focus is more effective than an individual approach. Fearful children seem more fortified to explore a fear through art if the group is attempting the same activity. One child, Anne, was terrified of imaginary monsters that appeared at night. A lesson was planned for letting each child in Anne's group create his own monster out of paper scraps, buttons, macaroni, etc. This activity motivated all the children to talk about monsters they have seen on TV or in the movies. They talked about being scared and about how it was make-believe. Anne listened intently and participated silently at first. As she created her monster she too began to talk about her fears, and when the children put their monsters in a box together at the end of art time, she rejoined the group with relief on her now-smiling face.

A TYPICAL STAGE TWO ART EXPERIENCE

The art therapist narrates a typical Stage Two art experience on the following pages. As in the previous chapter, the narration is cross-referenced with particular developmental objectives in the margin.

C-9
to exhibit a receptive vocabulary
no more than two years behind
chronological age expectations.

C-8
to answer a child's or an adult's
questions or requests with recognizable, meaningful, relevant
word(s).

B-9
to wait without physical intervention by teachers.

A-17
to recognize several colors.

B-9
to wait without physical intervention by teachers.

C-11
to use simple word sequences to
command or request of another
child or adult in ways acceptable
to classroom procedures.
A-17
to recognize several colors.

B-9
to wait without physical intervention by teachers.

"Who knows what this is called?" I ask as I hold up a #7 paint brush for the children to see.

"Brush, stupid," says Billy.

"A brush" chime in the others.

"Right," I smile, *"And what kind of paint is this? It's name has to do with the water in the jar."*

"Jar paint, Miss Williams," says Billy. He uses my name this time.

"Terrific guess, Billy. That's close, but what's in the jar?" Billy examines the baby food jars filled with water from where he sits. He has answered wrong. Can he try again?

"Water," he says softly.

Wanting to reward this difficult reaching out he has done, I explode with happiness, *"That's right! These paints are called water paints. They won't work unless you use water!"*

All the children are anxious to begin but they continue to watch me. *"I'll dip the brush in the water so quietly you can't hear me moving the water,"* I say. Hopefully, this will deter splashing and tipping the jar over, because the game of getting water without a sound is usually a challenge.

"Now what color should I choose?" I ask as I open the brand new paint set in front of the children. Everyone gets to examine the many colors. *New* paint sets are so wonderful!

"Blue! Red! Purple!" holler the children.

As they become excited, I lower my voice and appear to be sharing a top-echelon secret and only they are to hear my next sentence.

"I like all those colors. I heard blue first. Who can point to that color for me?" Faye, the shyest of the children, is picked out to do this as I put the set in front of her. *"Faye, can you point to blue for the class?"* I do not ask her to tell me the color because this would provoke too much anxiety now. Hesitantly, the timid child moves her small hand to the blue paint. Later in the lesson I will have the opportunity to discuss her work with her and work on several communication objectives.

As I demonstrate the painting procedure, I do it with exaggerated concentration. Carefully I wash my brush each time to change colors. When I do this I comment to the children about this but continue to focus on painting. *"I'm

going to paint a person in a red outfit, so I'll wash off the blue to change colors. Red makes a nice color for clothes. Now, the hair will be black. That's good."* Looking to the children at each step, I quickly execute a simple, basic version of a human figure in a red triangle.

"This person is standing . . . where? In a house or outside?" Outside is the considered opinion of the children, and so again the brush is washed off carefully and green is chosen for the baseline of the picture and appears to be grass to the children.

"Now what did I forget?" I ask the class. *"A face"* is the cry.

"Well, how many eyes should be in the face?"

"Two!" they respond with great enthusiasm as they feel the control they can exercise over the content of painting.

"Eyebrows?" I ask as I touch mine to make clear the meaning of the word.

"Two!" again is the answer.

"What else does she need?"

"A nose. A mouth. Ears!"

"Fantastic! I can finish quickly now." The ears and nose are added but I stop again.

"How should I draw the mouth? Should I make this face look happy or sad?"

"Happy! Happy!" is the cry and so the figure in the picture becomes happy with the addition of the last upward curved line to the face.

The kids are bursting to paint and know it's nearly time. Almost three minutes have elapsed and now I ask two more questions.

"Should I make it day or night in the picture?"

"No" says Mary. *"It would be scary. Make it day time."* And so a sun is added in the upper left hand corner where the children advise the sun has to be!

The creation of this smiling figure standing on grass outside in the day time has given: 1) a model for children to use in their work (whether it is used or not is up to the children), 2) a motivating demonstration of how to use the art materials in a step-by-step process, 3) opportunity for all the children to be part of an art experience that ended well (so they will have had some success that day), and 4) successful experience with a multitude of developmental objectives in communication, behavior, social interaction with an adult, and cognition.

Now the final question, *"Who's ready for art?"*

Hands shoot up. *"Me! Me!"* The supplies are handed out with maximum personal contact to each child.

"Joshua, you have waited so patiently. Here is your paint set, water, #7 brush, and paper. If you need any help, let me know."

He smiles and immediately begins his task. Carefully he dips the brush in the water as he saw me do it and chooses a color. He is on his way. I'll give him a chance to work on his painting before coming back to elicit comments from him on his creation. By the end of this art lesson (in about five to eight minutes) he will have experienced successfully a number of developmental objectives on his own and had fun with his paints!

The other children will all work in ways reflecting their individual development. With each, I try to maintain a high level of involvement. When frustrations seem to be arising (too much water on the brush or colors running into each other), I intervene and redirect the child's procedure in a way to bring success. I also help when a child asks me to show him how to make something necessary for his design.

"Mary, I don't know if I can make a flower, but I'll try and then we'll see if you can do it."

A simple tulip is attempted and then the brush is placed in Mary's hand. Mary imitates my simple strokes.

"You've just learned to do a tulip!"

"I can do one! she exclaims, delighted with her new ability. *"Josh, look at my flower. You want me to draw you one?"*

As all the children complete their work and while interest is still high, gently I remind the children that art time is nearly over. Then I end the lesson, giving clean-up instructions to help the children end successfully. (Waters jars are put away first; the last drops of paint on the brushes are used by each child to write his name on his picture, then brushes, paint sets, and finally papers are placed aside to dry.) Commenting on each child's work, I find a place in the room to put the wet pictures to let them dry. Getting the children ready for the next activity is easy if I quiet them with a softly spoken summary of what they accomplished.

The lesson has gone well. The next time water colors are used, the children will need only the briefest review on using the material. More time can then be devoted to the actual work experience, and there will be more opportunity for interaction between the children and me.

Although water color is a fairly skilled activity for Stage Two children, the step-by-step demonstration can provide tremendous encouragement for trying. For most of the children, it is an adventure into something new. Sharing "the secret of painting" with the children is a good motivator. Make each step an adventure: dipping the brush in the water and making sure it is clean; wiping it on the jar's edge so it will not drip; making the first beautiful line. All of these "secrets" become very important steps to master. How prolonged you want to make the demonstration and how much interaction you request from each child in the initial lesson are determined by each child's developmental abilities. Not only can interest be maintained by involving the children in the demonstration, but many developmental skills can be exercised in the three or four minutes it takes to do the demonstration.

Not all of the Stage Two art experiences need to be at the skill level of water color. A favorite lesson for Stage Two children is "free-tear" mosaics. Lots of fun and numerous developmental objectives can be a part of this art experience. This lesson is described in greater detail in the following section. The narrative under "Step-by-step motivation" shows how to encompass developmental

B-12
to spontaneously participate in routines without physical intervention.

B-10
to participate in sitting activities such as work time, story time, talking time, juice and cookie time without physical intervention by teacher.

C-13
to use words spontaneously to exchange minimal information with another child.

objectives in the fifteen-minute art lesson. In Step 1 the demonstration of tearing the paper is done dramatically, with exaggerated gestures to keep the children's attention and to help them attend and wait without physical intervention. By immediately handing out paper to each waiting child, sustained attention and participation are encouraged. Tearing is a wonderfully motivating activity and one that can be accomplished successfully by every child. At the same time, it develops hand and finger strength and dexterity. Asking for additional paper stimulates the use of words to request from an adult. By asking questions of a child about the process, the teacher also stimulates the verbal exchange of information. *"Did you draw that circle by yourself? Do you like drawing big or little pictures best?"*

The following suggestions for using art materials with Stage Two children represent only a few of the possibilities for helping these children develop further.

Perhaps there is no stage of development that equals Stage Two in the possibilities for using materials creatively and divergently. Because these children have few highly developed standards for their products, they can truly enjoy the creative art experience.

By the end of Stage Two, children should be able to identify primary and secondary colors, be able to use a paint brush, handle a container of glue, use scissors, choose colors for various projects regardless of the material being used, and follow a series of directions. There should be evidence of self-awareness in a child's art products and in his verbalizations. Finally, the child should participate spontaneously in cooperative activities with others.

ART ACTIVITIES FOR STAGE TWO

Medium	Special Preparation	Suggested Content	Step-by-Step Motivation
Acrylics	Not applicable at this stage		
Art Appreciation *Lesson 1*	1. Several prints of varying subjects. Tapes of music that might be associated with each print (e.g., a picture of a snake, Picasso's "Harlequins" and "Blue Guitar;" music from "Carousel"). You will need: 2. Drawing paper, pencils, or crayons for each child. *Note:* This lesson is particularly effective with verbal Stage Two children.	Music and art can go together	1. Show three pictures. Obtain each child's interpretation of what he sees in each picture. 2. Play the tape and ask each child to select the picture they think fits the music best. 3. Respond favorably to all answers. 4. This can be repeated with another set of prints and music but end before children get restless. 5. Follow with free art time, while replaying tape.
Art Appreciation *Lesson 2* *Drawing from real objects*	You will need: 1. Pictures, photos and prints of flowers, objects, fruit, etc. 2. Objects that are close facsimiles. 3. Drawing paper, pencils, and crayons.	Comparing reality to photos and prints	1. This art "game" involves each child matching a real apple to a photo or print of one; an orange to an orange, etc. 2. As a child matches, he keeps fruit, flower, or object. 3. Have a free drawing time; encourage them to draw their object or print. 4. If the objects are fruit, they can be eaten during snack time; if objects, incorporate them in play time later.
Batik	Not applicable at this stage		
Beadwork	You will need: 1. A variety of beads, cut plastic straws, bamboo pieces, thread spools, macaroni, or pipe cleaners. 2. Plastic-coated wire or a stiff waxed twine cut in 12″ to 14″ lengths. *Note:* This lesson is particularly useful with children just beginning Stage Two.	Making necklaces, tiaras, bracelets, holiday decorations, mobile designs	1. Show children a selection of materials and demonstrate "threading" process, putting objects on one after another. 2. Let each child ask for wire or twine. 3. Let each child choose five of each object for a necklace. 4. Assist those who can't do it; encourage those trying. Have the first child who finishes model it for the group. Then another creation can be made! And another. And another! 5. These may be used each day at play time or dress-up time!
Candlemaking	Not applicable at this stage		
Cast Stone	Not applicable at this stage		

(continued)

ART ACTIVITIES FOR STAGE TWO (continued)

Medium	Special Preparation	Suggested Content	Step-by-Step Motivation
Charcoal	Not applicable at this stage		
Clay	Use the general procedures described in Stage One clay lessons. However, more time should be spent in demonstrating the "pulling out" method to make legs and arms for animals or people. If the basic form is made by a child, then the teacher should encourage the child to decorate it. *"Shall we put eyes on your person? O.K. How many? Two! Good idea. What else? Right; mouth, nose. How many buttons on his shirt? Four! Four buttons it is!"* etc. If bowls or pots or even simple "pancakes" are attempted, textures and design can be encouraged by describing polk-a-dots, stripes, flowers, shapes, etc. See Chapter Five for more details for using clay with Stage Two children.		
Clay *Pinch Pots*	Same as in Stage One. *Note:* This lesson is more successful for Stage Two. However, children beginning to accomplish the last of the Stage One objectives may be ready for this. For greater details about using clay, see Chapter 5.	Pinch pots; music can help in motivating this activity	1. Teacher tears and slams clay ten times in hands (this softens clay and gets rid of air bubbles), counting aloud with each hit. 2. Children repeat this with their own clay. Form clay into round shape. (Teacher helps each child if necessary.) 3. Use pointing finger and put one hole halfway through clay. 4. Use two pointing fingers inside hole and gently pull wide. Turn clay; pull wider, etc., until bowl emerges. Pull to $\frac{1}{4}''$ to $\frac{1}{2}''$ width. 5. Use pencil to decorate inside and out (any attempt acceptable). 6. Teacher can help each child through this experience as much as he needs it. But praise any positive attempts regardless of quality of product! 7. Help each child write name or initial or sign on bottom of pinch pot. 8. Products can be fired.
Collage *Lesson 1* *Magazine*	You will need: 1. Magazine for each child (censor beforehand to get rid of disturbing pictures). 2. Glue for each child (2-oz. bottles). 3. Scissors (left and right handed). 4. Assorted sheets of colored paper. *Note:* There is no right or wrong way to tear out pictures, and the final product is not as important as children verbalizing in this activity and enjoying the experience. So this lesson is useful with a wide range of Stage Two children.	Free choice design or mood-feeling pictures	1. Each child gets to choose his own magazine! After choice is made, he chooses any color paper he wants and gets scissors. 2. Ask each child to tear out three pictures (five, ten, or as many as you think the child can handle). When doing mood-feeling pictures, discuss a certain feeling and show examples. Then ask children to look for other pictures with the same feeling. 3. When a child has completed this task, he obtains glue by handing back his magazine. Children can be given

(continued)

ART ACTIVITIES FOR STAGE TWO (continued)

Medium	Special Preparation	Suggested Content	Step-by-Step Motivation
Collage *Lesson 1 (cont.)*			suggestions such as where to place cut out pictures on the paper. This help may ease frustration before it causes a child unnecessary problems. *"Johnny, one drop of glue on each corner will do just fine." "Mary, I think that torn edge looks fine! Glue it as it is!"* 4. When each child finishes, he can have free art time or can look at magazines.
Collage *Lesson 2* *Scraps*	You will need: 1. Paper scraps of different textures and colors. 2. Glue for each child (2-oz. bottles). 3. Scissors (left and right handed). 4. One box of crayons for each child. 5. Lots of white drawing paper (cut to 3 sizes: $8\frac{1}{2}'' \times 11''$, $12'' \times 16''$, $18'' \times 24''$). *Note:* This lesson is very successful for children with poor hand skills.	Free choice (two- or three-dimensional)	1. Show group the materials to be used. Demonstrate how to cut a simple flower, shape, or 3-D circle; fold paper or make a quick design verbalizing on proper use of glue and how there is no right or wrong art today will be enough to start the lesson. 2. Encourage each child to ask for paper. 3. Offer a choice of the three sizes of drawing paper as a base for gluing the scraps. *"Do you want big, medium, or small paper?"* 4. Pass out glue and scissors to those who are ready. Encourage each child to ask for glue and scissors. 5. As the children work, verbally reflect the children's positive activities, *"Joe, you are making that square with no help. Tony is using his glue beautifully. Mary, I love the way you are making that face with those tiny pieces of black paper and no one is helping you! Did you think of that by yourself?"* 6. As the children are involved with their creation, motivate them to verbalize on what they are doing whenever possible. As the majority of the children near completion, start the count-down, *"We have two minutes left until art time is over. Joe, you will have time to glue that last scrap on because everyone else is finishing with the crayons. When you put your name on your work, I'll know you are ready to help clean up."* By setting this structure, children know what is expected to end art time.

(continued)

Medium	Special Preparation	Suggested Content	Step-by-Step Motivation
Copper Enameling	Not applicable at this stage		
Crayon	At Stage Two, each child should be given his own box of crayons to use daily. As the crayons break and wear down, the children will not be as thrilled with "their" crayons as they were initially. As they lose colors or use up certain colors, sharing with their friends can be the natural solution to the problem! Crayon work should be highly pleasurable and successful for the children now. The teacher should select the day's subject until the children come up with ideas on their own. *"I thought we could make some happy pictures today. What makes you happy, Tony? Flowers? Well, let me see if I can draw a happy flower. What color should I use, Mary? Red. Is red your favorite color? Good! Joey, should I make a big or little flower?"* As you demonstrate a simple flower, such comments keep their interest and provide a model for connecting ideas and words to art expressions.		
Crayon Resist	Use the same procedures as in Stage One, with focus on specific developmental objectives for Stage Two.		
Craypas and Craypas Resist	Use the same procedures as in Stage One, with focus on specific developmental objectives for Stage Two.		
Découpage	Not applicable at this stage		
Diorama	Not applicable at this stage		
Etching	Not applicable at this stage		
Finger Painting	Not recommended beyond Stage One unless developmental objectives are still focusing on arousing and responding. Finger paints tend to stimulate regressive, freeing behavior in most children, and at Stage Two the goal is to strengthen skills and ego processes, not loosen them.		
Leathercraft	Not applicable at this stage		
Lettering	Not applicable at this stage		
Macramé	Not applicable at this stage		
Magic Markers	As in Stage One, free use of magic markers is usually rewarding to Stage Two children. At this stage, children should be able to remove and to replace tops alone or with minimal help. Allow a child to use one color, close it up, and ask for another and then another. This procedure can set up good social interaction in a group during art. Eventually, give two or three colors to each child and then motivate them to exchange among themselves. Subject matter can be chosen by teachers or individuals. Having a "Design-a-line time" to the rhythm of different records can be fun also.		
Metal Work	Not applicable at this stage		
Mixed Media	Use the same procedures as in Stage One, but a more "sophisticated" approach is usually more motivating. *"Today each person gets to choose any two of the following art supplies to work with for art time! Yes—two!!"* Name each item; hold it up to show the class; then let each child make his own selection and combinations of media. Encourage exchanges and sharing to meet developmental objectives.		

(continued)

Medium	Special Preparation	Suggested Content	Step-by-Step Motivation
Mobiles	See Stage One		
Model Building	Not applicable at this stage		
Mosaics *Lesson 1 (precut)*	See Stage One		
Mosaics *Lesson 2* *(free-tear)*	You will need: 1. $8\frac{1}{2}'' \times 11''$ assorted colored construction paper. 2. Glue for each child (2-oz. bottles). 3. Crayons for each child.	Free design	1. *"Who can tear up this sheet into tiny, tiny pieces?"* Make a game of this and compliment those who are "great tearers." 2. As they finish, encourage them to glue the pieces in a design on a second sheet of paper *"One drop of glue to a scrap!"*. Your most creative child will attempt a design or ask for different colors of scraps. *"See if Tony will trade some of his blue for your red!"* Your less organized children will slap down piece after piece, but these too should be welcomed and praised! 3. For children with perceptual problems, draw a straight line on their base paper and ask them to place mosaics on the line. Also, predrawn squares, names, faces, or shapes can be used for less skilled children.
Natural Materials	See Stage One		
Oil Paints	Not applicable at this stage		
Papier Mâché	Not applicable at this stage		
Pastels *(color chalk)*	Use the same procedures as in Stage One, but with more demonstration of subject matter; give each child his own box of pastels.		
Pen and Ink	Not applicable at this stage		
Pencil	Use the same procedures as in Stage One, but with more emphasis on creating controlled scribbles, human figures, houses. Encourage appropriate verbalizations from children using their personal experiences as cues to how they see their world as they create their pictures.		
Plaster	Not applicable at this stage		
Play-plax *(crystal climbers)*	Use the same procedures as in Stage One, except show the entire collection to students. Demonstrate two or three different possible structures; break down your demonstration; replace in the box. Each child is given eight to twelve pieces. The whole class can help count out the number to each child.		

(continued)

ART ACTIVITIES FOR STAGE TWO (continued)

Medium	Special Preparation	Suggested Content	Step-by-Step Motivation
Pliable Plastics or Plexiglass	Not applicable at this stage		
Printing	Use the same procedures as in Stage One, but allow the children more access to preparatory steps: choosing a vegetable for a vegetable print; cutting a design in paper for a sponge print; cutting string for a string print. Use more than one color and choose different colored papers to work on. Also, encourage putting more than one print on a page to achieve a pleasing design.		
Rubbings	Not applicable at this stage		
Sand Castings	Not applicable at this stage		
Sand Designing	Use the same procedures as in Stage One, but more subjective designs can be attempted if you demonstrate while explaining the process.		
Sensory Lessons	See Stage One		
Shell Jewelry	Not applicable at this stage		
Soap Carving	Not applicable at this stage		
Stitchery	Not applicable at this stage		
Styrofoam (and toothpicks)	Use the same procedures as in Stage One, but have separate containers of picks for each child (20 to 30 per child). Let each child choose three to five pieces of assorted sizes and shapes to work with. Anyone who wants more needs only to use up what he has in order to obtain additional supplies. Motivation should focus on what they can make; while they are working, encourage the children to describe their creations as they work.		
Tempera Paint	See Stage One, Tempera Paint Lessons 2, 3, and 4. Each child should have his own supplies. Varying the colors, sizes of paper, and brushes will provide for different manipulative and conceptual experiences for the children. Children moving from one developmental level to another are especially in need of this medium.		
Tie-dyeing	Not applicable at this stage		
Tissue Paper Design Lesson 1 See-through	You will need: 1. Assorted colors of tissue paper. 2. Glue for each child (2-oz. bottles). 3. Scissors (left and right handed). 4. $8\frac{1}{2}'' \times 11''$ sheets of black construction paper. 5. Tape and string. *Note:* This lesson is for highly skilled Stage Two children. Some children at this stage might need precut construction paper because cutting	Free design or precut geometric shapes	1. Demonstrate how to put two sheets of black paper together; fold once; cut into different sizes for different designs. Open and on inside of one, cover holes with tissue. Glue other black sheet to this one. Insert string on one edge and tape together to hang up. 2. Encourage children to ask for scissors and two sheets of black paper. (Black or any dark color is good because it contrasts with the pastel colors available in most tissue paper.)

(*continued*)

ART ACTIVITIES FOR STAGE TWO (continued)

Medium	Special Preparation	Suggested Content	Step-by-Step Motivation
Tissue Paper Design Lesson 1 (cont.)	will be frustrating and may result in lack of success.		3. Children will need help in cutting out holes through two folded sheets. *"If you can fold it by yourself, I'll help with the cutting."*
			4. When cutting is done, each child can choose two or three favorite colors of tissue. When they have placed small pieces of the chosen tissue over the cut-out holes, excess tissue can be collected and the glue distributed.
			5. After the child completes gluing, assist him to insert string and hang or tape the designs for display.
Tissue Paper Design *Lesson 2* *Flowers*	You will need: 1. Wire (plastic-coated). 2. Precut circles of tissue. 3. Scissors (left and right handed). 4. Green construction paper. 5. Florist tape (green). *Note:* This lesson is especially suitable for developing manipulative skill. The bunching process can be an art lesson in itself for very low Stage Two children.	Flowers	1. Demonstrate how simple flowers can be made by "bunching" several pieces of round paper together and tying with wire at the base.
			2. Demonstrate taping precut leaf patterns or motivate the children to cut their own leaves. Help them to tape leaves down each stem.
			3. Each child can make as many flowers as time allows. Praising any original flower designs is helpful to your less secure children to attempt something other than the demonstrated model.
Vocational Art Studies	Not applicable at this stage		
Water Colors	You will need: 1. Water color paint sets for each child (eight-color sets). 2. A #7 paint brush for each child. 3. White drawing paper ($5'' \times 7''$ and $8\frac{1}{2}'' \times 11''$). 4. Baby food jars one half full of water for each child. *Note:* This lesson is effective with almost all children at Stage Two.	Free experimentation	1. "Gingerly" demonstrate how to open paint set; wet brush; wipe on edge of jar *carefully*; choose a color; then paint anything the children want! Line drawings of a simple subject can be demonstrated while you make children aware of what a *joy* this art experience can be.
			2. Washing the brush off before a new color is chosen each time is the hardest point to make. As you mix a primary color on your paper into a secondary color, "catch" yourself and remember to wash *your* brush! (The excitement alone in watching the water

(continued)

ART ACTIVITIES FOR STAGE TWO (continued)

Medium	Special Preparation	Suggested Content	Step-by-Step Motivation
Water Colors (cont.)			change from one color to the next is a treat for most children!)
			3. Encourage each child to ask for his supplies.
			4. As the children paint, use praise abundantly. Emphasize that they remember "how to paint with water colors."
			Caution: As confidence in the medium increases, Stage Two children will attempt "splatter painting," which can get on clothes and start fights! The structure described above can prevent this.
Wire or Pipe Cleaners and Spray Paint	See Stage One		
Wood Structures	Not applicable at this stage		
Woodwork	Not applicable at this stage		
Yarn Design	You will need: 1. Elmer's glue for each child. 2. Yarn (assorted lengths and colors). 3. Poster boards (12″ × 12″). 4. Scissors for each child. *Note:* This lesson is excellent for practice in eye-hand coordination but with severely delayed children it can become frustrating if glue gets on their hands.	Free design	1. Give children opportunity to verbally describe how the glue bottles open while the teacher demonstrates their directions. 2. Demonstrate how to "draw" with glue. Use a simple subject (fish, basic shapes, flower, etc.). Then choose a piece of yarn. "Think out loud" while demonstrating: why you chose a specific color; the length to cut the yarn; how it feels to lay it on the wet glue; the importance of keeping glue off of fingers. 3. Ask each child to think of a shape and encourage verbal descriptions. 4. Distribute poster board, scissors, and glue to each child. Put yarn within easy reach. 5. Structure the steps verbally as needed to encourage each child. 6. Discuss the shapes as they emerge and display each finished product.

chapter 4

Stages Three and Four: Learning Skills for Group Participation to Enhance Self-Esteem

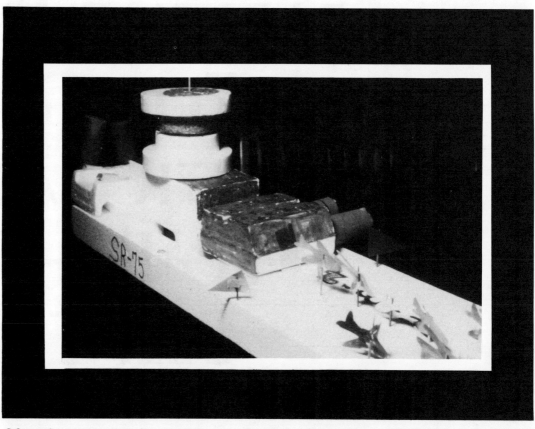

Often the most rewarding artistic experience for Stage Three children is one in which they become involved in a group project which turns out well. The exchange of ideas, helping each other as the project grows, and solving problems all extend the potential in each child.

Bette is an unusually bright seven-year-old referred to us by her school for bizarre behavior and unmanageable tantrums. She is vivacious, verbally precocious, and totally inept with her peers. She refuses to participate in all art lessons and begrudgingly uses each day's art materials *only* if she can draw her own private brand of animal friends. To lure her into participating in the group, art lessons had been planned for this low Stage Three group to include her special drawings as a part of each lesson. But, as her participation progressed, it was decided Bette was ready to be confronted with a new expectation.

"Today, each of you gets to draw any person you want in your family. Then we will put our work together in a mural so our family people can be the audience at the circus we are planning."

As the children start, a lot of reassurance and support are necessary to help them into the lesson. Bette is strangely quiet but drawing intently. As I move over to her drawing board, I quickly see the reason for her contented action. She is intent upon drawing a "no such animal" (as she calls all her animal drawings).

I kneel beside her and, as I begin talking, I move my hand near her drawing to be in a position to control when the confrontation occurs.

"Bette, you draw the best 'no such animals' I ever saw, but today everyone has to draw people."

With one hand I quickly remove her drawing from view and with my free hand hold her as she begins to scream in frantic frustration. The other children ignore her noise. They are used to her episodes.

I stay kneeling next to her and repeat over and over, *"You can finish your animal as soon as you do today's lesson."* My voice is soothing and gentle. About the fifth time I say this, she takes a deep breath, chokes down her next set of tears, looks at me hard, and says, *"OK"* in the smallest voice I ever heard.

She quickly executes a remarkable sketch of her mother and asks if that was what I wanted? *"Yes,"* I answer, *"and it's very good work, Bette."*

"Now, can I finish the 'no such?'"

"Of course," I say, *"as soon as you put your name on your fine art work."*

In one swift stroke she obliterates her mother's face and in another writes her name. After all, I didn't stipulate she had to leave her person intact!

Bette goes back to her animal this time, but she has turned an important corner. Even though her animal world is still her security blanket, people have been admitted into her world—a big step forward!

THE CHILD AT STAGES THREE AND FOUR

Bette is an example of an emotionally disturbed child just beginning to grow into the middle childhood phase of development. Normally, this period is associated with children between ages six and twelve. Within this period, there are such startling changes that it is easier to grapple with the differences in two therapy stages. Thus, Stages Three and Four emerge. The overall goal of therapy for Stage Three is learning skills for successful group participation; in Stage Four, learning to value group membership. Together these stages incorporate sequences of developmental milestones that result in self-esteem.

A child in Stage Three is quite distinct in actions, conceptual abilities, and social preferences from children in previously discussed stages of development. And as the Stage Three child progresses into Stage Four, there are other distinct differences. However, the transition between Stages Three and Four is often so gradual and subtle that it may be difficult to recognize the Stage Four characteristics as they first emerge. Also, there will be intermittent regression to lower levels of functioning during periods of stress. Because the stages flow from one to the other, Stages Three and Four have been combined in this chapter. In combination, these two stages span the normal developmental period of the middle childhood years.

The relationship of Stage Three to Stage Four can be described best as an expansion of the basic theme in which the group can enhance a child's own self-esteem. While the overall Stage Three therapy goal is to learn skills for successful group participation, Stage Four expands basic group skills into valuing the group, identifying with characteristics of other group members, and thereby coming to accept one's self as a valued individual and a significant member of the group.

Highlights of therapy in Stage Three are:

1. Expressions of feelings are coming through verbal and symbolic means, rather than through physical means as in previous stages.
2. The child is learning to regulate his own impulsivity and therefore needs fewer outside controls.
3. Basic processes for group interaction are being learned; for example, rights of others, social cooperation, participation with others, rules, expectations, and results.
4. The child is forming a sense of his own adequacy in the eyes of peers.

Among the major elements of therapy in Stage Four are:

1. Yielding personal will to the group decision.
2. Valuing the group activity and finding pleasure in it.
3. Becoming aware of different values and feelings in others.
4. Developing awareness of an ideal self and valuing the real self.

As the normal child moves into middle childhood, he brings with him a fairly well developed sense of his own worth and his own autonomy, which has developed within the limited confines of his prior experience. The handicapped child seldom has developed these attributes. Now, middle childhood exposes him to the ever demanding, ever broadening reality of the world beyond his immediate grasp. Erikson (1963) has described middle childhood as a time when self-esteem develops through industry and activity, within ever expanding social contexts. This is a time when there is a gradual shifting in the balance from dependence to independence. Loevinger (1976) describes this same period as a time when the child develops control of impulses but still views interactions with others from a self-protective viewpoint. Then, as ego development continues, Loevinger reports the emergence of a new, conforming stage in which the individual accepts rules and expectations for the security of social acceptance.

Six major forces impact upon the psychological development of a child during these middle childhood years: parents, peers, and the development of ego processes, conscience, cognitive structures, and motor skills. While each of these forces is significant, relationships with parents permeate the child's attitudes, his feelings, and his behavior with others.

Identification, the process by which a child assimilates the characteristics of another, is among the most dynamic forces at work. While the preschool child identifies with his parent in order to feel secure and to associate himself with feelings of protection, in middle childhood the personal characteristics of parents become significant in the dynamic process of a child's identification and modeling. If a parent's own conscience, moral standards, emotional responses, and behavior are mature and reasonable and if a parent deals with a child in a helpful and approving way, the child takes on many characteristics of the parent. He then takes these same characteristics and tests them in peer groups and with other significant adults. This testing may be a large part of the behavior teachers see.

There is abundant research on personality characteristics of parents and how they influence children's developing personalities. If a parent deals with a child aggressively, he offers a model for aggression. The result may be hostility toward the parent, rejection of the parent, or modeling in which the child assimilates the parent's aggressive patterns of behavior himself. Some children may be forced into passive aggression; that is, they are too afraid of losing a parent's love to oppose a parent openly and so they cause the parent disturbance in covert ways.

Direct physical aggression toward parents or teachers is practically absent in children under ten years of age and is even rare in later childhood and among young adolescents (Mussen, Conger, and Kagan, 1969). Direct verbal aggression, including cursing and bad words, is the most common form of open hostility. This is one of the most effective ways for a child to feel relief from hostile feelings toward parents or teachers.

Perhaps the most dynamic aspect of this entire process is the child's fear of loss of love or approval from the parent. This permeates and influences the entire development of the middle years. It also may contribute to some of the alienation that is experienced by many adolescents. It is easy to see how a child in the middle years, seeking parental love and striving to emulate parents, is in conflict when parental discipline is overly harsh or unfair. Harsh discipline is an assault on a child's real need for parental approval and makes it very difficult for him to identify with the parent. The conflicts that can arise from this are enormous. Behind such conflict is the child's guilt that he is inadequate in the eyes of the parent. Discipline, therefore, becomes a major input into a child's developing sense of self-esteem.

Conflict and guilt result when a child has anxiety about inadequacy, punishment, or loss of love. It is reported that guilt feelings normally are acquired by age six or seven and continue to change and develop as the child develops. Some amount of guilt about transgressions is associated with high conscience development. Carried to an extreme, it results in an overly anxious, superego-dominated child whose autonomy, self-esteem, and self-reliance are severely impaired.

In contrast, peer relationships are a means by which children in the middle years develop independence from parents and learn to relate to many different types of people. It is easy to see how successful peer relationships can contribute significantly to high self-esteem.

Conversely, failures in peer relationships can produce lowered self-esteem and a turning inward.

Characteristics of peer relationships change dramatically from the beginning to the end of the middle years. Selections of a "best friend," small groups of friends, and enemies are characteristics of six- to eight-year-olds. By age ten or twelve the group expands, becomes more tolerant, and identifies with heroes and other admired adults. This is an important preparation for identification with adults in society and an ingredient in the successful transition from adolescence to adulthood.

Changes in attitude toward rules is dramatic. Rules for the six-year-old represent order, security, and the only way to govern the actions of people. "Tattling" is a common characteristic. It represents a child's plea to adults to maintain security through order in face of a possible transgression. Between ages eight and ten children are very concerned about cheating and nonconformity in others. It threatens their own sense of security and order. But as cognitive skills increase, the older child is able to see reasons, relationships, cause and effect, alternatives, and new ways to use rules (Piaget, 1932).

Quarreling represents the child's great concern with right, wrong, and fairness. These concepts coincide with the child's cognitive maturation and the state of his own self-esteem (Kohlberg and Turiel, 1971). As children mature, quarreling tends to drop off. Group spirit and comradeship tend to be prominent. Children are learning to solve problems through verbal exchange. Competition and boasting are other manifestations of the same maturation process. Gradually these become sublimated as identifications with groups become stronger. Team pride and group identification are the capstones of the middle years.

Throughout this period of development, children are experiencing a significant increase in their ability to use words for social power. They use words for shock effects with their families and to maintain status with their peer group. The school, too, is a fertile ground for the shock effect of words. The type of words and the way they are used are influenced by a child's identification, modeling, and cognitive development.

At the beginning of the middle childhood years, the child relies on powers outside himself to solve problems. He does not see actions related to consequences (a cognitive function). Magical solutions, fantasy, and wishes are characteristic ways children cope with problems before age ten, and they still rely on adults or significant others to solve problems for them.

Systems of impulse control are changing also. The middle childhood years are dominated by the need to develop competence, to do, and to meet the expectations of others. Underlying these demands a child experiences many feelings that cannot be expressed or fulfilled. Because he is so aware of society's expectations and rules (and still accepts them) he is directed toward winning approval, characteristically explaining away his slips with, "I forgot" or "I don't know." Beneath it all, he worries about feelings that cannot be controlled, that he may make "mistakes." Fears are the result of this struggle for impulse control and meeting the standards of others. Fears that are common among many children of this age result from:

Their sense of responsibility to meet standards

The possibility of letting out hidden secrets or unacceptable drives

Concern that others will disapprove

Frustration over unfulfilled feelings, often the need for nurturance and love

Hostility toward a parent, often because of unmet love needs or because of "unfair" discipline

The impact of the irreversible nature of death and adults' inability to control it[1]

All of these fears add up to many potential problems for children, whether handicapped or not, before age twelve. Characteristically, fears take three forms: *realistic fears* ("It could happen"), *remote fears* ("It might happen"), and *mystical, symbolic fears* ("Wouldn't it be awful if this happened?"). The shape and form of the fears usually depend upon the child-parent relationship, past experience, ego processes, cognitive maturation, and conscience development. Most characteristic fears are expressed through nightmares, school-related fears, death fears, obsessions, compulsions, and through symbolic play, art, and other creative activities.

As he matures, a child becomes increasingly well equipped to cope with the stresses of middle childhood. His ability to perform many complex mental tasks, using symbolic forms, is among his most useful assets. So, too, gross motor development serves most children well during the complex development of peer social exchanges. The effectiveness, or lack, of motor skills also influences the child's acceptance of himself as an esteemed, competent person. Perhaps the normal need for physical activity among children during this period of development is among the major culprits in pro-

ducing many classroom behavior problems: restlessness, lethargy, or apathetic attitudes.

A handicapping condition, whether mental or physical, adds another complexity to the problems of middle childhood. But even if the handicap results in developmental delay, the same dynamic changes can be seen. The significant milestone may not occur at the same chronological age as with normal children, but the sequences of unfolding events are similar. For this reason a dynamic art therapy provided to handicapped children within a developmental framework can be responsive to the highly individual needs of each child as he progresses through the social and emotional experiences of the middle childhood years.

DEVELOPMENTAL ART THERAPY FOR STAGES THREE AND FOUR

In children's art processes the dramatic changes of middle childhood are clearly evident. Cognitive maturation enables the Stage Three child to leave the pre-schematic stage and to produce art with organized form concepts. The art work of this *schematic stage* is typically a decorative alignment of forms along a single ground line.[2] Each image or form the Stage Three child produces has meaningful representation and is repeated again and again. Sky, earth, trees, people, and familiar objects are developed with ever increasing skill and elaboration of detail. Forms are generally stereotypes and fairly simple. Yet the concepts a Stage Three child has about his art forms are apparently much more complex than is his skill in expressing

---

[1] Anthony (1967) terms this developmental milestone the "existential crisis." Through actual experience with the death of a pet or someone they know, through hearing and observing the reactions of adults to death, the child grapples with this complex entity, usually alone.

[2] According to Lowenfeld and Brittain (1970) this "schematic" stage of art work is evident in children from appproximately six to nine years of age.

them. Personal exchanges between an adult and child in front of the group is more difficult at this stage of development so it is necessary to use the group's *strengths* to make art therapy vital for all.

As a child emerges from Stage Three into Stage Four, a degree of awareness and skill is developing so that representational products become increasingly important as means to express *dawning realism.*[3] At this point, inability to make it look "right" is a frequent problem for children. It takes a sensitive and skilled teacher to plan art experiences that stimulate Stages Three-Four children to participate with enthusiasm to new art experiences. Children who feel inadequate at portraying reality often change from being previously enthusiastic participants to derogatory or withdrawn dissidents in the group. When this happens it is a sure indication that the teacher must avoid art experiences that emphasize the representation of reality.

The Stage Three child usually will be familiar with a limited range of art tools, art terms, and art experiences. He is becoming more conscious of his peers and wants to "draw better." He wants to have his work gain recognition and praise from others, but accepting help from a "dumb" teacher is difficult to do.

Current fads, TV programs, and movies are important to most Stage Three children. As they grow into Stage Four, these children gradually develop considerable interest in outside peer activities and the exciting "real" world. Making use of these interests to motivate art experiences is a real challenge for the therapist. One Stage Four class used squirt guns loaded with water colored by food dyes on a sheet pinned to a clothes-

line to create a mural in the manner of the famous artist of the 40s, Jackson Pollack. The art time was fantastically successful both motivationally and developmentally. As the children are maturing socially, it is imperative that the art therapist be "tuned in" to what is really exciting to them. What is the biggest rock group now? Who has the best football team? What did they think about the big storm last night? By sharing this information with the entire group during snack or talk time, all the children learn about the topic and then everyone has the same basic information to use as a base in the subsequent art activity.

It is easier for some children to succeed in art work than others, but it is essential to create the attitude that no one fails in an art attempt. Every attempt is an artistic expression. This sets up a degree of safety for all members of the group. Their art work reflects a more realistic world. Sky is blue for day, multicolored for sunsets. Smoke comes out of chimneys in a certain way. These children are curious about how things work, where animals live, what a Chinese family looks like; all are useful subjects for art. Children who have collections can share their experiences and treasures with the class as part of an art experience.

Providing Developmentally Suited Art Sessions

As with the other stages, to provide therapeutic art sessions for Stage Three and Four children, the sessions must be developmentally suitable. They must also build upon a base of 1) trust in the teacher, 2) trust in themselves, and 3) a sense of value in the art activity. At the beginning, art lessons often are individually planned. The structured time is followed by a "free" art time with crayons

---

[3] "Dawning realism" is the description given by Lowenfeld and Brittain to the stage of development usually occurring between ages nine and twelve.

and paper for anyone who finishes the day's assignment. This allows the most insecure child to attempt the day's lesson with the promise that he can then draw his favorite car or scene to his heart's content.

At Stage Three, art lessons are "open-ended" art times, not product-oriented. For instance, one effective lesson is, "What can you do with a large sheet of colored construction paper, scissors, and glue?" No sooner does the Stage Three teacher have the words out than the majority of the children are clamoring for supplies and shouting a hundred ideas. This same question used with Stage Two children would cause anxiety and result in restless, defensive behavior. When Stage Two children are grouped with Stage Three children for this particular lesson, special adaptations must be made. For example, a child who cannot creatively handle the materials should be given support, such as suggesting that he cut the strips and make rings for a three-dimensional design on a second sheet of paper or turn the rings into a paper chain. This open-ended approach assures everyone success on their level because there is no right or wrong.

With subsequent lessons, the Stage Three children begin to feel confident in themselves and can begin to reach out to others. It is not unusual to see a new friend helping a child at art time. The significant socialization process of middle childhood is at work. As the children become used to working with one another, large sheets of butcher paper can be rolled out. This gets everyone involved in coming up with a topic for "today's mural."

This is not to say there are no blow-ups, spilled paint, or torn art work. There are. But these disruptions lessen with each day of success and with gains in developmental milestones. Some

of the most disturbed children can emerge as leaders during different art experiences. For example, a child, living in a bizarre fantasy world, was able to transfer his imagined friends and pleasures into beautiful art work and show others in the group the techniques to produce the same dramatic effect.

The art supplies that prove most successful should be used each day. Crayons, pencils, magic markers, and water colors should always be available along with an endless supply of 12″ × 18″ sheets of white drawing paper. A roll of butcher paper serves the same purpose but also conveys a sense of abundance. As the children become used to the expectations and routine, more supplies can be provided for the children to choose from each day. More time may be needed to help them clean up, but the processes of sharing, following directions, and self-direction have begun.

Dramatic changes in socialization and behavior controls can be observed week by week. For example, one Stage Three group began each art session sitting around one large table for the introductory discussion, instructions, and demonstration. As soon as everyone understood the lesson, each child got his supplies and went anywhere in the room he chose. This led to children isolating themselves in corners on the floor, or one or two at each table working on individual projects. Such isolation is not a desired outcome for Stage Three children but is often necessary during the early part of Stage Three.

By the fourth week a few children elected to stay at the main table together, and several went to a corner to work together. Group murals were good for encouraging such activity. At first the children drew individual pictures, cut them out, and each placed his picture on one large sheet. Another version was a very quick attempt with magic markers to make an "Instant Design" on white butcher paper. The children then selected their favorite medium for free art time. This seemed to drain off the tensions surrounding the unfamiliar process of group collaboration.

Art, music, and drama are important vehicles for emotional growth during the middle childhood years, and, when combined, they can be most effective (Purvis and Samet, 1976). One Stage Three group put together a play and variety show during special activity times. Art time was used to make a backdrop and props. The children were so motivated by this venture that socialization skills emerged at a great rate! The play emerged into a unique version of "West Side Story" involving music, movement, and art. The group decided to interpret "The Rumble" and described it as "a riot with guys getting creamed." The backdrop was a highly successful city skyline, the first completely satisfactory group mural, according to the group's judgment. Subsequently this group produced artistic versions of the overture to "Carousel" interpreted through dance and art as a circus; "I Heard it Through the Grapevine" with an elaborate grapevine mural; and "The Blue Danube" with water scenery and swinging body motions. Each member of this group made significant strides toward emotional maturity through these intensely satisfying group collaborations.

Another aspect of combining art and music can be the creation of musical instruments. Stage Three children have great success with this activity. Maracas can be made from "L'egg" plastic containers filled with dried beans or rice. Using masking tape, attach a toilet paper roll to the end of each container and then apply papier mâché over the entire object. Another lesson can involve tempera painting and shellacking the maracas. Simple drums can be made from coffee cans or dried oatmeal containers, decorated around the sides with colorful construction paper.

One advanced Stage Three group dyed T-shirts for their costumes, painted a poster naming their musical group "The Aces," and, after many rehearsals, their teachers video-taped a performance of their best number, "Jeremiah Was a Bullfrog," dancing and using their handmade instruments. They were so pleased with the tape that they invited the director of the center and other guests for a replay, with popcorn served to all!

For Stage Four children, combined creative activities can lead to exciting dramatics, original stories, choreography, and art work. Richard Crosscup (1966, p. 200) describes one way in which art can be part of a complex, creative production appropriate for Stage Four children.

> Following a discussion of what a scene should contain, it is sketched in with charcoal or chalk. Then the drawing is painted with tempera. The less the adults do, the better it will be. Very seldom do children get a chance to paint in such a large way and anyone acquainted with children's art work—the color, the impact, the two dimensional force—will understand that this is an opportunity for magnificence which children will not fail to take advantage of.

The Stage Four child is becoming a creative, functioning member of his family, school, and community. He is eager to accept guidance in extending his own talents and life experiences. The structure of the art class can be modified to enhance these new interests and abilities. One student may work slowly, meticulously, while others produce results quickly. Art projects can be designed for individuals or the group. Praise is less contrived and more reality-oriented than at previous stages. Where praise was used before to motivate a child to continue participation in art, now praise for art work can be on genuine artistic merit. Stage Four children function within a reality context, and it is up to the teacher to maintain and enhance this contact. This is the opportune time for self-evaluation to begin. *"You know, Joey, you are really best in art when using paints. Some people are good using oils, others do their best work using water colors. Of all the media you use now, tempera is definitely the best! Do you know why you are so good with it? Have you always liked it? Would you consider working with craypas today, even if the results aren't as good as your paintings?"*

Corrections and suggestions should be given to Stage Four children routinely. It is not always necessary to accept a first attempt. Stage Four children are eager to add improvements to their work. Constructive criticism from the teachers and the group can be encouraged. *"At the end of class today, I would like to put everyone's art work on display and discuss them. I've noticed some good things happening in each person's work and I want to share it with the class."*

There should be no art lesson a Stage Four group cannot attempt. The fun of trying new projects can take precedence over easy art lessons that always ensure successful results. Field trips to museums and libraries, nature walks, excursions to the zoo to draw animals or to a junk yard to paint abstract impressions are highly productive for Stage Four children. Art lessons drawing "unusual" sights can help students see their world more clearly. Drawing the pipes under a sink, the design on a butterfly's wing, or the motor of a car allows for new insight and awareness.

There is the opportunity to teach techniques and art methods upon re-quest. A Stage Four child trying to draw a boat in the background of his picture asks how to make it look far away. Now is the teacher's opportunity to tell him the "secret," *"If you draw something smaller than other objects in the picture, it will make it look like it's farther away."*

Conducting the Art Sessions

Each child's abilities, likes, and dislikes are important in setting up valuable group art experiences with successful outcomes. In Stage Three, the children's verbal skills are developed enough to allow for some discussion before each group art project begins. You need to guide this discourse and lead the group to choose an appropriate subject and project in which each child is able to contribute successfully. The main emphasis at Stage Three is the involvement of the children with each other through the art medium. The demonstration, the subject to be painted, the work time, all need to motivate the group interaction— not focus on individual art products.

At first, minimum verbal instructions should be the rule. This helps anxious students to settle into each lesson easily. Demonstrating while talking proves most effective. For example, while making a clay animal, you could say, *"If you watch my hands while I talk, you can see how to do today's lesson."*

Gradually, lessons can be introduced on a more complicated verbal basis. *"Today, we will try making mobiles. First, cut out a tag board shape any way you want it to be. Then get a supply of mosaics and glue to decorate the shape. When you get this step done, we will use a hole puncher to make a hole for string. Decide where you want your shape to hang on this wire frame. When we finish, we will have a group-made mobile."*

Lessons can be planned to last over twenty-minute periods as long as the teacher has prepared the students for this plan of action. *"To make these models today we will need more than one art session, so we'll work for the entire time today. When art time is over, put your name on your model kit. Put all your model parts back in the box, close the glue, and store it in the box too. I'll save them for you for the next time. Our last lesson will be to make an airport for the finished model planes."*

As lessons begin, actually use art terms and call tools by their proper name. Use the art terms appropriate to each art lesson: "background," "designs," "texture," "dark colors vs. light colors," "pastels," etc. *"How is a water color brush different from a tempera paint brush?"* As the group progresses, make lessons into more involved procedures. Instead of finishing a lesson each day, plan a lesson that requires one day for half the procedure, and the next day to finish up. Always briefly "talk through" the art lesson for that day. Then start the class off step-by-step. Compliment creativity and emphasize design in any picture that looks as if a child needs encouragement.

Stages Three and Four children eventually should be able to use all art materials, even the messy ones such as pastels and craypas, with minimum trouble. The children should be able to prevent smearing their own work with minimum frustration as they use these tools. A verbal cue to the children should be enough to prevent them from smearing their work. *"Hold your arms off the paper so it doesn't get on your forearm."* Directions to, *"Keep the paper steady by holding it where you did not put any coloring"* should be acceptable to the children.

Stage Three children have become accustomed to most of the art materials that are available, and now it is up to you to suggest original art lessons. Materials such as styrofoam and aluminum foil offer many new ideas, such as making animals and figures from styrofoam pieces and toothpicks. You can also use needle and thread to string foam pieces for necklaces, or make "windchimes" that are silent but move beautifully in the wind. Draw on foil with a pencil, lightly so as not to tear the foil. Coat it with a thin layer of India ink and then gently rub off the ink, leaving the patina finish as thick or as light as desired.

By Stage Four, children should be able to critique their own art work under *careful* supervision and be able to point out the best features of each person's art work that day. Leave negative criticism alone. However, they should be able to go back and elaborate on it with suggestions from you. Children who cannot or will not do this should be allowed to do free art lessons of their own choice as long as they have tried the assignment. Some standby art tools that all children like to use should always be available for these "free" lessons because if the child has failed on a new lesson, he should have a good lesson with a trusted medium such as crayons or pencil and paper. This will allow him to save face and to regain his position in the group.

If the group is responding well to art sessions, the children are quick to prepare for art each time. The "I can't do it" moans should not be heard anymore except as an occasional habit response. If you are still getting it from any of your students, reply immediately, *"You might be right and if this lesson is too hard, I'll help you when you get in trouble!"* Or, *"Let me get the rest of the class started and I'll give you help."* Or, *"Let's begin and then see where it gets tough."* The objective here is to stress how we can learn from one another. Whatever response you give, the point is to agree with the child and relieve his symptoms, give yourself time to start the lesson for the others, and finally allow the child the chance either to wait for your help or to change his mind and try it on his own. If you find it necessary to help him, do it quickly just to get him going. If he is especially fearful, find something to praise right away. *"I like the way you are holding your crayon, now make a circle to start your drawing."* Here you have praised the child and instructed him in his first step in one sentence. The minute he continues by himself give him some privacy to create on his own. *"Great! You continue for awhile by yourself while I see what John and Sue are doing. I hope they are doing as well as you."* This brings you back to the other children, and the focus is once again on the entire group.

Even at this stage of development there will be children in Stage Three who, because of individual problems, are still unable to draw on the level of the other children. These children will become more and more frustrated unless they learn to feel that whatever they try to do is as good as the work done by the other members of the class. The Stage Three goal stresses the individual child learning to function as part of a group.

Some children finish every art lesson in two or three minutes, while everyone else is just beginning. When a child does this, compliment what has been done and suggest that he now use two colors in place of the one color or repeat a design in three places instead of the one area on his sheet of paper. If the child is still distressed by his inability to make anything out of his work, then you should help him "see" things in his work. *"Hey, look over here at this loop you drew; this looks just like the head of a horse!"* You can ask permission to

draw on his paper and then turn the loop into a horse's head and see what reaction you get from the child. He might be overwhelmed with what you have done and reject it. If he does, challenge him to see what he can do with another part of his drawing; or he might find this fascinating and go right into changing the other parts of his drawing into animals or objects. He might also fall back on this in the next art lesson and use you as a crutch. If this should happen, give him a few ideas but do not draw them for him; or say you are really intrigued by his picture today and think it makes a beautiful abstract design just the way it is!

With Stage Four children, risking failure is feasible. Allow them to choose the subject matter of the day and the art materials they wish to work with. If the children make creative use of this free choice, then allow it to continue. If, on the other hand, they continually fall back on old art lessons (peace signs, trees, flowers, houses, etc.) then intervene and try to stimulate their imaginations. This can be done with stories, pictures, incidents that may have happened in class, current events, TV, and their own lives. These children should be adaptable enough now to attempt any art lesson you put in front of them. They may not succeed, but they should have learned from you that the *attempt* is the important part of each art lesson. This attitude hopefully should be carried over to other activities and to the children's attitudes about themselves, helping them to begin to emerge as *healthy* individuals.

**Managing Behavior
Problems in a Therapeutic Way**

At the beginning of Stage Three, children often attempt to test limits to establish their positions in the group and to test the adult's control. *"I don't want to do this." "That's dumb kid stuff."*

This is a general reaction to insecurity about new situations. Any negative responses must be dealt with immediately. Sometimes simple redirection works. *"Oh, you don't want to work with tempera; I can understand your feelings. Let's see if you can start your picture with a pencil first. Sometimes that makes for a better picture."*

Reassurance and constructive help can often do the trick. *"Well, this is a hard lesson. Would it help if I draw the first part of the animal and see if you can finish it from there?"*

Being creative and flexible is imperative now. *"Oh, you don't want to draw today? That's too bad. Do you feel well? You do. Sometimes we all don't feel like doing certain things, but we do them."* [In confidential tone] *"Do you see what a fantastic monster Ted is drawing? I wonder if you know how to draw that kind of animal? Since that's the lesson today, once you've done your best, I'll let you draw anything you want. As a matter of fact, as soon as you complete today's lesson, we'll have a free-choice art time."* Always having a back-up art lesson will also save many a disastrous situation!

The decision as to when to continue to redirect negative behavior, when to confront the child with his action, and when to interpret are delicate questions. The main factor to be considered is whether the entire class is disintegrating because of the acting-out behavior or whether they can ignore the behavior and continue on the project, enhancing their own strengths and controls in the process. The question is, will ignoring the disturbing child result in his coming back into the group spontaneously, or will he cause further disruption because of his isolation? Keep in mind it is through willing participation that developmental milestones are mastered.

The teacher's role is not only as an authority figure helping the group maintain expectations but also an advocate and supporter for the child in crisis. Helping the child to begin making positive social overtures to other classmates is important now. Praise for all positive artistic efforts, behavior, and outward social actions is often effective. Redirection and remotivation to a highly desirable art experience may be productive. The key is understanding the child's feelings and aligning with the child to work through the crisis. With such an attitude of trust and mutual respect there are few rules needed to govern behavior during art time. Five basic rules for Stage Three are listed below:

1. In art you can talk all you want, but some art work has to be done. (Doodling is accepted as art work.)
2. If you use supplies, you put them back.
3. You don't mess with anyone else's art work.
4. If you mess up something, don't throw it away. Put your name on it. Give it to the teacher and tell her if you want it shown or put away. Then you can have another sheet of paper. There is no limit to the number of pictures you can do.
5. Anyone who wants to be "mean" during art time, can—away from the art class!

If a student does not like his own work and has a history of destroying his work, be alert. When the first sign of frustration is shown, two alternatives are available:

1. Be at hand to remove the work just before the destruction occurs. When this is done, always admire the product and tell the child you value it because it is something he has done. Be sure to save each work removed this way. There will be a time when the work can be reviewed to show accomplishment.
2. Tell the student he can start again on the back of the drawing or by tearing down the clay or other three-dimensional material and starting again. This is the way many artists work.

If you are too late to prevent the destruction, always gather up the pieces. Whenever possible, see that the child tapes the pieces back together. Then put the paper safely away because it is the child's work and what he does is important. Try to avoid displaying these repaired papers. Such a move would display the child's inadequacy to the group.

When the destroyed product of one day's art session is to be the basis for the next day's session, it is important to prepare another for the child before the next lesson occurs. This procedure conveys a sense of security to the child. He can trust the teacher not to embarrass him further. It also permits the child to participate in the group activity as an equal.

Each student must learn that the smallest attempt is valued. Insist on keeping all art work (including the rejects) and verbalize the reason. *"What's important is that you try, and when you try it's part of you. That's important."* Hopefully this approach will be accepted by the students in time and will encourage them to do their best in each art experience. Eventually, these ideas should become part of each child's own outlook.

A TYPICAL STAGE THREE ART EXPERIENCE

A memorable water color lesson with a Stage Three class illustrates a typical Stage Three art experience. The group, five boys, is volatile and aggressive. The boys have limited manipulative and artistic skills, and yet within this group emerging personalities are becoming evident. John is the most artistic of the group. He is twelve years old, unable to read on a third grade level, soft spoken, and a "model" for the group. Alfonso is an impulsive thirteen-year-old. If he does not get what he wants immediately, he acts out to destroy the activity and to get the needed attention. Eleven-year-old Ken is the smallest of the five boys physically but functions at the highest level intellectually in the group. When unable to do a task he withdraws, but as soon as supportive help is provided he is able to continue. Jeff, age twelve, seems the ideal child to the casual observer, especially at art time, which he loves dearly. However, when he wants attention or is displeased with his work, he either baits the nearest child to start a fight or attempts to destroy the group project. Francis, an insecure eleven-year-old, is a child who fluctuates from being teacher's pet, cry baby, the class scapegoat, or the class clown.

When the group was first formed, no group art lessons worked. Each child had individual supplies and an individual but parallel project. They succeeded individually because of the personal attention given to each boy and because they were allowed to do favorite drawings using "easy" art supplies. Gradually, the teacher planned art activities in which the boys on one side of the table would make one section of a project and the boys on the other side the remaining

S-21
to suggest activities or preference for play materials to the teacher for group activity.

S-18
to participate in cooperative activities or projects with another child during organized class activities.

B-13
to verbally recall group rules and procedure.

C-14
to accept praise or success without inappropriate behavior or loss of control.

C-14
to accept praise or success without inappropriate behavior or loss of control.

part. Eventually several murals were attempted, with all of the children working side by side. These efforts usually ended with lines being drawn by the boys so "no one will draw on my place!" If their territory was violated, fights insued.

Water colors often have a calming effect, and with this group a little calm was needed. One day, as the group returned from outside game time, the art therapist went to the easel in the corner of the room, placed a sheet of paper on it, quickly sketched a bunch of flowers, and began to paint quite intently. She describes what happened in the following narrative. As in previous chapters, development objectives are referenced in the margin.

The boys are saying things like,
"What the hell is she doing?"
"She's painting, asshole."
"Miss Williams, is it art time?"
"I ain't going to do it!"
Ignoring the verbal barrage, I ask, *"Who knows what kind of paint I am using?"* This verbal redirection takes back the control of the class.
"That stuff's called water colors."
"Right, John! I guess you all know how to use these paints."
The others see he is interested in what I am doing, so I have a chance to get them all involved. *"The hard thing is to decide what we should draw with pencils, first, and then paint, to look real good."*
Nervous stares and anxiety begin to build in the room. I either get them with me now or we'll be back to the same familiar projects again.
"I know three guys in here who are sensational at drawing cars... no names mentioned." A few smiles begin to show, and knowing looks are exchanged among the boys. *"I know another guy who can draw people and one who is great at drawing trees. How could we put all that together in a big picture?"*

"We could draw a road in the country and put cars on it," offers John.
"Yeah, I'll draw cars," says Jeff.
"So will I," says John.
"I'll do the people," says Francis.
"I don't want to do it," says Ken dejectedly.
Alfonso offers no comment, so I decide to make him my helper. This will get him involved in the group and functioning rather than allowing him to isolate himself.
As Alfonso hands out pencils, the boys help to spread the large butcher paper on the table. To prevent any immediate frustrations, I put some structure out for all to hear.
"All you boys know how to use pencils really good, but what should you do if you have a problem?"
Francis immediately responds, *"You should ask the teacher for help!"* Before anyone can pounce on him, I compliment his recall and ask if they want to use chairs or stand as they work.
They agree they need their chairs. Now the five boys, close to each other, are staring at the white paper.
The usual *"Don't-you-draw-over-my-line"* is heard from two of the boys, and I ignore this by setting up the procedure to obtain paint.
"O.K. guys. I know you are ready to start drawing. Oh, Jeff, you've already begun—all right!"
"Now when you think you need paint, brush, and water, turn in your pencil to me and you'll get your water color supplies."
They are working now, all except Ken. Alfonso has begun a car next to Jeff who is hard at work. Francis is working on people along the bottom of the paper.
Each child is talking about his work or experiences, and I respond where I think a response is necessary. One child actually listens to another and responds as he works. Another compliments this part of a drawing or that, and they are all succeeding to some degree. Except Ken.
I walk down the line behind them as they work, giving an idea here, a compliment there, and a reminder out loud to no one in particu-

lar: if anyone needs help, all they need to do is ask for it. I continue down toward Ken, stopping for a final word to Jeff who is next to him.

"Jeff, where did you learn to draw so good?" I inquire.

He beams and snuggles down closer to his work and shrugs delightedly.

"I bet Ken would like to draw a car like that. Gosh, that'd be too much to ask of you, though." Jeff is interested. Ken is looking at him. *"What?"* he asks.

"Why, to take the time to start a car for Ken! Would you want a car or a person, Ken?" (I'm giving Ken a way to ask for help from Jeff, not from me.)

"A car," Ken says.

"Sure, I'll do it. Come here, kid. Move over and I'll start it. Now watch this." Jeff's directions are masterly, and so Ken begins. I come back later to redirect Jeff back to his own drawing and compliment Ken into finishing his part of the project, which he did quite well.

When verbal interaction becomes too involved and begins detracting from the project, I notice aloud that two boys are ready for paint. The timing is critical. They take the cue, turn in their pencils, and obtain their paint supplies. This in turn motivates the others, and soon everyone is painting.

I have purposely set out only two containers of water for the five boys, to motivate sharing. This proves successful.

When some splashing takes place and water gets on one child's work, I ask, *"How can we keep this from happening again?"*

John suggests they get water slowly. I ask if everyone can do this?

"Of course."

So back to more painting.

Then it happens. Black paint from Jeff's road somehow found its way to Alfonso's side of the paper. Instant profanity and pseudo-slugging at one another. Those not involved watch intently. John keeps painting.

I move between the two and put an arm around Alfonso, reflecting, *"That black paint sure did go over the line."*

"Yeah, you dumb head!" agrees Alfonso.

"But you know what I think the paint is telling you? It wants to become a road the

whole length of the picture! Everybody stop! Has everyone got black paint?"

"Sure" chime in the others.

"O.K., John, start a black line from your end to Francis." John quickly complies. (I picked the one I knew could set a model for the class.)

The black painted line is now a road! *"Francis, connect your road to his and paint it to Ken."*

"Ken, you are ahead of me. It's already connected up to Jeff's road! All right! Looking good! Now, Jeff, finish it to Alfonso's part."

"Now, Alfonso, you're O.K. and don't need help. Now where's your brush?" I help Alfonso to find his brush. He picks it up defiantly (one has to save face, you know) and struts back to the table. As no one is paying attention to him, he sits down meekly and finishes the line from one side to the other.

"Guys, you can go back to finish your work because we've got five minutes left. You all worked that road out together really nice!" I encourage them to finish specific parts of their art work. Alfonso needs the structure on what to do to finish successfully. When he is involved again, I reflect to the class how neat it is when everyone works together to solve a guy's problem!

A few affirmative nods and comments on their "bad" cars. We display the picture together, and everyone reflects on their "tough" picture. The clean-up time goes smoothly because each child helps. One collects paint sets; one picks up the brushes; another puts pencils on my desk; and the other two wipe off the table.

When they are back at their chairs, I reflect how good they did that day with only one accident!

"Yeah, Alfonso was mad!" said John. *"But he did good, teacher."*

"He didn't hit Jeff 'cause then he'd get in trouble!" said Francis encouragingly. Alfonso looks like he'd enjoy pushing Francis through the wall.

"You guys know it's not cool to lose your temper and end up hurting someone. It isn't easy to remember, but I'm sure proud that you

B-12
to spontaneously participate in routines without physical intervention.

B-19
to maintain self-control and to comply with group procedures.

C-19
to use words or nonverbal gestures to show pride in own work, activity, or to make positive statements about self.

S-24
to recognize and describe characteristics of others.

can do just that. Now, what's the next thing we have on our schedule for today?"

The teacher quickly changes the subject because the point has been made and a lecture is unnecessary. A number of significant developmental objectives have been involved in this group project. On another day, after a similar experience, the boys were led through a discussion asking each other about different ways to handle the problem of someone getting mad. This verbal interchange led them to fuller understanding of the feelings and consequences of their actions. Each contributed what he was able to do. The group became stronger, and each child was lending support and skills to each other.

A STAGE FOUR ART EXPERIENCE

As children master the Stage Three developmental objectives in behavior, socialization, communication, and academics they may be ready for placement in a Stage Four group or for termination from therapy. It is always a focus of therapy to help children function in the mainstream as efficiently as possible. Sometimes a therapy class will serve this purpose. In other instances work with the child's regular school will best achieve the acquisition of developmental objectives at the next stage.

The art therapist provided such a transition for Wendy, a thirteen-year-old Stage Four girl. Wendy had been referred to the center for aggressive, destructive behavior. She was unable to cope with any stress. She had experienced immense family upheaval from the days of her infancy; as a result, her coping responses to any stress were to throw tantrums or beat up someone until she got her way or got out of the situation.

After a year in a Stage Three developmental therapy group, she had learned to manage her impulses in much more acceptable ways. She had gained a better self-image; her parents had been helped to establish a more structured home environment; and she was functioning in a middle school on a half-time basis.

Wendy had achieved most of the Stage Three developmental objectives and needed a Stage Four group. Because successful school adjustment was critical, a Stage Four group was formed at her school. Three girls from the school who would be appropriate models for Wendy wanted to participate in this special high school preparation/art class. The three girls were academically superior, socially adept, and found this course interesting. The art therapist hoped that Wendy would see positive characteristics in the other three girls that she would like to use herself.

This school had several other high school preparation classes, and the art therapist's visit three times a week was viewed as simply another group. Using art lessons as the focus of each one-and-a-half-hour session, the art therapist was able to maintain Wendy successfully in her middle school. As she found acceptance in this group, Wendy gained status for the first time in the school. The girls in this group *never* would have associated with Wendy under other circumstances. Her reputation had preceded her everywhere in the community. However, as the group was helped to discover the positive attributes and skills in each other, she was acknowledged openly as something other than an aggressive, hostile girl. Her art skills, acting ability, and love of children were carefully brought out during the sessions.

All the activities planned for each art session were fun, very "cool," and for girl's only! In addition to art projects, the girls did charades (*"To help gain poise for high school"*), dancing, cooking lessons, field trips to the local high school (*"To see what it'll be like when you are there next year"*), and a tour of a restored historical mansion (*"To study interior decoration and history"*). For one unit, each girl was teacher for the day. Each chose what she would like to teach the others. Wendy chose child care, and the teacher helped her to write questions, prepare displays, and finally on "her day" drove her to her sister-in-law's house so Wendy could get her two-year-old nephew for a live demonstration in class! Everyone was impressed with Wendy!

For another unit, the girls became very interested in embroidery and diligently worked on their own beautiful floral designs. The group all enjoyed this particular art activity, but Wendy resisted when her first attempts failed. While the others did their art work, Wendy wrote a story. She was proud of her handwriting and quite skilled at creating stories. The group agreed to this when the art therapist explained that writing was an art form.

As each member worked on her own project, Wendy wrote with great gusto. The art therapist encouraged the girls to examine each other's work. This led to compliments and expanded discussions of what each liked, their family experiences, and, in general, discovery of one

another as interesting people. Wendy's story was woven into these discussions by the art therapist. Finally, the breakthrough came when the group leader offered to show Wendy how to embroider, and the offer was accepted!

Wendy's growth is typical of Stage Four children. They are able to learn to deal with their own temper tantrums, frustration, and anxiety on more of a verbal level and with less acting out. Self-esteem grows from a successful group's interactions. Art is a most effective means to ensure that these developmental milestones emerge. Sometimes, individual projects are needed; sometimes, group projects. One child may need to attempt an art lesson that he has never done before. Both success and failure can now be therapeutic and both are important parts of the Stage Four experience.

The following section contains materials and activities suggested for use with Stage Three followed by a section applying to Stage Four. The lessons in these sections are not explained in as much detail as in the previous stages where basic structures of the lessons, supplies, and step-by-step procedures are outlined. In the following sections, attention has been given to adaptations in motivation and content that directly involve the developmental objectives of the middle childhood years.

As Stage Three children develop greater self-esteem, they become increasingly free to respond to membership in the group. "A quality of groupness" begins to emerge. As children are able to sit next to one another with minimum negative exchanges, work together as a group, share supplies, and find success in their mutual effort, you know your Stage Three children are making significant developmental progress.

The exact point at which a Stage Three child moves into Stage Four is usually difficult to determine. The transition often is obscured by intermittent episodes of regression followed by spurts of new skills, sometimes appearing when you least expect them. One thing you can be sure of, when children care enough about the group to sublimate their own needs to the group welfare and when the group accepts and respects the individual differences of each group member, the Stage Four goal of increased individual self-esteem has been met.

ART ACTIVITIES FOR STAGE THREE

Medium	Special Preparation	Suggested Content	Step-by-Step Motivation
Acrylic	Not applicable at this stage		
Art Appreciation	Discussing art work can always be a filler before, during, or after a lesson. A game can be made of showing pictures: "Who can name what they saw?" This can be done with photos, prints of old masters, or matching posters or pictures with music, as described in the Stage Two list of art activities.		
Batik	Not applicable at this stage		
Beadwork	This activity is not generally motivating because it often is viewed as tedious by Stage Three children. One exception is to use beadwork as part of a unit lesson on Indians, etc. The group can recreate original Indian designs or make up their own if interest is sufficient.		
Candlemaking	Not applicable at this stage		
Cast Stone	See art lesson for plaster with vermiculite		
Charcoal	This activity is not generally applicable at this stage because it usually frustrates children due to its "messy" results.		
Clay	Use the same basic procedures described for previous stages. However, more time should be spent on creating objects and textures. Determine subject matter for each lesson through group discussion. This discussion and subsequent lesson can encompass a wide range of social, behavior, and communication skills. Also see Chapter Five for a detailed description of clay lessons for Stage Three children.		
Collage	You will need: 1. A mixed selection of different types of papers and colors: newspaper, paper towels, tissue paper, napkins, cardboard scraps, construction paper, paper chains (pre-glued surface), paper cup cake liners. 2. Glue and scissors (left and right handed). 3. Mural-size paper for a group or individual. 18" X 24" sheets of construction paper. (Some children cannot work together early in Stage Three, and separate work is better than no participation.) *Note:* This is a nonstructured lesson to encourage manipulative and conceptual experimentation.	Free choice by group or individuals	1. Discuss and demonstrate how to tear, cut wiggly lines, fold, crunch, and curl paper; then challenge the class to see how creative they can be with the materials and these basic techniques. 2. Control supplies by specifying three selections to start. When these are used, three more selections may be made. 3. Follow up the lesson with a group discussion of various ideas, designs, color relationships, and patterns that emerge from the collage.
Copper Enameling	Not applicable at this stage		

(*continued*)

ART ACTIVITIES FOR STAGE THREE (continued)

Medium	Special Preparation	Suggested Content	Step-by-Step Motivation
Crayon	You will need: 1. One box of crayons per two children (to encourage sharing). 2. Assorted sizes of paper to allow each child the size paper he wishes. (Small sheets would help insecure children. The bigger sheets would take longer to fill up but would be indicative of a child's bravura or security!)	Any subject (class can decide on subject, or each child can do his own design)	1. Demonstrate how to use crayons to produce a *heavy* line (more pressure), a thin line (light pressure), a *quick* drawing (with different areas colored in), or *outline* (with black for a dramatic effect). 2. Distribute crayons to every two students to share, and ask each child which size paper he wants. 3. Compliment each child's effort *no matter* how he is using the crayon (except in a destructive manner). Especially remark on those who use all four techniques in one drawing! 4. Finish the lesson on a positive note if at all possible, and display one work by each child. 5. Any fast workers can be allowed to do as many pictures as they want to do or have time to do! 6. A critique can be led at the end to discuss the four techniques used that day.
Crayon Resist	Use the same procedures described for Stage One, but allow for more interchange of ideas for subjects and work time with crayon; motivate more variety in designs.		
Craypas and Craypas Resist	Use the same procedures described for Stage One, except provide more time for planning and work on the project. Group discussion of subject matter can be used to achieve social and behavior objectives.		
Découpage	Not applicable at this stage		
Diorama	You will need: 1. Oak, tag, poster board (9″ X 12″), or large box for group to work on together. 2. Scraps of all colors of construction paper. 3. Glue and scissors for each student. 4. Crayons to share. 5. Magazines, Christmas cards.	Any subject	1. Display several finished dioramas. 2. Demonstrate how to make "prop-up" sticks to hold shapes upright and give the three-dimensional effect by gluing prop and picture to tag board. 3. Distribute magazines or Christmas cards and encourage each child to choose a subject and cut out objects, people, etc. With advanced Stage Three, the group can decide on a subject and then the teacher helps

(continued)

Medium	Special Preparation	Suggested Content	Step-by-Step Motivation
Diorama *(cont.)*			assign work roles to come up with finished product.
			4. Watch for original ideas and provide encouragement.
			5. Plan a display area with title cards for each diorama.
Etching *(with crayons)* *(two parts)*	You will need first day 1. Liquid soap mixed into black tempera ($\frac{1}{4}$ to 1 cup paint) in a container. 2. Sheets of white drawing paper. 3. A box of broken crayons for everyone to share. 4. A #12 brush for each child. 5. Newspaper spread on desk area. You will need second day: 1. Scissors or pencil for each child to use as an etching tool.	Free design	On the first day 1. Demonstrate and explain the process: a) Paper is completely filled with different colors of crayon applied as *heavily* as possible (no black is used) b) Paint with soapy black tempera to cover the coloring completely. (If paint resists the crayon, add more liquid soap until it sticks.) c) Use a previously completed painting and etch through the dried black paint to reveal crayon colors 2. Explain to children that this is a two-day art lesson; distribute paper and crayons; encourage designs using bright, shiny colors. Be sure each child's name is on the back of his art work. 3. As each child completes coloring, pour a small amount of black paint and liquid soap mixture into a cup, provide a brush, and encourage him to cover the paper. 4. Remove brush and remaining paint immediately, and put painted paper in a safe place to dry. 5. Provide extra paper for coloring more designs while others finish. On the second day 1. Ask children to think of their favorite shape or design while looking at their black, painted paper. 2. Encourage them to imagine how they would draw that design. (They may want to use their finger to point it out.) 3. Distribute tool for etching and

(continued)

ART ACTIVITIES FOR STAGE THREE (continued)

Medium	Special Preparation	Suggested Content	Step-by-Step Motivation
Etching (with crayons) (cont.)			encourage children to repeat the design they just thought of. 4. Display etchings and ask each child to make up a title and tell it to the group.
Finger Painting	Not applicable at this stage		
Jewelry Making	See the wire or pipe cleaner lesson		
Leathercraft	If *easy* kits are available and students *express an interest*, this could be attempted late in Stage Three.		
Lettering	If students have a group play or project coming up and signs are needed, a lettering project using rulers, magic markers, or crayons on poster board could be attempted by the group. Stencils could also be used to ensure success.		
Macramé	Not applicable at this stage		
Magic Markers *Lesson 1* *On glass or plastic*	You will need: 1. Three to five magic markers per child (their choice of colors). 2. Large, mural-size sheet of plastic or a glass window that is easy to reach.	City; circus; underwater scene	1. Lead group into discussion of procedures for using magic markers (caps on back; do not press too hard on felt tip or it will go in and isn't usable). Discuss how to assign glass area for each child and how to work with the persons on either side. Before anyone begins, discuss what the group should draw. 2. Once everyone has agreed on a subject, suggest starting points for your insecure students, praise your early starters, and constantly monitor individual progress. *"Joe is drawing a nice outline; he can fill in later; Tom's trees are drawn right next to Mary's house. It looks like a friendly neighborhood."* 3. As the basic drawing is completed, start motivating children to color in specified areas, exchange colors, add details. Stay on guard for signs of frustration in any of the children. 4. When the project is nearly completed, let the entire group admire it and discuss what it needs to be finished. If a lot of work is needed, this can be delayed to a second lesson. If the

(continued)

Medium	Special Preparation	Suggested Content	Step-by-Step Motivation
Magic Markers *Lesson 1 (cont.)*			group's interest is invested in finishing it, and it can be done within the time limit, encourage completion so it can be put on display.
			5. At the end of the lesson or when time is up, appoint someone to help collect magic markers.
			The group can tape the project up for display and make a sign telling about it.
			The transition time from ending an exciting, fun art project to moving into another activity is usually chaotic and difficult. Praise the children who are leading the way; also begin to introduce and motivate for the next activity.
Magic Markers *Lesson 2* *Student* *outlines*	You will need: 1. A six-foot length of butcher paper for each child. 2. Magic markers for each child to select a variety of colors as needed. 3. Masking tape.	Teacher draws outline of each student	1. Explain that each child is going to have a "figure portrait" done. Choose your most positive, nonacting-out student to demonstrate.
			2. Have the student stand up flat against paper taped on the wall. As he takes a "pose" quickly draw an outline around him.
			3. Have the child describe what he is wearing and use Magic Markers to color in his figure to make it look like him. Involve the group in this discussion if necessary.
			4. The hardest part of this lesson is the waiting required of the children not participating yet. Compliment their "waiting" ability. If you have more than one teacher, outlining the activity will be smoother.
			5. End the lesson when majority of the work is done. Have the children step back and look at the "together group" on the wall.
Metal Work	Not applicable at this stage		
Mixed Media	Use the same procedures as described for previous stages; however, more planning, time, and variety can be used now by group to achieve Stage Three objectives.		

(continued)

ART ACTIVITIES FOR STAGE THREE (continued)

Medium	Special Preparation	Suggested Content	Step-by-Step Motivation
Mobiles	You will need: 1. Wire coat hangers 2. Assorted objects 3. Glue 4. String	Free design	1. Demonstrate how to unbend a coat hanger; tie two together in an X shape; and suspend free-form shapes. 2. Assign children to work with partners. 3. Provide each pair with two or three hangers, a selection of objects, styrofoam, toothpicks, glue, string, and wire. 4. Provide a place in the room to hang each mobile. A clothesline from one wall to the door works well. 5. Assist any pair that runs into a balance problem. 6. An advanced version is an "ultimate mobile" that the entire group develops.
Model Building	This is an individual activity that should be given a group focus. Each child makes a model airplane, and then the group can make an airport to display the models.		
Mosaics	Use the same procedures as described for previous stages, but attempt a group project or do mosaic pictures with a partner.		
Natural Materials (twigs, rocks, shells, leaves)	You will need: 1. Containers of collected materials ready for the class. (A field trip could have been made previously to collect them.) 2. Glue and scissors for each student. 3. Scraps of colored construction paper. 4. Sheets of tag or poster board (18″ × 24″) for "partners" or large mural sheet for entire group. *Note:* There are two approaches to this lesson. For lower Stage Three children allow each to keep the natural materials he has found for use in his own collage. For more advanced children, put all materials in a common pool for sharing as a group. The teacher should be the dispenser of the common pool.	Collage of any design or subject	1. Encourage children to place a few pieces at a time. 2. Comment on emerging designs, line, form, color, and texture. 3. Encourage the use of as many materials as desired. 4. Children can be cautioned against using too much glue. This will ruin a really good collage! 5. Everyone helps to clean up.
Oil Paints	Not applicable at this stage		

(continued)

Medium	Special Preparation	Suggested Content	Step-by-Step Motivation
Papier Mâché	This material can be used now, but is more valuable in the next stage where students can do the entire project. At Stage Three the teacher has to make the chicken wire form, mix wheat paste, and supervise the covering process. These steps are more valuable if the children have the skill and behavioral controls to do it all.		
Pastels *(color chalk)* *(Wet or dry method)*	Use the same basic preparation as described in previous stages, but lead a class discussion to choose a subject for a class mural. Have one box of pastels for every two children to encourage sharing.		
Pen and Ink	Not applicable at this stage		
Pencil	See procedures described for Stage Two, but elaborate on detail and realistic representation.		
Plaster *(with vermiculite)*	You will need: 1. Plaster (1 to 1½ cups per 2 to 3 cups of water) mixed and poured into cut-off quart-size paper milk containers. Add ½ to 1 cup vermiculite. This softens the dried plaster for easier carving. 2. A dull dinner knife or scissors with rounded edges. 3. Crayons and paper as a standby art lesson for those who finish carving early. 4. Pictures of carvings by famous artists (Verrochio, Bernini, Moore). *Note:* If there are any children in the group who could be dangerous to themselves or others with the above tools, do not use this lesson. This lesson also is more suitable for advanced Stages Three and Four children.	Animal or human forms	1. Demonstrate and make the plaster molds as the first lesson. 2. At the next session, let each child tear off the milk container from his mold. 3. Discuss the pictures of carvings. 4. Convey that this is an experiment, and if nothing comes out at least they will enjoy themselves today! 5. Reflect various carving strokes as the children experiment. 6. Put all carvings on trays for display, and lead the group to discuss the shapes, forms, and patterns.
Play-plax *(Crystal climbers)*	Use the same procedures as described in previous stages, but with more varied and sophisticated structures made individually and by the group.		
Pliable Plastics or Plexiglass	Not applicable at this stage		
Printing *Lesson 1* *Found objects*	You will need: 1. Containers of objects (spools, bolts, model parts, macaroni).	Free design	1. Let students choose and arrange objects on own sheet of paper. 2. Spray over the entire area. Let it

(continued)

Medium	Special Preparation	Suggested Content	Step-by-Step Motivation
Printing *Lesson 1 (cont.)*	2. Spray paint (fast-drying). 3. Construction paper of opposite color to paint (white paper, black paint). *Note:* This is a highly successful lesson with beginning Stage Three children.		dry for one or two minutes. Child can remove objects and check design. 3. Discuss pattern and design effects with each child. 4. A group mural also can be done, or as many different individual prints as time allows.

Printing
Lesson 2
(two parts)
String and glue
	You will need first day:
	1. 4″ X 4″ cardboard for each child.
	2. Twine or string
	3. Scissors and bottles of glue for each child.
	You will need second day:
	1. Printing ink (dark colors).
	2. One brayer for each two children to encourage sharing.
	3. Large sheets of light colored paper.
	4. Sheets of oakboard for spreading ink on. (Tiles or glass can be used.)
	5. Crayons
	Note: This lesson is most successful with advanced Stage Three children. It can be used for individual or group projects.
		Any subject	On the first day
			1. Be sure to establish this as as two-part lesson.
			2. Demonstrate how to "draw" with glue, making simple lines. Place string carefully over glue "trail."
			3. Provide supplies and encourage children to make simple lines.
			4. Let work dry overnight.
			
			On the second day
			1. Demonstrate and then assist children in these steps:
			  a) Squeeze out small amount (one tablespoon) of ink on oakboard; roll brayer back and forth, coating it completely.
			  b) Roll brayer over string design until string is covered with ink.
			  c) Place inked card face down on large sheet of paper. Press firmly. Do not move it!! Rub back of card with heavy object like wood or jar to achieve a clear print.
			  d) Quickly remove card. Repeat as often as the child wishes.
			  e) Fill in background with crayon when ink dries.

Printing *Lesson 3* *Vegetable prints*	Use the same procedures described for Stage One, but do it as a group project, filling in the background with crayons or craypas after prints are dry.		
Printing *Lesson 4* *Stencil* *and tempera*	You will need: 1. Paper cut to 9″ X 12″ size for stencil.	Free design	1. Demonstrate these steps: a) Fold 9″ X 12″ paper two or three times and cut out intricate pieces.

(continued)

ART ACTIVITIES FOR STAGE THREE (continued)

Medium	Special Preparation	Suggested Content	Step-by-Step Motivation
Printing *Lesson 4 (cont.)*	2. Paper 18″ X 24″ for printing. (Larger paper is used if a mural is attempted by the group.) 3. Sponges and different colors of tempera paint to be shared. 4. Scissors for each child.		b) Unfold paper and place over 18″ X 24″ paper. c) Dip sponge lightly in paint. Lightly apply paint in cut-out areas. Do not let stencil move. d) Replace sponge. Lift stencil quickly and carefully. 2. Provide supplies and encourage children to experiment. 3. Children can do as many different prints as time will permit. 4. A second lesson can be done when paint is dry by using crayons to color unpainted areas.
Rubbings	You will need: 1. Pencils, crayons, or craypas. 2. Newsprint or onion skin paper.	Any interesting surface	1. Demonstrate the process in the room, using ordinary surface (wood grain of a table top, vinyl patterns in floor, metal ID tags, license plate, coke bottle bottom, coffee cup design). Place a sheet of paper over the area to be reproduced and crayon back and forth in smooth, even strokes until the area is covered. As you do this, the design will emerge. 2. Describe the problems that may come up as you work. *"If the paper moves, the design is changed; so grasp the paper carefully." "The paper tears if the pressure is too hard."* 3. Help each child to select a surface for his rubbing. Then distribute paper and crayons. 4. As each child finishes one rubbing, encourage him to find another surface so he can have practice with several rubbings. Interest can be heightened by suggesting that each rubbing be done in a different color. 5. For advanced Stage Three children, group rubbings can be very effective. Structure it carefully so there is adequate surface and work space for all of the children to work simultaneously (such as parquet floors, brick wall, or

(continued)

Medium	Special Preparation	Suggested Content	Step-by-Step Motivation
Rubbings *(cont.)*			a local architectural bas relief or frieze.
			6. The rubbings can be matted or can become part of a larger picture using water color paints.
Sand Castings	You will need: 1. A large supply or area of sand (such as a sand table). 2. Plaster (quick-setting). 3. Gallon cans to mix plaster and water. 4. Drawing sticks. 5. Selected objects (bolts, nails, metal taps, broken glass, shells). 6. Outside water source to clean up. (If you use water supply inside, plaster can clog pipes! Use hose outside.)	Free design	1. Demonstrate the dipping process to create a design in the sand in reverse so that when plaster is poured into it, the hardened result will be the desired form (e.g., for a protrusion, scoop out a hole in the sand). 2. Encourage each child to make a design in the sand. 3. Mix three parts of plaster to one part of water in gallon can. Pour slowly, covering sand designs. 4. Cover sand area with table cloth. Allow to harden for a minimum of one hour. 5. Assist each child in pulling out plaster mold at end of class day. Brush loose sand from surfaces.
Sand Designing	Use the same procedures described in Stage One, but spend more time on subject matter. Instead of individual designs, partners can do one large design, or the entire group can do a mural.		
Sensory Lessons	As previously discussed in Stage One, all of the senses can be used as part of other activities (e.g., work time, art, snack, recreation, etc.). Suggestions:		
	1. For work	List all the senses and discuss how spices can be used in foods the children like to eat.	
	2. For snacks	Use fresh fruit; identify by smell and taste, and discuss countries they came from.	
	3. For games	Use spices and fruit names for a word game.	
	4. For art	Use glue to create a design and use oregano, garlic salt, and parsley flakes to finish the creation.	
Shell Jewelry	Not applicable at this stage		
Soap Carving	Not applicable at this stage		
Stitchery	A group embroidery project can be attempted if interest can be held over weeks. Burlap and yarn are best. A Stage Three group can achieve many social and behavior objectives in determining the subjects to be embroidered, how to begin it, colors to use, etc.		
Styrofoam *(and toothpicks)*	Use the same procedure described for Stages One and Two, Lessons 1 to 4, except focus on the group creating one large structure instead of individual creations.		

(continued)

Medium	Special Preparation	Suggested Content	Step-by-Step Motivation
Tempera Paint Lesson 5 Mixing primary colors	You will need: 1. Large sheets of 18″ X 24″ white drawing paper. 2. A #12 bristle brush for each child. 3. For each pair of children, a set of three containers, each holding $\frac{1}{2}$″ of primary color tempera paint and a container of water. 4. Crayons for standby.	Any subject	1. Pair the children before the lesson begins. 2. Explain that the purpose is to create new colors. 3. Demonstrate how to dip brush in paint; wipe carefully on edge of container; paint design; choose second color *but* wash out brush first before changing color. Paint with new color. Then mix secondary color directly on paper. Wash brush; go for another primary color; etc. 4. Encourage children to experiment with paint mixing until everyone has had the opportunity to mix all three secondary colors.
Tie-dyeing	You will need: 1. String or rubber bands. 2. Length of muslin or cotton T-shirts. 3. Three containers of cold water dyes (primary colors). 4. Newspapers *Note:* This lesson should be used only if a group has developed a high degree of impulse control.	Free design	1. Show students how to "bunch" up fabric and tie it. 2. Let each student tie and dip different fabric parts into each color, or use only one color. 3. Spread dyed fabric on newspapers to dry. 4. Dry overnight and untie next day.
Tissue Paper Design	Use the same procedures described for Stage Two, but establish the expectation of sharing supplies and ideas.		
Vocational Art Studies	Whenever the group shows interest in a famous picture, art displays, famous artists, designers, etc., discussions can insue about careers in the arts.		
Water Colors	Use the same procedures described for Stage Two, but elaborate to the degree that the children feel successful.		
Wire or Pipe Cleaner Sculpture (with or without spray paint)	You will need: 1. Assorted lengths of wire for each student. 2. Enamel paint (quick-drying). 3. Newspapers	Any subject	1. Prepare wire animal or human figures for display ahead of time. 2. Demonstrate twisting and turning techniques, and then let each student experiment with a piece of wire. 3. Discuss the variety of shapes produced by the children. A student who hesitates to make anything can be encouraged to make flowers, rings, or free designs.

(continued)

Medium	Special Preparation	Suggested Content	Step-by-Step Motivation
Wire and Pipe Cleaner Sculpture *(cont.)*			4. Distribute more wire. 5. Finished wire projects can be sprayed if desired. (Teacher should do this activity for the children.)

Wood Structures *(two parts)*	You will need:
	1. Various sizes and shapes of soft wood and balsa scraps.
	2. Glue for each child (6-oz. size).
	3. Supply of toothpicks (preferably in colors).
		Free design, geometrics, boats, cities of the future	On the first day
			1. Bring several examples of completed three-dimensional construction from wood scraps for the children to examine. Be sure they understand that the lesson will take two days.
			2. Demonstrate making a triangle shape. Construct it flat on the table on a small tray, heavy cardboard, or board. Use the following steps:
			  a) Select two pieces of wood, commenting on grain of the wood and smoothness of the ends, and arrange them in an L shape.
			  b) Test the fit of the ends. If the pieces seem to fit together, apply glue to the ends that will touch. Keep the glue $\frac{1}{2}''$ from the outer edges so that it will not ooze out.
			  c) Select a third piece to form the L shape into a triangle. Quickly apply glue to each end that will touch another, Press the pieces together.
			  d) Move the piece, on its tray, to a safe shelf so that it can dry overnight, undisturbed.
			3. Distribute supplies to each child. The number of pieces of wood scraps for each child will depend upon the work space available (approximately five to twenty pieces).
			4. Encourage individual designs based upon the shapes and patterns in the wood pieces (geometric shapes, boats, free designs, etc.). Allow approximately fifteen minutes for the children to work. Encourage making more than one shape, if time permits.
			5. As each shape is completed, store on shelf to dry.

(continued)

ART ACTIVITIES FOR STAGE THREE (continued)

Medium	Special Preparation	Suggested Content	Step-by-Step Motivation
Wood Structures *(cont.)*			On the second day toothpicks can be glued flat on the finished structures to decorate. Provide a glue bottle for each child and as many toothpicks as each child wants.
			On the third day with Stage Three children who have learned to work as a group, the individual projects can be glued together to form a single, spectacular construction!
Woodwork	Not applicable at this stage		
Yarn Design *(glued on cardboard)*	See the procedures for the string and glue printing lesson, except omit printing with ink and provide many colors of yarn for design work.		

ART ACTIVITIES FOR STAGE FOUR

Medium	Special Preparation	Suggested Content	Step-by-Step Motivation
Acrylics	Any content suitable for a painting lesson can be adapted to acrylics. Acrylics go on quickly and dry fast. Thick coats of paints can be used instead of building up layer upon layer, as with oils. Techniques of current artists who use acrylics can be discussed.		
Art Appreciation	Plan a field trip to an art show; watch a beautiful movie; take a nature walk; or study famous artists, past and present. The art of oriental artists, black artists, impressionists, and old masters can be discussed; techniques and colors compared; and the idea of art as a reflection of history can be introduced.		

Batik	You will need:
	1. Muslin or any fabric that will absorb dyes.
	2. Hot plate.
	3. Sauce pan.
	4. Wax or cooking paraffin.
	5. Metal spoon with hole or funnel-like attachment to "drip" or pour wax designs onto cloth.
	6. Three vats with primary color dyes.
		Any design or subject	1. Demonstrate the process, discussing each step:
			  a) Heat wax in saucepan.
			  *b) Drip wax on cloth in design desired.
			  *c) After wax cools, totally or partially dip into color vat.
			  d) When using more than one color, work from light color to dark color in dyeing process.
			  *e) After cloth dries, use more wax. Dip totally, or go to darker color over original wax design.
			  f) Let dry and iron off wax.
			2. After each step marked with an asterisk (*), stop the demonstration and assist the children in repeating that step.

Beadwork	You will need: 1. Various types of colored beads. 2. Rawhide strips or string to use for stringing.	Indian beadwork designs	1. Begin with an in-depth study of American Indian culture. Be sure to include pictures of the various tribes' art work using beads. The meaning of the symbols and the religious connotation used by various tribes can be discussed. 2. Let each student create his own design or copy illustrations. 3. Plan a display to culminate the unit.
Candlemaking	Kits are available for this lesson, or scrap crayons can be used. This can be an extensive art experience for a group: searching for and making use of different cans and jars to be used for molds; finding references for the process; using different scents and colors; and using sand, pebbles, or different textures.		
Cast Stone	See the procedure for plaster with vermiculite described in Stage Three. This art activity offers excellent opportunity for Stage Four children to plan a group theme for their sculpture and to share ideas about what forms are emerging.		

(continued)

107

ART ACTIVITIES FOR STAGE FOUR (continued)

Medium	Special Preparation	Suggested Content	Step-by-Step Motivation
Charcoal	You will need: 1. Charcoal sticks. 2. Charcoal paper 9″ × 12″ or larger. 3. Gum erasers. 4. Wet paper towels to clean up.	Sketch a shoe	1. Demonstrate how to draw with charcoal; how different pressure causes light or dark lines, thin or thick widths; how to smudge with fingers to achieve different colors. 2. Demonstrate how to erase charcoal lines. Use gum eraser or "smudge" it away with fingers. 3. In doing the "shoe" lesson, demonstrate how to look at shoe. Select a volunteer or your own shoe to study. *"This shoe is great to draw because of all the creases and smudge marks. Notice the lace torn here. This shoe has great character."* 4. Place the shoe in front of your paper at the angle you wish to draw and quickly demonstrate how to start "contour drawing" from one side of shoe to other. 5. Ask each child to take his own shoe for study. "O.K., off with a shoe!" (Ignore "pee-yew" remarks!) As they go through these "antics," use supplies as a structuring device. *"Yes, there is a new odor in the room. Now who is ready for paper?" "Joey, you have your shoe off and are ready for your charcoal and paper."* 6. Praise children who start by themselves. Make the first mark to start off insecure children. *"I'll do the first line and see if you can go from there."* 7. As children complete their basic outlines, start describing what detail each child should be looking at next. *"Tom, that's a great outline of your sneaker! Now are you going to start the drawing of the U.S. Ked insignia at the back or start from the front with the wrinkles and then the laces?"* 8. Encourage the children to complete repeated attempts. As each child finishes his best attempt, allow for free time. Have famous charcoal

(continued)

Medium	Special Preparation	Suggested Content	Step-by-Step Motivation
Charcoal *(cont.)*			sketches of Old Masters available, or materials for a charcoal sketch of anything in the room, etc.
			9. Let each student use fixative to spray their final results.
Clay	See the procedures described in the three previous stages. Larger quantities of clay can be given to each child in Stage Four to experiment with life-size head portraits, "slab" constructions, or human figures in action. Trips to a local college to have the class watch college students work on the "wheel" or hand-building pottery can serve as a motivating force for art or career plans. Also, see Chapter Five for more details about using clay with Stage Four children.		
Collage *(paper)*	Use all available types of paper (tissue, construction, newspaper, etc.) and motivate children to think of all their previous experiences with paper for art projects. Each child's ingenuity and creativity will be the only limit for their art achievement. Using *scraps* invariably leads to sharing of ideas and group problem solving. Free designs or three-dimensional structures can be attempted individually or in a group project.		
Copper *Enameling*	This is a very complex and expensive process that is feasible at Stage Four but more realistic for older high school age students in regular art class.		
Crayon and *Crayon Resist*	Children probably have had so much crayon work by this stage that it will be the least appealing medium to use. However, crayon engravings and resists can be planned if the group shows an interest.		
Craypas and *Craypas Resist*	This medium should be available to be used in similar manner as crayons or in connection with other materials.		
Découpage	There is little art value in this activity, but if interest is expressed, kits could be used for Stage Four children.		
Diorama	See the procedure described in Stage Three but have higher expectations for final products from the children. More difficult subjects can be attempted and with all working together on one display, numerous socialization, behavior, and communication objectives can be accomplished.		
Etching *(with crayons)*	Use the same procedures described for Stage Three, except encourage more planning on the part of the children. Have them begin with sketches before the crayon work is started. Also encourage more detailed etching.		
Finger Painting	Not applicable at this stage		
Leathercraft	Leather work generally is frustrating to Stage Four children. The problems that arise when working with leather usually require adult assistance. The needed strength or skill to complete an item comes through practice which children at this stage do not have. This activity does little to promote feelings of group cohesiveness which are so vital for Stage Four children.		
Lettering	Not applicable at this stage unless interest is shown by the children. It is an exacting, isolating exercise needing great concentration. Using lettering to promote a group project could be meaningful if all are able to contribute to the final product.		

(continued)

ART ACTIVITIES FOR STAGE FOUR (continued)

Medium	Special Preparation	Suggested Content	Step-by-Step Motivation
Macramé	This is a very repetitive, difficult art activity even when the simplest knots are used. However, produced work is exciting and beautiful. If instruction books, different types of yarn, twine, string, and cord can be purchased, then this lesson could be planned for this stage. Headbands, wall hangings, belts, necklaces (with shells and beads) are all possible. It would be ideal if one child in the group had previous macramé experience. He could be a resource to the others.		
Magic Markers	See Stage Three procedures for magic markers, Lesson 1. Magic markers are generally of less interest to Stage Four children than to children at previous stages.		
Metal Work	This is an art experience best left to high school classes.		
Mixed Media	Use the same procedures as described for previous stages. Mixed media lessons can be used for accomplishment of many developmental objectives at this stage if group planning, decision making, and problem solving are emphasized.		
Mobiles	Use procedures described at Stage Three, but encourage Stage Four children to gather their own objects for the mobile. These can range from pictures of favorite rock stars to airplane models. Each child can do a personal mobile, or the group can work on a single, group project.		
Model Building	If several children in a Stage Four group already build models as a hobby or if the group shows interest in the activity, it can be motivating. However, model building can use up many class hours. Structuring the time to accomplish specific developmental objectives is difficult but possible.		
Mosaics	Use the same procedures as described in previous stages, but use more complex materials in place of paper (tiles, flat colored stones, rug scraps, colored glass). Group preplanning can develop drawings. Transfer the drawings, apply glue to board, and then apply mosaics.		
Natural Materials (rocks, leaves, branches)	This lesson can be set up as previously described in Stages Two and Three. However, instead of the teacher providing the materials, the group can collect their own materials during field trips for individual or group art work, decide on design or subject, plan the construction details, and develop a way to display the final product which communicates their ideas.		
Oil Paints	If children express an interest in this media and if funds are available to secure oils, canvas, palettes, linseed oil, brushes, easels, and turpentine, oil painting sessions can be planned for this stage. To motivate children to attempt simple still lifes, landscapes, or designs, plan visits to museums to see actual oil paintings or to visit a local college to see college students working in oil.		
Papier Mâché	You will need: 1. Chicken wire or wood for form. 2. Newspaper. 3. Wheat paste and water. 4. Tempera paint and brushes. 5. Lacquer (not mandatory).	Any animal or human form	1. Demonstrate or simply describe the steps for making a papier mâché form: a) Bend chicken wire and tie into rough shape (or wood pieces nailed together to create base for mâché work). b) Tear newspaper into strips. Dip strips into paste mixture and lay them over and around form to build up desired shape. Build layer upon layer to required thickness.

(continued)

ART ACTIVITIES FOR STAGE FOUR (continued)

Medium	Special Preparation	Suggested Content	Step-by-Step Motivation
Papier Mâché *(cont.)*			c) Each thick layer should dry overnight. When finished, let it dry thoroughly before painting (several days for large pieces). 2. Let class do all the work (if possible). The form construction is a crucial part of conceptual learning for the children.
Pastels *(color chalk)* *(wet or dry method)*	Any subject is suitable for pastels. Encourage experimentation with the chalk (on the side, using it like a pencil, coloring through wet areas into dry areas, etc.).		
Pen and Ink	If India ink and pen (with changeable points) are used, experimentation with texture and line drawings can be tried for any subjects. India ink will not come out of clothes so accidents can be traumatic!		
Pencil *Lesson 1* *Drawing* *from a model*	You will need: 1. Drawing boards (18″ X 24″) with white paper tacked to each board (two or three sheets). 2. Soft lead or #2 drawing pencils for each student, with extra ones for children who break the lead during drawing time. 3. Gum erasers.	Model in class	1. Choose a child for the model who can sit still for five to eight minutes. (Usually the "show off" types are best for a model because it is very satisfying for them!) This job has to be structured so the model will know the limits *"You can't talk because a model cannot move at all! It's a hard job. Be sure you're comfortable because it's very hard to sit still. It looks easy but it's not!"* 2. Place the child in a seated or standing position and draw a quick sketch, demonstrating to the class how to do a light outline of the entire figure; then go back to fill it in with details, or start with the head and put in details and work down to neck, shoulders, etc. 3. It usually proves helpful to talk as you demonstrate. *"Well, he is looking at the wall and so from where I stand I can only see half of his head. I will only have to draw one eye and part of the mouth and nose and ear with a side view of his hair. Is his hair long or short? Short? Where does it end? Yes! Just below his ear. I can make his straight hair with a few lines. Now, I will go to the neck and shoulders, and, because I can only draw what I see, I will only draw half of the front of his*

(continued)

Medium	Special Preparation	Suggested Content	Step-by-Step Motivation
Pencil *Lesson 1 (cont.)*			*shirt and only his arm that is against his side. How many buttons on his shirt? Short-sleeved or long? What kind of a design does it have?"* *"Now no one expects perfect drawings, just interesting ones. If you can't draw a part of our model, just leave it off!"* (Be sure your demonstration is a very rough sketch!) 4. As soon as all the children have pencils and boards, tell them to write their names on each sheet. When they have done that, you'll know they are ready for the model to begin posing. 5. Make sure your model is comfortable and usually looking at a wall so eye contact will not be with the other students. Be very "serious" about this drawing exercise. Watch for anyone who starts by himself and praise this; but immediately go to the nonparticipators and try to: a) Motivate them to make a few quick lines. b) Use their pencil to start them off by doing a circle for the head. Ask *"What should be drawn next? Hair? Eyes? Ears?" "Good, now you continue it and I'll come back in just a minute."* 6. It should be emphasized to the group that you do not expect any one to do perfect drawings. If a child cannot do the model at all, having tried, he should be allowed to draw the wall behind the model or anything else in the room. (*"Some people are good at drawing walls, plants, copying pictures, but today we want to see if anyone can first draw people!"*) 7. To further aid a very insecure child, you can stipulate before beginning that no one will see another's work *unless* he gives permission! 8. Praise all positive efforts. Give honest appraisals, but end all critiques

(continued)

ART ACTIVITIES FOR STAGE FOUR (continued)

Medium	Special Preparation	Suggested Content	Step-by-Step Motivation
Pencil *Lesson 1 (cont.)*			on a positive note. (*"Yes, hands are hard to draw but you did your best." "I think the way you made John look happy is the nicest part of your picture!" "O.K., so the model drawing isn't that great, but the way you drew that window is terrific! Have you ever thought of studying to be an architect?"*)
			9. End the lesson when each child has shown some investment in his work, and before your model becomes too uncomfortable. Compliment the entire group's particpation and your model's good posing. Collect their work in a special artist's portfolio.
Pencil *Other lessons*	Anything children are interested in can be planned for a pencil lesson: studies of still life arrangements, cars in parking lot, microscopic drawings of insects or flowers, etc. Encourage children to try out different pencil textures (shading, cross-hatching, use of contour drawing, quick-motion sketch, etc.). If one child is especially good at this, allow him to assist the others to stimulate use of social and communication objectives.		
Plaster *(with vermiculite)*	Use the procedures described for Stage Three.		
Play-plax *(Crystal climbers)*	Use the same basic procedures described for Stage Two, but have group decide what to build and how to end the activity (display, take down, etc.). This activity is generally not too motivating for Stage Four children unless they have a highly creative plan for using the material.		
Plyable Plastics *or Plexiglass*	These materials present many of the same problems as creating with wood or leather. Any three-dimensional design can be constructed. However, there is some difficulty in connecting pieces with epoxy or plastic glue for children who are not extremely patient and careful. Instead of hammer and nails, epoxy or a nonintoxicating plastic glue would be used to connect pieces together.		
Printing *Lesson 1* *Found objects*	Use the procedures described for Stage Three. Let each student gather objects he thinks will make a good print. When each student has the number of objects he thinks will do for an interesting and varied design, printing can be done. Sharing of objects and ideas should be encouraged.		
Printing *Lesson 2* *String and glue*	Use the same procedures described in Stage Three, but require children to prepare more elaborate designs and finished products.		
Printing *Lesson 3* *Vegetable prints*	Use the same procedures described in Stage Three, but require children to prepare more elaborate designs and finished products.		

(continued)

ART ACTIVITIES FOR STAGE FOUR (continued)

Medium	Special Preparation	Suggested Content	Step-by-Step Motivation
Printing *Lesson 4* *(two parts)* *Cardboard*	You will need first day: 1. Sheets of oak tagboard for each student to cut out shapes for printing. 2. Tag board sheets (9″ × 12″ or smaller) to use as base. 3. Glue and mat knife for each student. 4. Shellac and brush. You will need second day: 1. Brayer and printing ink. 2. Absorbent paper (rice paper or construction paper). 3. Spoons or jars. 4. Newspaper. *Note:* This is a basic printing lesson that can be used early in Stage Four. It is important to be certain that there are no children in the group who would be dangerous with a mat knife used under these conditions.	Any subject	On the first day 1. Explain that this activity requires two days. 2. Encourage each student to draw and cut out any shape desired from oak tag board using mat knife. Demonstrate safety procedures in cutting by making cuts away from body and hands. 3. Glue cut out shapes on tag board base. 4. When glue dries, paint on one coat of shellac. Dry overnight. On the second day 1. ink the brayer, roll ink onto shapes, press inked design onto paper, press, and rub (without moving) design with jar or spoon. 2. Remove cardboard design and examine print. 3. Title prints, discuss, and display.
Rubbings	Use the same procedures described for Stage Three, except that the children can play an active role in planning field trips to discover sources for rubbings.		
Sand Castings	Use the same procedures described for Stage Three with less teacher direction.		
Sand Designing	Use the same procedures described for Stage Three, but the sand or gravel can be collected from local areas by the children for different textures and colors.		
Sensory Lessons	At this stage, a more mature approach to the physical world can be enjoyed and explored by the students. Instead of just going outside to find objects for a collage, the group can sit quietly for one minute for *listening* (birds, branches moving in the wind, leaves rustling); *touching* (feeling the bark on the trunk of a tree, scooping dirt from the ground and letting it trickle through your fingers); *smelling* (earth, weeds, leaves); *seeing* (the vein design on a simple leaf, patterns of fern fronds, variation of colors in the earth). In class, cooking experiments, music studies, folk dancing, would all afford the students valuable sensory experiences.		
Shell Jewelry	You will need: 1. Various types and colors of shells. 2. Plastic backs for pins or earrings. 3. Metal clasps and glue (nonintoxicating). 4. Tweezers.	Flower or free design	1. Show examples of finished shell jewelry. 2. Demonstrate how to place shells on glued area to build up a design. 3. Encourage students to create their own jewelry designs.

(continued)

ART ACTIVITIES FOR STAGE FOUR (continued)

Medium	Special Preparation	Suggested Content	Step-by-Step Motivation
Shell Jewelry (cont.)			4. Encourage use of reference materials to expand interest into the study of shells or the study of cultures' uses of shells. 5. Assist children in planning and implementing an informative and artistic display of their work.
Soap Carving	This activity could precede carving plaster molds and would be a good practice lesson before going to work on any serious sculpture work.		
Stitchery	You will need: 1. Kits (crewel or any simple embroidery projects); or 2. Burlap nailed to wooden frame and yarn and needles. 3. Crayon or magic markers.	Any design	1. If kits are used, children can follow color instructions or create their own color pattern. 2. If burlap is used, drawing can be done directly on burlap (or planned first on paper and transferred to burlap). The stitchery is done with yarn by individuals or as a group project. 3. The products can be framed, displayed, mounted, or used to make pillows.
Styrofoam (and toothpicks)	Use the same procedures described for previous stages with more intricate structures.		
Tempera Paint	Encourage children to mix colors, try abstract designs, paint "emotions" (by using "sad" or "happy" colors), make dramatic lines, or choose dramatic subjects. Stage Four children can be given several size brushes, mix their own colors, and experiment with painting to music, copying famous prints, or doing impressionistic or cubistic style paintings.		
Tie-dyeing	See Stage Three.		
Tissue Paper Design	See Stages Two and Three.		
Vocational Art Studies	Jobs that make use of artistic talent are of interest to most Stage Four children. They might study car designs, fashions, fabrics, newspaper layouts, advertisements, television graphics, cartoons, food labels, etc. Field trips and creative design projects of their own are generally successful at this stage.		
Water Colors	Use the procedures described for previous stages. Content and motivation can be generated by the children themselves.		
Wire or Pipe Cleaner Sculpture	Use the same procedures described for Stage Three.		

(continued)

115

ART ACTIVITIES FOR STAGE FOUR (continued)

Medium	Special Preparation	Suggested Content	Step-by-Step Motivation
Wood Structures	You will need: 1. Various sizes of wood blocks to provide each child with a good selection. 2. Hammer and nails for each child. 3. Enamel or flat paint and brushes (not necessary). *Note:* This lesson is an expansion of the Wood Structures lesson for Stage Three.	Three-dimensional structures	1. This should be a free experience with structural materials to exercise each child's manipulative and creative abilities. 2. No directions are necessary for using the tools, other than cautioning the children not to hurt themselves or others.
Woodwork	If you have access to woodworking equipment, simple products (book ends, plaques, boxes) can be attempted by Stage Four children, after they have had success constructing simple wood structures described above.		
Yarn Design (glued on cardboard)	Use the same procedures described for Stage Three, but expect more intricate designs. Drawings are done before the yarn work is begun. Mexican yarn work can be used to illustrate the many possibilities.		

chapter 5

CLAY . . .
THE SUBLIME
MATERIAL

The simplest clay forms created by Stage Two children take on new beauty with the proper display.

Why is clay[1] so desirable as an art medium for children? The answer is as basic as the joy children get from playing in mud. Manipulating a pile of sloppy clay into a creative form offers endless opportunities for exploration, imitation, and fantasy. Dramatic responses are nearly always evident. In the process, developmental skills are also stimulated. It is not at all unusual to see a child take a blob of wet clay, reject or abuse it, and then begin to find security and creative expression from it.

As you watch children work with the clay, you should be alert to the possible benefits to be gained from the lesson. For each child these benefits will be unique and distinctly reflective of a developmental stage. Is a child actively enjoying the sensory experience or is he getting "lost" within it? Is the clay activity helping a child work through some problem or is he killing time? Is a child accomplishing specific developmental objectives or is he simply using it because it is today's lesson? At Stages One and Two the sensory experience would be the most important aspect of a clay lesson. To respond to the squashy mess with pleasure is the first step. Even rejection of the clay (throwing it, destroying it, or refusing to touch it) could be enough of a response, negative as it is, to let you know that the activity is reaching the child. At Stages Three and Four clay gives children a healthy way to work out aggression and frustrations while also learning artistic skills for manipulating the material to a successful and satisfying outcome.

The most important thing to remember during clay lessons (or any art experience for that matter) is that if working with clay is not *the most exciting, fun thing you have ever done in your life*, then the children will sense your boredom and the lesson will lose most of its effectiveness. Our own attitudes are easily read by children. So, as art is usually a joy for most children regardless of age or handicap, make the most of each art opportunity. Keep it a joy! Keep it exciting! A teacher unable to do this should either skip art so as to avoid ruining the experience for the children or expect a low level of responsiveness to art activities. This is particularly true when it comes to using clay. Children will be excited and invested in a beginning lesson with clay. Some teachers make the mistake of pulling back assuming the children will do well on their own. In the first three to five minutes of the lesson this might be true, but with each subsequent minute frustrations begin to arise. Suddenly stereotyped art forms begin to emerge along with nonproductive behavior and antisocial talk. For a successful lesson, it is critical that you stay tuned-in, constantly motivating and directing the movement of the lesson from beginning to completion, including the important clean up phase.

A FEW TECHNICAL TIPS

White clay is hard to come by, but the search is well worth the trouble. It fires to a fine, white surface. It also lends itself to water color or tempera painting, with or without firing. As you watch children experience the fun of painting

---

[1] For this chapter, clay has been selected as the medium to best illustrate the way an art material is adapted to each developmental stage. For a full description of the changes in teacher techniques across stages of development see Wood (1975), Chapter Five, "Management Strategies and Verbal Techniques Which Bring Therapeutic Results." Also, steps for the three basic clay lessons are outlined in Chapter Two of this text.

their products, the value in this form of elaboration is evident. However, make sure the children have used water colors before they paint their clay work. This will ensure a successful end to the clay lesson.

Before you start a clay lesson it should be well established that the clay products will need to dry out for one or two weeks to ensure that each piece is thoroughly dry for the firing. Keep the children informed as to the progress of the drying clay if you have removed it from the room. 1. *"They're drying nicely; let's hope none of them cracks."* 2. *"I plan to fire them today and tomorrow, so we should have them in three days."* 3. *"If we can finish our regular art lesson today, we can discuss how we should get ready to paint all the clay animals for the farm diorama."* Hand-built clay work, if thoroughly dried, can be fired for two hours on *Low* and two hours on *Medium* with the lid propped open. Then close the kiln and fire to approximately 2000° for four to six hours. Leave lid closed until kiln has completely cooled. An alternative method is firing on *Low* for an eight-hour period with the top open. Then shut off the kiln and leave over night with the lid closed. The next day continue with the first process described above. This combination proves best for minimum breakage.

Always include in the firing a few extra pieces you have made. There may be breakage, and it is bitterly disappointing to most children to have a broken product. If glazing or painting is to follow, this compounds the frustration because the child with the broken piece has nothing to do.

For glazing, have three large cans, each with a different glaze in it, and a brush for each child. They can paint on the glaze, dip their prefered clay pieces

into the glaze (really the best way), or drip glaze over their work with a second container under it to catch the glaze (messy and hard to control). Glaze should be applied in two layers as smoothly as possible. The bottoms of each piece should be kept clean. Let the pieces dry overnight before firing. **Note:** Fire most basic glazes for two hours on *Low,* two hours on *Medium* always with the kiln lid open, then close and fire on *High* until automatic shut-off at approximately 2200°. Leave lid closed until kiln has cooled completely.

NOT SO SUBLIME!

Not all children like using clay or become proficient with it. Through careful observation you can determine who is making use of this medium and who is not. If it is not useful, drop it quickly from the curriculum. Some children do not like to touch it at first. Most developmentally advanced children do not usually like the results after firing. They usually expect something miraculous to happen to it in the kiln! Or if they do like the results, they will rarely tell you. However, with each succeeding clay lesson, children of every stage should be more comfortable with clay and more daring with what they are making.

For the teacher or therapist, the most challenging part of a clay lesson is being constantly on guard to prevent the overwhelming frustration that can occur when a child is using clay. Clay can be a vehicle to transfer everything failing in himself to the blob of clay; then the child can reject the clay product as he rejects himself. Invariably, destruction of the product follows, and the child is left with a devastated feeling. This can be avoided by close observation of each child during the clay lesson to see that the procedures are followed as they were outlined in the preliminary demonstration. The smallest deviation from the expected procedure by a child should serve as a warning that possibly something is starting to go wrong. At this point, intervene, physically helping the child to form the particular shape he was attempting. Such intervention serves to redirect the child back to the art process and away from the destructive feeling. Sometimes simple verbal cues serve the same purpose, redirecting the destructive behavior. For example, a child is pounding his clay wildly and you realize that within the next few strokes he will be out of control. So, tell the child that he has done a marvelous job of wedging the clay. In fact, he has hit it so hard that he can pat it and then rest!

CLAY FOR STAGE ONE

The most important decision to be made before you plan a lesson with clay for Stage One[2] is whether or not the children are ready for it. That is, there must be some degree of relationship between the teacher and each child. If not, the clay is not usually an effective arouser because of its color, coldness, and inert appearance. To begin, clay can be physically placed in a child's hand. Observe the child for any reaction, negative or positive. Any degree of response can be a clue to begin the next steps. Place your hand over the child's hand while holding the clay; show him how to roll, pound, squeeze, and eventually pinch the clay.

The most important technique for introducing clay is to get the child's attention quickly by showing the magic of changing a lump of clay through the act of touching. If the child is able to stay with the clay for as much as a minute or two, take the opportunity to help him continue his exploration of the material. If the child refuses to manipulate the clay but is watching you handle it, return the clay to him to see if further interest is there.

"You have clay." Move his hands to the clay but pull back and allow the child to make any further response. The final move at this point is to ask the child to hand you the clay. If the child can do this, then some contact has been established. If, after repeated lessons where you have aided the child in grasping the clay, pressing his hands into it, making hand or finger prints, and rolling balls, the child still shows no response, then clay should be left out of the curriculum until later. Trying to force a response or participation from such a child can be detrimental to his entire art therapy program.

However, if the child is attracted to the clay after the initial introductory steps, assist him to continue rolling "logs," making clay balls, and pounding pancakes. Then, to vary the approach, introduce a pencil to make designs on the clay. This increases manipulative skill. Another idea is to have prepared slabs.[3] Hand prints, cookie cutters to cut out shapes, and foot prints produce stimulating sensory experiences for Stage One children. The three clay lessons described at the end of Chapter Two outline these sequential steps.

Making shapes of animals, people, insects, or objects is too much to expect

B-0
to indicate awareness of a sensory stimulus with any responses away from or toward source of stimulus.

B-2
to respond to stimulus by sustained attending to source of stimulus.

C-2
to respond to verbal stimulus with a motor behavior.

B-3
to respond spontaneously to simple environmental stimuli with a motor behavior: object, person, sound.

B-4
to respond with motor and body responses to complex environmental and verbal stimuli.

---

[2] See also the outline for clay lessons for Stage One contained in Chapter Two.

[3] Slabs of clay are ¼″ to ½″ thick squares of clay. A slab is prepared beforehand by the teacher in a procedure similar to rolling dough for a cookie cutter.

for Stage One children, but if a child is ready to respond to his environment, he can collect pebbles, sticks, and other objects to press into the slabs. Or if a child can obtain satisfaction and success out of the wedging[4] process, then this in itself is a wonderful learning activity for Stage One. Clay also can be watered down to a soupy consistency, giving the children a different tactile experience. Play-dough left out in the room for use during play or free time can provide opportunity for spontaneous, unstructured experimentation with this medium and carry over from the art lesson.

To summarize, the quality of any work done at Stage One is unimportant. The interest and response the children express toward the clay are the major focus. Through interest and simple responses the Stage One child will begin the gradual process of mastering sequential developmental milestones. When he is responding spontaneously to the material, the Stage One child is on his way.

S-16
to participate in a verbally directed sharing activity.

B-4
to respond with motor and body responses to complex environmental and verbal stimuli.

B-6
to respond independently to several play materials.

CLAY FOR STAGE TWO

Before presenting a clay lesson to children at Stage Two,[5] lay the groundwork with the children ahead of time. *"I hope we will be able to use clay soon. Has anyone ever used clay before? You have? It's lots of fun!"*

Have painted clay pieces displayed around the room from time to time. Also display pictures of ceramic works and talk about how much fun it is to work with clay.

Before you begin the first clay lesson, have everything ready ahead of time. Divide the clay into palm-size balls

C-8
to answer a child's or an adult's questions or requests with recognizable, meaningful, relevant word(s).

C-12
to use words to exchange minimal information with an adult.

[4] Wedging is the term applied to pounding and rolling the clay to remove air bubbles before a form is made.

[5] See also comments about clay lessons in Chapter 3.

and wrap each in a wet cloth or store inside plastic bags to ensure having soft clay when it is time for the lesson. Also have a supply of pencils, cookie cutters, found objects, or marking tools. Early in Stage Two, each child should have his own tools. However, sharing materials and tools is a developmental objective that comes at high Stage Two and should be introduced as a natural part of the art lessons as soon as possible.

Working on a bare table is best because it can be easily cleaned. Paper or plastic on a table usually becomes shredded into the clay during the lesson; this proves to be frustrating and ruins the clay.

When the day arrives for the clay lesson, prepare the children for the experience that lies ahead. *"The clay you will be using is grey right now, but when I cook it in the kiln, it will turn pure white! A kiln is like a very hot oven. When your clay goes into the kiln, we call it 'firing the clay.' When it's done, I'll bring it back, and you can paint it."* Take time to answer any questions, but as you do, remove some clay from the storage container and start working it. This will help hold their attention and will illustrate what you are saying. *"At first the clay will feel cool to your touch, but you will get used to it. The reason it is wet is to keep it soft. See how it turns grey on my hands as it starts to dry out. When we finish our clay lesson, we will wash hands, so don't worry about it getting on your hands at all!"*

You can also discuss where clay comes from, what objects around the room or at home are made out of clay, how Indians used clay for pottery, etc. As long as you think this information is of use to the children and their interest is held, such information can be helpful. Your introduction to the lesson should be as quick and as exciting a demonstration as you can present to the children. If you observe any of the children getting restless as you demonstrate, it might be wise to reflect this, *"I know you get tired of hearing teachers talk sometimes, so if you do, just watch my hands and you'll be able to learn just what you need for today's art lesson."*

The demonstration should be structured to encourage the children to participate verbally in the discussion. First, demonstrate how to wedge the clay. This is a great activity for overly aggressive, withdrawn, or bored children. For Stage Two, splitting the clay in half and slamming the two halves together in air in front of you is a good way to wedge. The clapping motion is easy to imitate and prevents it from sticking on the table. It also prevents a high noise level in the room, which occurs when children discover the great slamming sound clay makes on a hard surface! You can usually help hold their interest by conducting this action together, counting to ten with each hit. This gives each child a structured procedure to start his clay work.

The most successful forms to make at this level have proven to be simple pinch pots or four-legged animals. The "pulling out" method to form figures is sometimes beyond the skill level of children at this stage. A pinch pot is more suitable. On their own, Stage Two children usually produce lots of "pancakes" or "hotdogs." These shapes are very satisfying to them. Making these forms also is conducive to many Stage Two objectives. Demonstrate whatever the group can do best. Remember, success is the overall goal for Stage Two.

As you complete your demonstration, take the forms you made and roll them back into a ball; or if you think the children could use your model for their clay work, ask them where you should put it so everyone can see it.[6]

As each child receives clay, you can provide extra motivation by assuring them that when they finish one shape they can have extra clay to make whatever they want. Also verbally structure the first step, *"What is the first thing you have to do? Right! Wedge the clay at least ten times."*

Your main task at the beginning of the lesson is to watch for the children who will be totally frustrated or overly powerful with the wedging. Get potential problems under control early and gently. Sometimes verbal restructuring of the process is enough. Another strategy is to remove the clay from the child's hand and to show him again how to do the particular step. Compliment the children who are able to work on their own spontaneously. Try to stay away from them as they work but stay within range to prevent problems before they happen. If a child works especially quickly, have him attempt his name or initials on the finished piece. Then allow him a choice of 1) starting another shape, 2) cleaning up and watching the others, or 3) working with crayons and paper until art time is over.

As all the children experience some degree of success, start to clean up. This process can be chaotic, so prepare ahead of time for the steps you expect the children to go through and the standard of accomplishment they can meet. Establish a level of accomplishment that gives each child a sense of success. Clean-up is an important activity in its own right, and it can lead to many developmental skills.

---

[6]Whenever a teacher-made model is used for demonstration, be sure that the final product is *below* the skill level of the children. This protects the children from feeling inadequate to meet the standard the teacher has set.

C-12
to use words to exchange minimal information with an adult.

B-12
to spontaneously participate in routines without physical intervention.

B-11
to participate in movement activities such as play time, mat time, games, music, or art time without physical intervention by teacher.

B-9
to wait without physical intervention by teachers.

S-13
to participate spontaneously in specific parallel activities with another child using similar materials but not interacting.

S-18
to participate in cooperative activities or projects with another child during organized class activities.

As you get the children ready for the next activity, tell the children that in three or four weeks, after the clay has dried out thoroughly and is fired, you will bring the pieces back for the painting lesson. A trip to see the kiln might be a good idea for a field trip for the group.

On the day for painting the fired pieces, have water colors, containers of water, #6 brushes ready for each child, plus sheets of paper. Quickly demonstrate how to paint with the water colors first. Involve the children in describing each step as you demonstrate: wet the brush; wipe it off on the container to prevent it from dripping; wipe the brush in the chosen color; paint the clay piece; as the brush goes dry, wet it again and continue painting. Remind the children that if they want to change color they have to make sure their brush is clean by thoroughly washing it in their water container without making splashing sounds or making a mess! Right? Right!

Next, hold up each fired piece and appreciate its beauty. If you show that you are impressed with their work, the children will be that much more happy with it. Such attention also motivates them for the painting process; as a result, handing out supplies will go smoothly.

As the children paint, be sure to watch for those who are becoming dissatisfied with the way their art work is looking and who start to mess it up on purpose. If this begins to happen to a child who has a history of doing this with various other projects, stop him and compliment what he has done well. Remove the object and let him work with standby paper and his paints. In other instances, a child may begin to work out an inner frustration through painting. You may want to allow this to continue for as long as you can protect the child from regressing severely or from destroying his work.

The painted clay forms can be shellacked for a glossy appearance, but this should be done by the teacher at Stage Two and only if the children want it done! They can watch you do it, but, because the fumes can be harmful, it is best done after class.

If you wish to glaze their products, instead of painting them, have some previously glazed pieces to show the children the final results. This process will not be as satisfying to Stage Two children because there is another long delay between activity and outcome. This type of decoration is better for Stages Three and Four but can be used with advanced Stage Two children who can accept delayed gratification.

To summarize, Stage Two children are striving for a sense of self, attempting to master basic manipulative skills and to assert themselves successfully in the art process. The product is not the focus, but the process is! Participation should ensure success, and it is the teacher's responsibility to see that each Stage Two child's participation is successful. This sense of individual success through participation is the goal for Stage Two. With such a feeling about his own skills, a child is ready to progress to Stage Three.

CLAY FOR STAGE THREE

Basically, the same lessons and approaches described in Stage Two can be used, but at Stage Three the teacher should demonstrate more elaborate forms, allow more work time, give out larger amounts of clay, and encourage making several pieces.

The major focus for art time at this stage is to set up lessons that encourage group interaction. Keep this focus in mind throughout every step of the lesson from your introduction to the clean-up time. As you are demonstrating the day's lesson, show the children how to make figures with the "pulling" method and the "additive" method.[7] Ask for responses from the children as you work. *Purposely* run into "trouble." Destroy the work and start over with a statement about how great it is that when you work clay you can always start over if you make a mistake or get a better idea. Remind them that as the clay starts to dry out they will not be able to start over. So, advise them to watch the condition of the clay as they work with it. By emphasizing the condition of drying out, you have a way of determining when a particular child's clay has reached its "bad" period. This will provide a means to structure his activity so that he can finish successfully and be a contributing member of the art project.

It is usually a good idea to demonstrate two projects for each day's lesson. Three or four choices would be too much and one is sometimes too little to motivate all of the children in a Stage Three group. During your demonstration, encourage the children to reflect on prospective problems and ideas they have.

After the clay has been handed out and each child has wedged his clay ten times (as described previously for Stage Two) have the tools ready but purposely be short of some items so that the children are forced to share with one another.

At Stage Three, the children can go through numerous clay exercises using the slab technique. These activities could vary from building a house or animal to cutting out shapes with cookie cutters and adding designs and textures. The children can learn to use slip to seal clay edges together. They can collect objects and print on slab tiles with them. A tongue depressor can be a handy tool to cut out various shapes. Put a hole at one edge of each piece before they dry. After firing string them together for a wind-chime or a mobile. Among the popular clay lessons at this stage is making animals or figures for dioramas (jungles, circuses, underwater scenes, family in a house, etc.).

Bring in real vegetables, fruits, and flowers and see if the children can duplicate them in clay. Also try giving each child a model of a car, airplane, or boat and see if he can recreate it from clay. These activities should always be planned to stimulate group interaction, collaboration, and problem solving. Here is an example.

"As I work on this dragon . . . isn't that what everybody decided to make today? Good! Well, I'm thinking, what should we do as each guy finishes his dragon?" [No response.] *"Where can we put the dragons to dry for at least a week?"* The group gives several suggestions, some profane.

One child takes the cue correctly and suggests the teacher's desk. *"Fantastic idea! On my desk. O.K., then, should each guy take his dragon to the desk when he is done or ask me to carry it?"*

After the group thinks through this problem aloud, several suggestions are offered mainly concerning it being too small a room for a lot of people to walk around at once. The children suggest that they might drop their work and then someone would get mad. This might lead to trouble, whereas if the teachers carried the pieces it would be "cool." If the teacher dropped any of the work, the group decided, the child

A-38
to perform eye-hand coordination activities at the six-year level.

C-17
to contribute to making group expectations of conduct and procedure.

S-21
to suggest activities or preference for play materials to the teacher for group activity.

---

[7] The pulling method: From the original piece of clay small amounts of clay are squeezed out to make heads, legs, etc. These forms are never separated from the original piece. The additive method: Role legs, handles, etc., separately and then use water with a piece of clay as "slip." The new piece is attached to the main form using the slip as a glue.

B-14
to contribute to making group expectations of conduct and procedures.

C-19
to use words or nonverbal gestures to show pride in own work, activity, or to make positive statements about self.

S-21
to suggest activities or preference for play materials to the teacher for group activity.

S-30
to participate in group planning and constructive problem solving.

B-21
to spontaneously participate in activities previously avoided.

C-23
to recognize and acknowledge feelings in self: sad, happy, angry, afraid.

who had created the work would get more clay or the teacher would have to do one for him. This discussion, of course, is guided by the teacher.

"Guys, you solved that problem beautifully. I've finished my dragon. What do you think?" The general consensus is that it is "tough." (This is a smart group, the teacher acknowledges!)

"I see everyone is anxious to start. Joe, you hand out the marking tools; Tom, roll your sleeves up and see if Eddie needs help to roll up his."

"Paul has long sleeves on, too, Miss Williams," says Tom.

"Good, help him, too."

The previous dialogue is a typical exchange among children and teacher in Stage Three. The need predominates for establishing the importance of oneself in the eyes of peers. Yet developmental skills are scarcely adequate for the challenge. So, Stage Three children rely on the teacher to be the provider of structure, rules, procedures, and recognition. When the teacher has proven dependable, strong, and trustworthy, the children drop many defensive postures. Gradually, each Stage Three child opens himself to new experiences with the group. This is the goal: applying individual skills to group activities.

CLAY FOR STAGE FOUR

Children at this stage should have ample opportunity for exploration of the potential in clay. Demonstrations and tight control of procedures are not necessary. You should be able to introduce the lesson quite simply, allow the group to set the goals for the completed work, and then you should let it go.

Stage Four children should be able to attempt difficult projects with the clay, risking failure and yet feeling secure enough to do so. If a child wants to

try something completely new to him, then you might have to start him off, but once he is into the lesson, he should be able to finish by himself. You can either accept whatever he produces or provide helpful criticism. Your strategy should be determined by the amount of self-esteem the child has developed. Another approach would be to praise what the child has done and then to suggest improvements, refinements, or elaborations. *"That is a gorgeous tiger, but you know what I think would make it even better? Well, what design is on the fur of a tiger? Right! Could you draw stripes on his coat and maybe even add whiskers?"*

"George, Mary is making a beautiful bowl. Show her your bowl and see if she wants to add a design in the middle like yours."

At Stage Four, each child can be asked to go beyond his original effort. There is always something new to try. Sometimes the best motivation for this comes from the other children. This can lead to achievement of many developmental objectives for everyone. Maybe just saying, *"No, I like it this way,"* would be indicative of a child's progress.

The more complexities the children are able to handle, the more difficult the art lessons can be. Examples of advanced assignments are busts, sugar bowls with covers, prehistoric animals, fish or mask plaques, figures in motion, slab vases, three-dimensional geometric forms, etc. Let the children choose what they want to make, excluding easy things they have made in the past (snakes, cannon balls, peace signs). A Stage Four child can understand why you think he can do better than these basic lessons, and discussion about this can enhance communication skills.

In short, Stage Four children have developed to a level where their skills, emotions, behavior, and thought processes are functioning and well organized. They can, and should, bring all of these skills into operation during a clay lesson. Conducted within the context of freedom to explore and express, the clay lesson can be an incredibly effective means to assist the child in seeing himself as an esteemed and worthy individual. This accomplishment in time leads to a satisfying position in the group, which is the Stage Four goal.

CLAY FOR STAGE FIVE

Developmental Art Therapy for Stage Five has not been discussed in this book, because it is a stage that does not require a treatment setting. The fifth stage of Developmental Therapy is a process for termination from a special program. During this stage, the child is no longer in need of highly specialized assistance, but he does need the same assistance from adults that all children need in order to continue to develop into the teenage years.

These children ordinarily do not have much opportunity to work with clay in regular schools or at home. The equipment is costly and some degree of expertise is needed in using, storing, and firing clay work. Some Boys' Clubs and Y groups offer ceramic lessons. Any child who has found satisfaction from working with clay in a therapy program should be encouraged to continue this art form in community programs.

There are "instant" clays available commercially through most art supply stores. These can be used by children at home. The whole family working together on creative clay work would be a wonderful extention of the therapeutic program into the home. Family projects in clay can have endless variety: wind chimes, ceramic forms, bowls, dishes, pots, Christmas and other holiday decorations, napkin rings, decorative free forms, family hand prints, plaques, etc. Whenever an art therapist can work with a family in their homes for special art times or in a public school with the regular art teacher, equally special bonds can be established between all those working together!

S-31
to initiate and maintain effective interpersonal and group relationships.

C-30
to use words to initiate and maintain positive relationships.

chapter 6

DEVELOPMENTAL ART THERAPY ON EXHIBIT

A Stage Two group assembled and decorated this twelve-foot dragon with the help of their teacher. They used glue-on stars, buttons, paper discs, sequins, craypas, and magic markers. Their creative use of these materials gave the dragon a vibrancy that made it the highlight of the art exhibit.

Within the framework of developmental art therapy, each child's art should be judged on one criterion alone: the art experience serves to stimulate the eventual achievement of developmental milestones. Both the art process and the product should serve this end. For this reason, an art exhibit in a developmentally oriented treatment center presents some unique problems but also many possibilities for further developmental gain.

Each year we have held an art exhibit and have found that the more carefully we plan ahead for the participation of every child, the more successful it will be. Simply walking around a room full of art work is an unrewarding experience. Therefore, special activities are planned for each group at each stage of development.

The exhibit is held in our large conference room, and all art work is matted on contrasting brightly colored paper with the child's first name and a code number printed on a strip of paper attached to the work. The code number is used by the children to aid in finding their own art work.[1] The art work is hung at a child's eye level on free standing pegboard screens, none higher than five feet tall. Too often art work is displayed for adults' eyes and children miss much when they must look up. The screens are placed to lead the children naturally from one display to another in a continuous flow. This helps teachers to keep their group together and also organizes what a child will see.

Each child should have a work on display. Most advanced Stage Two and all Stages Three and Four groups also should have a group project on exhibit. These projects mean a great deal to the children as they become increasingly aware of their group. We prepare an attractive mimeograph program listing each child's name, number, and a description of the work (e.g., 22. John. Water Color Scene). This provides tangible evidence for those children who want to show their friends or family that they have been in an art show! (usually children in Stages Three and Four). Taking home a program is also a great motivator to bring parents in to see their child's work. Because art work does *not* go home regularly, this is an important time for the parent's to see the work displayed in a setting that conveys its value.[2]

The art exhibit continues for two or three days, allowing time for each group to have a private visit. Then the exhibit is open to the public at a time when children and parents are not at the center. Late afternoon seems to be the best time for high attendance, but evenings and Saturdays have also been used. Special invitations are also mailed to community groups and individual professional and civic leaders who have supported the program every year. Throughout the year, local merchants, community groups, and people interested in the program accumulate art supplies for us (egg cartons, styrofoam, fabric scraps, wallpaper books, etc.), and we make it a point to invite them to see the results of their efforts. Seeing a battleship made out of packing pieces and toilet paper rolls can be awe-inspiring! Notes are sent

---

[1] In the case of a group product, the teacher's name is used (such as "Mural done by Ms. Smith's group"). In this way, children and their families are protected from identification. Perhaps some day the stigma of having an emotionally disturbed child will not require this approach, but today it does.

[2] We keep the children's art work at the center because in many homes their work would go unnoticed, ridiculed, or be destroyed quickly. In the rare instances we do allow art work to go home, the parents have been carefully prepared to receive and treasure the art work.

home to parents asking them to try and come to the show, but working parents often find it difficult to take the time. Publicity about the exhibit in the local papers is minimal. We make a point *not* to refer to "art work done by emotionally disturbed children," but simply announce that the exhibit is being held.

As soon as the exhibit is in place and all the teachers have double-checked the display and program to see where each of their student's work is located, the art therapist becomes the "tour director" for every group's visit to the exhibit. Each teacher picks a time and day for her group to attend the exhibit, and a schedule is set.[3] Discussions about the exhibit in Stages Two and Three are held before the big day. Often, to ease anxieties, these sessions involve role playing a visit to an art exhibit. Advanced Stage Three and Stage Four groups often have chosen which of their works they think should be on display, have helped in the design of the program cover, and may have assisted in the mimeographing and collating processes.

At the appointed time, for each group, the art therapist comes to the classroom to begin the art exhibit experience. The art therapist is dressed as for a special occasion and her attitude conveys that something very important is about to happen. Stage One children are told that the visit is a "special time," and they are lead out of their room to the exhibit. For Stage Two the art therapist brings programs into the classroom with her and goes through these steps.

1. Asks who has been to an art exhibit before. She builds a brief discussion about an exhibit from all positive responses the children offer.
2. She describes the step-by-step proce-

---

[3] Each group has a distinctly different experience during the visit to the exhibit.

dure to be followed. (Stay with the teachers; look for the work they did, touch exhibits that are "touchable"; refreshments will be in the room afterwards, etc.).
3. Each child is given a program and helped to find his name and code number. This is a good time to refresh the child's mind about his own art work.

In Stage Three, the art therapist enters the room as a "VIP" and introduces herself as the "tour guide" for the exhibit. The teachers have already reviewed the expectations for visiting an art exhibit. It always helps to have the group review them for the art therapist again.

"What will you need to do once you are at the exhibit? Right! Look for your work, ask questions, and enjoy yourself as the group tours together."
"If someone loses control, what should we do?" Let the group review the rule, such as, *"Yes, removing the person from the show seems to be the best thing to do."*

Stage Four children generally have been involved in the preparation of the exhibit and can have a group discussion with the art therapist about what they will look for throughout the exhibit (color, form, patterns, etc.).

WHEN STAGE ONE CHILDREN VISIT THE EXHIBIT

Words are minimal; experience is everything, even at an art exhibit. Soothing classical music is playing (thanks to our music therapist who prepared a forty-five minute tape for the exhibit). In each display area there are several art works that can be touched (sand design, styrofoam displays, rug collages). These have been carefully chosen especially for this tactile experience. Live plants are interspersed with art displays, as are an aquarium, soft pillows to sit on, and a colorful climb-over alligator. These additions to the art exhibit help involve the Stage One children in this special time. The children are led around and are helped to touch the displays. Often the teachers must turn a child's head to look at a color or object or assist a child in climbing on the alligator. At the end of the tour, the children go back to their room for a cookie and juice. For the Stage One child, the programs are meaningless, but the activity and snack have been arousing.

WHEN STAGE TWO CHILDREN VISIT THE EXHIBIT

Before they begin, Stage Two children are excited about going to the art exhibit. Once inside the show, they cluster at the first display with the tour guide and their other teachers. The art therapist, as tour guide, provides the needed structure. *"One of the three pictures you are looking at was done by someone in your group. Which picture is it? That's right, James, it's yours. What did you use to make it? Craypas, right! What a good memory!"*

This verbal structuring is continual as the group moves to the next display area. Each child is encouraged to answer a question. As they move through the exhibit, anxieties will usually decrease. This will reduce the amount of restless, inappropriate behavior. The restful background music is another calming factor. The result is a group of children showing pride in their own work and interest in the work of others.

As the group approaches the end of the exhibit, the art therapist asks if anyone wants refreshments? Of course, the

response is overwhelming. The therapist laddles out a pitcher of punch from the punch bowl and prepares a basket of cookies for a treat back in the room. This makes an easy transition to the room. Once back in the room their newfound pride can be used for continuing to expand upon the experience. (*"Did you see Johnny carefully hold that African drum? Didn't Sally's crayon etching have beautiful colors?"*)

WHAT DO YOU REMEMBER FROM THE EXHIBIT?

Because acting out by Stage Three children often occurs at the beginning of the tour, a specially structured activity is needed. As they enter the exhibit, they are asked to locate their name and code number on their own program. This brief assignment tends to calm them down and set a tone for the tour. Again, the art therapist is the guide.

Endless questions can be used to redirect behavior, focus on appropriate action, and build self-confidence in the group.

"What medium is this? Right! Crayons."

"One of these five pictures was done by a very young child, can you pick it out?"

"You mean all of you worked on this mural every day for two weeks? Fantastic!"

"You've identified every art medium we have in the show!"

"I wish I could let you handle that clay work, Billy, but who knows why the delicate displays can only be looked at?"

At the end of the exhibit, the children are asked if they would like refreshments. The group decides, and members of the group assist in dispensing refreshments. For a group in good control of themselves, the refreshments can be served right in the exhibit room. If the group seems volatile, the same procedures used for Stage Two children will work and the refreshments can be sent back to the room.

EVERYONE IS REPRESENTED

The art work pictured on the following pages illustrates a recent art exhibit. From among many art works, these were selected for this text especially to illustrate the developmental changes that occur across stages, evident through control of the medium; organization of shape, line, and form; increasing concern for naturalistic representation; and emerging sophistication in human forms, houses, and other symbols. The figures also present a variety of media at each developmental stage.

Art Examples

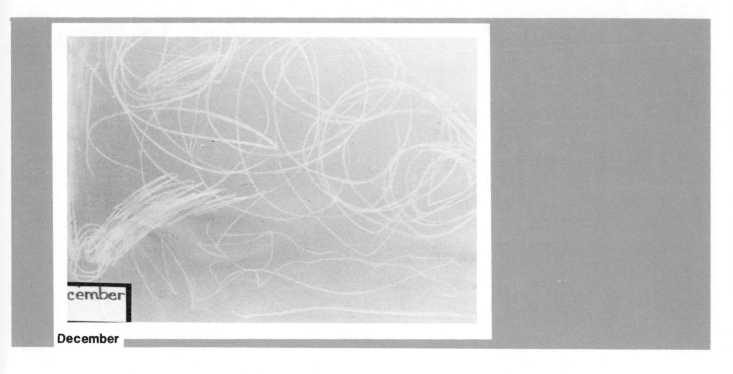

December

Figure 1.

These four figures illustrate the dramatic developmental changes occurring in one four-year-old schizophrenic child in a six-month period. Figure 1 shows a typical Stage One production: controlled scribbling. In Figure 2 forms are emerging from deliberate control of lines, space, and form. This preschematic work is typical of a low Stage Two art production.

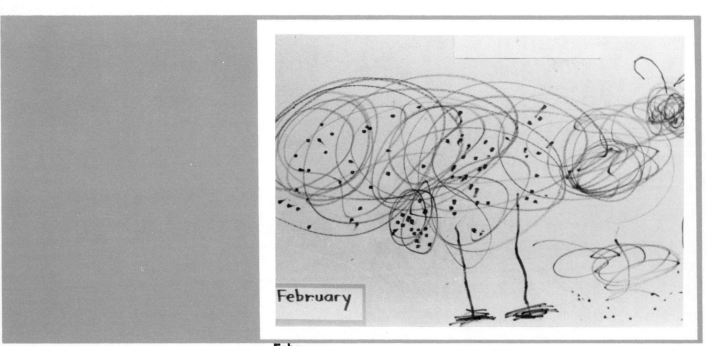

February

Figure 2.

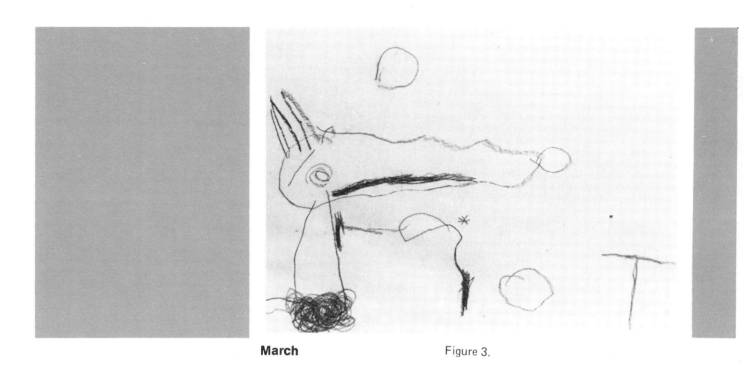

March   Figure 3.

Figure 3 illustrates a more organized, deliberate expression characteristic of children well into Stage Two. The switch in subject matter from animal to human form is the important change in Figure 4.

May

May   Figure 4.

137

Figure 5. *These three human forms were produced by the same child three years later. A discussion of this sequence can be found in Chapter One. The completeness of the human forms, elaboration of detail, and placement of the forms on the paper are characteristic of early Stage Three productions. Age-appropriate schematic conceptualization and representation has surely emerged!*

Figure 6. *This mass of blue fingerprints and smudges was produced by an autistic four-year-old after three weeks of careful, preliminary steps in which the art therapist moved the child's hands into the paint, onto a sheet of paper, and then into a bucket to rinse. This work was her first independent effort! She patted, fondled, and swirled her hands in the fingerpaint. Then she looked directly at the paper, rubbed her hands together to feel the paint, and finally made sounds of pleasure.*

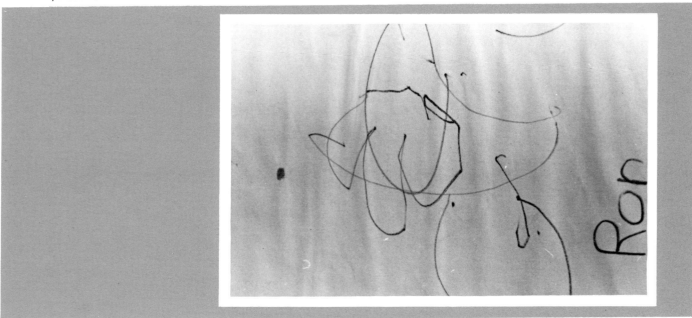

Figure 7. *A magic marker is particularly arousing for Stage One children. It is quick, responds to uncontrolled hand movements, produces a sharp, bright line, and has a unique sound and aroma as it is moved across paper. This work was produced with two colors. The first color was so pleasing to the child that he was able to sustain attention and the second color was provided.*

139

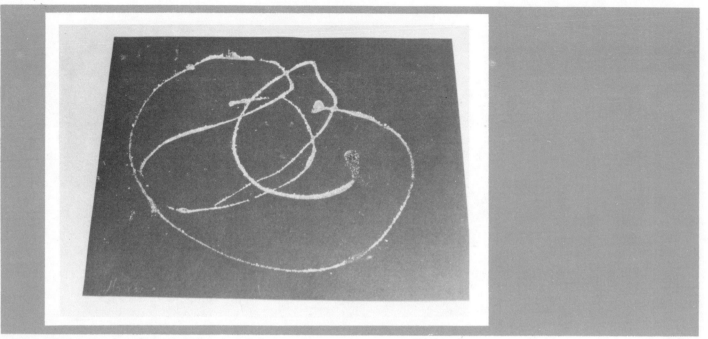

Figure 8. *A Stage One child used glue (a 2-oz. size container already open) to pour this design. Then she reached into a shoe box loaded with sand, grasped some, and poured it over the glue on black paper. Finally, with some physical assistance, she poured the excess sand back into the box and said the word every Stage One teacher hopes to hear, "More"!*

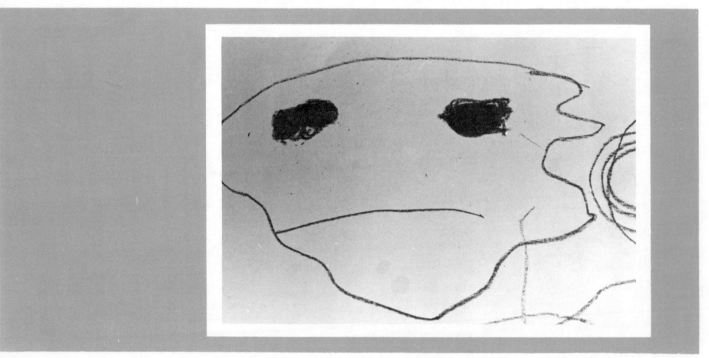

Figure 9. *Using craypas a high Stage One child spontaneously produced this circle form. Then he was able to carry out the representation of eyes and mouth with only verbal direction from the art therapist. This was the first time he had produced any elaboration in his controlled scribbling.*

Figure 11. *This tempera painting was done by another advanced Stage One child. The emerging preschematic pattern can be seen in the way the child has repeated the pattern all over the paper. The pleasure of color and movement stimulated the child to work on this painting for about five minutes. Such sustained attention to one work is extremely unusual for a Stage One child.*

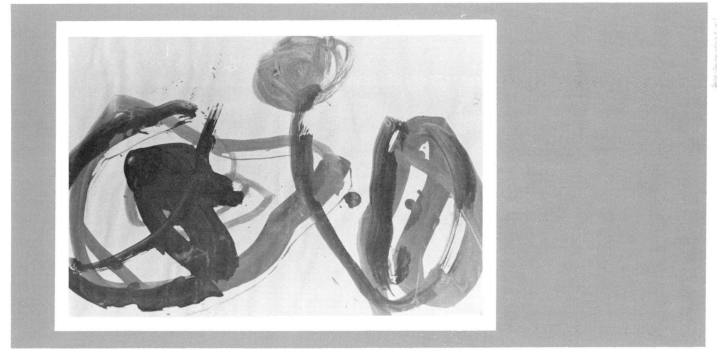

Figure 10. *As a Stage One child masters his eye-hand movements and develops the ability to control his scribbling, shapes and forms emerge rapidly. This tempera painting was produced by a child making the transition from Stage One to Stage Two.*

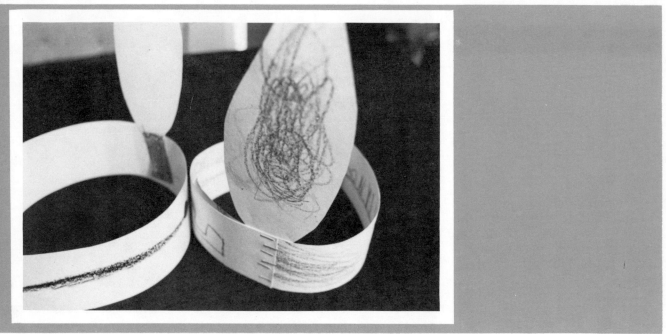

Figure 12.

Figure 13.

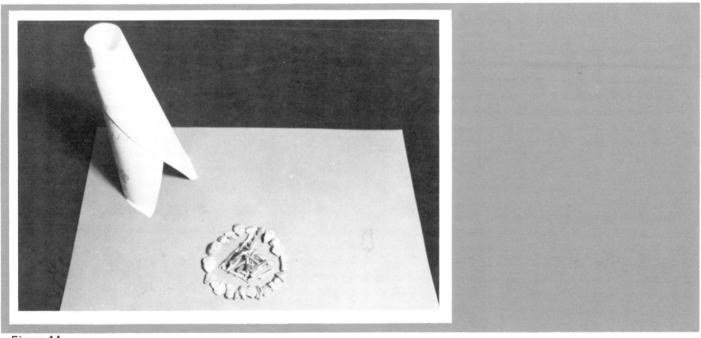

Figure 14.

A Stage Two group's interest in Indians and pioneers was the start of a week-long unit. The Indian headbands were made for a dance to be done at music time. Simple precut bands and feather shapes were given to each child to decorate with crayons. Then the headbands were created by stapling the two ends together to fit each child's head. To continue the unit the next day, a pioneer and Indian story was told and the children made individual covered wagons from precut styrofoam scraps which they painted. Precut cardboard circles and rectangles were provided for further elaboration. Figure 13 illustrates the work of one boy who produced this wagon using circles for wheels and a rectangle for the top. Figure 14 shows how one child arranged his collection of pebbles and twigs after an outside activity to hunt for materials the pioneers might use for a fire. The art therapist demonstrated how to role a teepee from a 9" × 12" paper. In the next step, each child was provided a green poster board for the base and glue to hold the natural materials. The culmination of this unit was a dramatic play, the children representing pioneers and Indians sitting around the campfire.

Figure 15. *A Stage Two child began this project as the others in her group did. She used a precut paper triangle and square and glue to make a house, as had been demonstrated by the teacher. Then she spontaneously asked for crayons and began her human forms. This was her real pleasure in this art lesson.*

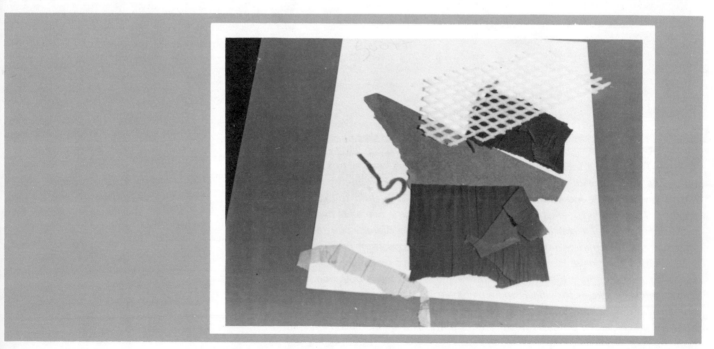

Figure 16. *This collage was produced with scraps of crepe paper, yarn, styrofoam packing, and construction paper. It followed previous lessons experimenting with tearing, folding, breaking, and bending these same materials.*

144

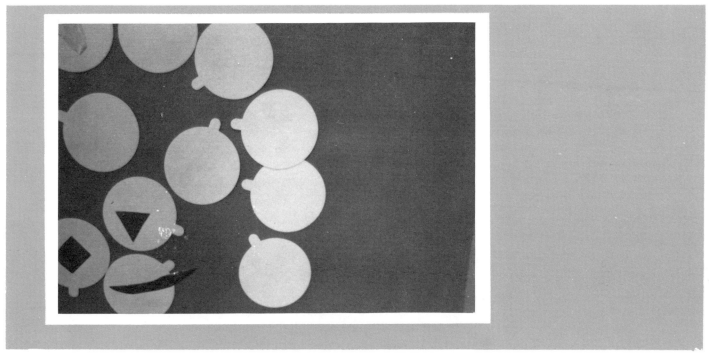

Figure 17. *To make use of donated scrap materials can be a creative challenge. One ten-year-old Stage Two child produced this satisfying design using specimen lids a local hospital had donated. After gluing them down, he used a few scraps of gold contact paper to finish the design.*

Figure 18. *A Stage Three group saved their cups, French fries wrappers, and hamburger papers from a successful field trip. These set the stage for the hamburgers and fries they made out of clay! The products were painted with tempera and shellacked, impressing everyone as looking very real and therefore very "cool"! Although there was a distinct group feeling beginning to emerge, it was evident that these youngsters found their satisfaction in the individual accomplishment.*

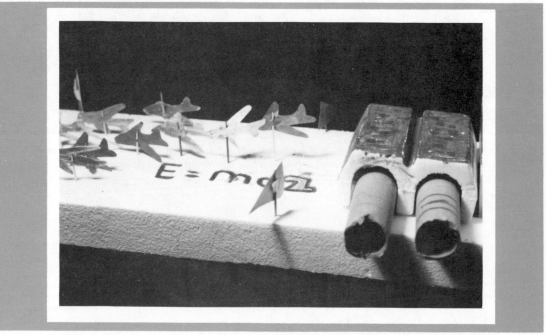

Figure 19. *After hearing a story about the Navy, the same group of boys together created this aircraft carrier from styrofoam, toothpicks, paper, magic markers, and toilet paper tubes. It was produced in a sustained group effort over three art periods. This work illustrates the level of collaboration and socialization skills that can be attained by Stage Three children.*

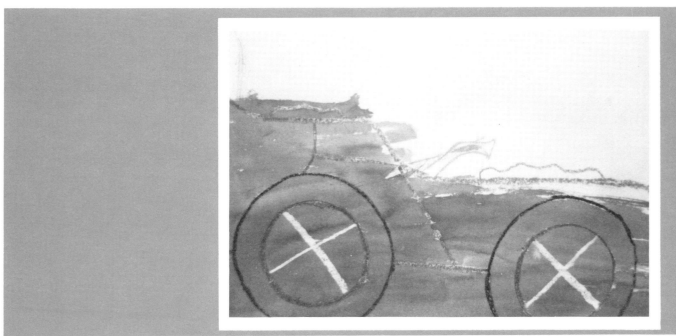

Figure 21. *Children in Stage Three rapidly become aware of what peers think. It is the final word on "cool" art projects. Vehicles were all-important to one group of boys. They produced cars with intensive care, exclaiming over each added detail and showing concern about what their classmates would think of the finished product. To ensure that the most delayed child in the group gained the necessary peer recognition, the art therapist provided precut circles to trace around for wheels and a ruler for straight lines. She even helped to draw exhaust pipes or spoked wheels whenever the child asked for this. This crayon resist work represented a typical Stage Three problem. When the child started to paint this hot rod, the youngster accidentally went outside the lines. This upset him and he proceeded to destroy the work by painting rapidly across the paper to obliterate it. The teacher intervened and interpreted the paint as being "exhaust fumes." His peers were impressed and the child was delighted!*

Figure 20. *The moon landing created space heroes for a Stage Three group and led to a unit on astronauts. This drawing, done with color pencils, is typical of a Stage Three child's ability to produce a complete human form from his imagination. Notice the interest in detail and the quality of power in the form.*

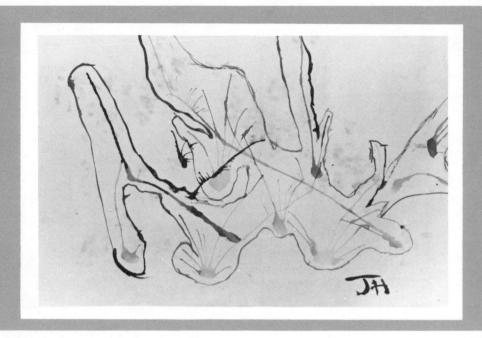

Figure 22. *Usually "blowing" water color paint is a rewarding art lesson for beginning Stage Three children. But one girl seemed dissatisfied after she blew her design. Using water colors and a brush, she began connecting one line to another until she remarked, "Now I like my design!"*

Figure 23. *This drawing with magic marker was done by a nine-year-old Stage Three child. It illustrates the details of animal life and nature that is typical of young Stage Three children. Notice also the decorative touches to the houses. This drawing was done over a 20-minute time span and, when completed, was shown to the class with great pride. The child was terminated from our program shortly after this work was done and continued to exhibit a healthy adjustment in his school and at home.*

148

Figure 24. *In a group making the transition from Stage Three to Stage Four, each child had the opportunity to select the topic for the daily art lesson. One inadequate, withdrawn youngster wanted to become a truck driver and clung to this dream tenaciously but with little peer recognition. On the day for his art choice, a truck was parked outside the building. The group agreed to have an outdoor art lesson, to sketch the truck from real life. They all made several free drawings but none satisfied this particular boy. He spent several days afterwards drawing (with pencil and ruler) from his original sketches until he produced this drawing which pleased him and drew admiration from the group. It represented a major milestone for him in socialization.*

Figure 25. *In the same transition group, another child was able to impress his peers with his "Tony Orlando" portrait. Although not his most creative work, he was pleased when his group suggested this painting for the art exhibit. This episode is characteristic of the child moving into Stage Four, developing greater skill with media and symbols, responding to folk heroes, and finding self-esteem through peer recognition.*

Figure 26. *A beginning Stage Four child who had always resisted art activities saw a picture of a clown and wanted to draw it. He was risking complete failure because he had never drawn anything spontaneously, always insisting on coloring predrawn forms. Using ink, pen, and crayon he produced this sensitive drawing. His first!*

Figure 27. *This eagle was drawn first with pencil by a twelve-year-old boy in a beginning Stage Four group. There were exquisite details of feathers on the wing shape but these were obliterated when he asked to paint it "so it will show up better." Artistically this was a mistake, but for the first time this child had asked to do something (in a proper way) and was so invested in it that he was willing to risk himself by showing his interest and involvement. The finished art work pleased him and brought greater admiration from his classmates.*

150

Figure 28. *This child carefully listened to a story on Japan and exclaimed over the beautiful pictures of houses and temples in the* National Geographic. *In art, she wanted to try to copy one. She worked on this tempera painting for almost an hour and was quite pleased with her results. So were her friends in this Stage Four group.*

Figure 29. *One Stage Four group was ready for a very advanced art activity, drawing a model. The group talked about who to draw; where to place him; and how he was to pose. There was also a discussion of whether the art work should be shown. It was agreed; everyone could take the criticism! They also decided that if you just couldn't draw a human figure, something else in the room could be substituted. This plate illustrates the arrival of the pseudo-naturalistic phase and a highly sophisticated ability to perceive and portray. Perhaps it is the most developmentally advanced product in the exhibit.*

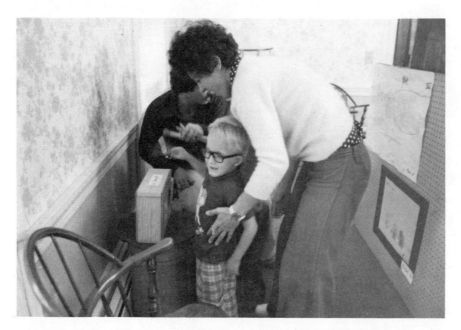

Figure 30. *What can a Stage One child experience from an art exhibit? Here an autistic boy is assisted by the art therapist to explore the sounds made from striking a drum made by a Stage Two youngster.*

Figure 31. *From the drum, the child moves on without showing any awareness until the huge, green, shiny alligator comes into view. He moves to explore it spontaneously, touching it on his own. The art exhibit is a success!*

Figure 32. *Guiding Stage Two children through an exhibit can be difficult. Each child wants and needs individual attention. In their anxiety they often are restless or stand rooted in one place until physical contact and restructuring of the procedure is provided.*

Figure 33. *These Stage Two children first clung to their teachers and the art therapist.*

Figure 34. *As they relaxed and began to see and experience the art work, the adults were able to pull back and let the children move and explore on their own.*

Figure 35. *As one child spotted his work or something of interest, individual questions were answered and discussion was stimulated. The exhibit became a fine place to extend verbal communication skills.*

Figure 36.

Figures 36 to 38. *The program serves to stimulate and structure the participation of Stages Three and Four children. The exhibit is an opportunity for the students to be ''grown up'' and to see their work displayed in ways communicating its value. Previous art experiences have provided them with the knowledge and words to have successful discussions with each other about the art.*

Figure 37.

Figure 38.

DEVELOPMENTAL THERAPY CURRICULUM OBJECTIVES

(Revised)

The Developmental Therapy objectives contained in this Appendix are 146 developmental milestones which promote emotional growth. They are sequenced for stages of therapy and according to four curriculum areas: behavior, communication, socialization, and (pre)academics. These objectives can be used to plan a developmental art therapy program for an individual child or for small groups of children. The objectives can be used also as an instrument for criterion-referenced evaluation. For specific instructions on this latter use, the reader is referred to Chapter Two of *Developmental Therapy*, Mary M. Wood, editor. For technical information concerning the validity of the objectives and other evaluation data, see Chapter Three in *Developmental Therapy.*

Behavior Objectives

STAGE I:
Responding to the Environment with Pleasure

STAGE I BEHAVIOR GOAL: TO TRUST OWN BODY AND SKILLS

■ 0. to indicate *awareness* of a sensory stimulus with *any responses* away from or toward source of stimulus (in situations with tactile, motor, visual, auditory, taste, and smell stimuli). Child must have two out of six modalities.
Examples:
Child responds when:
   a. Teacher touches child's cheek (tactile).
   b. Teacher picks up child (motor).
   c. Teacher claps hands out of sight (auditory).
   d. Presented with strong odor (smell).
   e. Child puts objects in mouth (taste).
   f. Child follows moving object with eyes (visual).

■ 1. To *react* to sensory stimulus by *attending* toward source of stimulus by body response or by looking (in situations using tactile, motor, visual, auditory, taste, and smell stimuli). (Same as academic objective A-1.) Child must have two out of six modalities.
Examples:
   a. After teacher blows bubbles, child attends briefly by looking or responding with body language (visual stimulus).
   b. When teacher starts to play guitar, child attends briefly by turning head to source of sound, looking at guitar or teacher, or smiling (auditory stimulus).
   c. When teacher places child's hand in water, child indicates awareness by splashing or clapping hands together, withdrawing hands, or looking briefly at water (tactile stimulus).

■ 2. to respond to stimulus by *sustained attending* to source of stimulus (continued looking at object or person after initial stimulus-response has occurred). (Same as academic objective A-2.)
Examples:
   a. After initial stimulus, child continues to watch teacher strum guitar during a song or continues to smile or move body to music.
   b. Child continues to look at or play in water.

■ 3. to respond spontaneously to *single* environmental *stimulus* with a motor behavior: object, person, sound. (Same as academic objective A-3.)
Examples:
   a. Child sees block, picks it up, and throws it.
   b. Teacher holds out guitar. Child explores it.
   c. Teacher turns on music box (out of child's view). Child comes to see.

■ 4. to respond with motor and body responses to *complex* environmental and verbal *stimuli* (through imitation, "Do this"; through completion of verbal direction; minimal participation in the routine; *given physical intervention and verbal cues*). (Same as academic objective A-4.)
Examples:
   a. Teacher says, "It's time to play in the water." Teacher puts her hands in the water and splashes (to show child what to do). Then child puts hands in the water and splashes.
   b. Teacher says, "This is a boat. Let's push it." Teacher pushes boat as example. Child does not respond, so teacher places child's hand on boat. Then child begins to play with boat. Teacher says, "Good, you're playing with the boat" and pats child on the back.
   c. Teacher announces, "It's play time." Child gets up but is not sure in which direction to move. Teacher steers child (with hand on back) to play area. Child sits down in play area but doesn't initiate play, so teacher hands child a toy. Child takes toy.

■ 5. to actively *assist* in learning *self-help skills* (toileting, washing hands, dressing, putting arms in coat when held [should be based upon chronological age expectations in combination with developmental expectations; mastery not essential]).
Examples:
   a. Child indicates need to use bathroom (verbal or nonverbal); tries to pull down pants.
   b. Child tries to turn on water; puts hands under water; tries to use soap.
   c. Child pulls up pants or tries to button pants.

■ 6. to respond *independently* to several play materials. (Verbal cues may be used; age-appropriate play is not necessary.) Perseverative or self-stimulatory behavior not acceptable.

Examples:

a. *Child spontaneously picks up a doll, holds it, rubs hair, moves doll's limbs (but does not rock baby, try to take doll's clothes off, or put baby in bed as would be expected of a child that age).*

b. *Child picks up block, puts it to his mouth, then throws it down.*

■ 7. to indicate *recall* of classroom *routine* by moving *spontaneously* to next activity area without physical stimulus; verbal cues or touch may be used.

This objective is intended to help organize a child to the extent that when the activity is announced, the child is aware enough of the routine to move to the next activity.

Examples:

a. *When teacher says, "It's play time," child moves to play area without having to be physically moved by teacher.*

b. *Teacher says, "It's music time." Child gets up, starts in wrong direction. Teacher touches child and says again, "It's music time." Child moves to music area.*

c. *Teacher says, "It's time to go." Child goes to closet to get coat.*

STAGE II:
Responding to the Environment with Success

STAGE II BEHAVIOR GOAL: *TO SUCCESSFULLY PARTICIPATE IN ROUTINES AND ACTIVITIES*

■ 8. to use play materials *appropriately*, simulating normal play experience.
Child plays with toys with awareness of their function, both as representative, real-life objects (play stove for cooking, as well as objects for pretending (play stove turned over makes a castle wall). He does not see toys as objects to be destroyed but as objects which he uses to facilitate his fantasy or to play out real-life situations. For a child who has difficulty discriminating reality from fantasy, it would not be appropriate for the child to continually pretend.
Examples:
  a. *Child drives toy car up to service station and pretends to get gas.*
  b. *Child feeds and dresses a doll.*
■ 9. to *wait* without physical intervention by teachers. (Verbal support or touch may be used.) (Same as socialization objective S-14.)
Examples:
  a. *Child races up to roll on the mats but is out of turn. Teacher says, "Wow, you are really happy about having mat time! I can't wait to see how well you do your cartwheel after Ricky finishes." Child goes in turn.*
  b. *Mike wants the cookies, and he wants them NOW. Teacher says, "You can have a cookie after John." Mike is able to wait.*
  c. *Child wants his turn first at kickball. Teacher says, "I remember that fly ball you caught yesterday. You were standing right here." Or, "Everyone gets a chance to kick and catch. It's your turn to catch now." Child moves to field.*
  d. *Child runs out of the room ahead of the group. Teacher says, "Wait at the door." Child waits.*
■10. to *participate* in *sitting* activities such as work time, story time, talking time, juice and cookie time without physical intervention by teacher. (Child is able to take part in the activities *by staying in the activity area, responding to materials,, and *following teacher's directions* when given verbal support or touch by the teacher. (Child's sitting per se is not the focus.)
Examples:
  a. *Child moves away from story circle. Teacher exclaims and points to the book, "Wow, look at that huge wolf's teeth!" Child moves back into circle.*
  b. *Child moves in and out of chair during work time. Teacher says, "This work is easy when you're sitting in your chair." (Important then to support child during completion of work.) Child continues work to completion.*
  c. *Child begins to pour milk on the table. Teacher says, "Kids drink their milk here." Child stops pouring milk.*
  d. *Child runs away from the table. Teacher says, "We sit for art time." Child comes back to table. Or, teacher gets up, touches child on the back, then points to the table. Child comes back.*
■11. to *participate* in *movement* activities such as play time, mat time, games, music, or art time without physical intervention by teacher. (Child is able to take part in the activities *by staying in the activity area, responding to materials*, and *following teacher's directions* when given verbal support or touch by teacher.)
Examples:
  a. *Child is reluctant to go through transition and, instead of going to play time, remains apart from group. Teacher says, "When you come to the play area, you'll get to play with the doll." Child moves to play area.*
  b. *Child loses control and threatens another child physically. Teacher moves between two children and says, "I know you want that truck, but I hear a big, red fire engine trying to get out of the toy cabinet." Child ceases fight and goes to toy cabinet.*
  c. *Child yells out words of a song very loudly, instead of singing, during music time. Teacher turns to other child who is singing appropriately and says, "Your soft voice sounds so pretty." Child stops yelling.*
■12. to *spontaneously participate* in routines without physical intervention. (Verbal support or touch may be used, but child indicates some personal initiative to comply with routine.)
Examples:
  a. *Teacher says, "It's work time." Child picks up work folder (if that is the routine previously set up).*
  b. *During snack time and before play time, children begin discussing what they will play during play time, indicating that they know routine. Child subsequently moves to play.*
  c. *Teacher says that play time is almost over. Child begins to bring his play to closure and realizes that it is time to put toys away. Child begins putting toys away.*

STAGE III:
Learning Skills for Successful Group Participation

STAGE III BEHAVIOR GOAL: *TO APPLY INDIVIDUAL SKILLS IN GROUP PROCESSES*

■13. to verbally *recall group rules* and procedure. (Same as communication objective C-15.)
Examples:
  a. *Before going outside to play the teacher questions the group about the rules of a game they have played previously.*
  b. *After taking 10 cookies at once during snack time, the teacher asks the child about the rule for taking cookies. The child responds, "Oh ya, only one at a time."*
  c. *During a talk, the child is able to verbally recall the rule he or she has broken. (May continue to break the same rule.)*
  d. *Before leaving the classroom, the group may review the rules for riding the bus or walking through the building.*

■14. to contribute to *making group expectations* of conduct and procedures. (Same as communication objective C-17.)
Example:
  During a group discussion on rules for the class, children might respond in the following ways:
  "We should walk down the stairs."
  "Children should stay in their seats while riding on the bus."
  "Work is done at the table, so we should stay in our chairs."

■15. to *verbalize consequences* if group's expectations are not reached. (Same as communication objective C-18.)
Examples:
  a. *When questioned about what is going to happen if a child continues to fight on the bus, child may say, "I won't be able to ride it anymore" or "The bus driver is going to kick me off and get mad."*
  b. *During a crisis situation, the teacher may ask the child, "Why are we in the quiet room?" The child responds, "Because I was kicking John, and I had to leave the room."*
  c. *When a child misses snack time because he was having problems during the activity, he can say, "I did not get my snack because I caused trouble in class, and I had to leave the room."*
  d. *Teacher asks the child, "What would happen if...." and the child can tell the consequences.*

■16. to give *simple reasons* for group's expectations. (Verbal cues from teacher may be used.) (Same as communication objective C-21.)
Examples:
  a. *A teacher may ask the question, "Why should we have a rule about hitting?" The child may respond in these ways:*
  "Hitting hurts."
  "When children are hitting it causes trouble."
  "Children don't like to get hit."
  b. *Teacher asks a question about the classroom rule on talking. The child may say, "One person should talk at a time, because if everyone talked it would be hard to hear."*
  c. *Teacher asks a question about the rule on walking down the stairs. Child answers, "After class we should walk down the stairs, because if everyone ran someone could fall and get hurt."*

■17. to tell other, *more appropriate ways* to behave in a given situation; individual focus. (May not be able to implement alternatives.)
Examples:
  a. *The teacher might ask, "What else could you do other than hit John?" Child responds, "I guess I could tell the teacher that he is making me mad."*
  b. *After shouting in class to get attention, a child might say, "I can raise my hand instead of shouting." (This may come after a question by the teacher.)*
  c. *A group of kids has been having a hard time coming up the stairs after recreation class; kids have been running around the building instead of going to the classroom. In group discussion about this problem, kids are able to say, "When we walk right up the stairs, instead of running around the building, we can get started sooner on our project."*

■18. to *refrain* from inappropriate behavior or breaking group rules *when others* in the group *are losing control* (given verbal support by teacher.)
Examples:
  a. *A child does not join two other children in name calling.*
  b. *A child remains in his seat when others are out of their seats fighting, running around, etc.*
  c. *A child remains involved in a recreational activity when others in the group are not participating.*

■19. to maintain *self control* and *comply* with group procedures (given classroom structure and verbal support by teacher).
Example:
  Child participates in all classroom group activities appropriately and according to structure established by the teacher (work, art, recreation, group games, snack, etc.).

STAGE IV:
Investing in Group Processes

STAGE IV BEHAVIOR GOAL: *TO CONTRIBUTE INDIVIDUAL EFFORT TO GROUP SUCCESS*

■20. to respond *appropriately* to choices for leadership in the group (either not being selected or being selected leader). (Same as socialization objective S-26.)

Example:

The group decides to role play a voyage on a ship. One child is selected to be the captain, and the rest of the children are to be the crew. The child chosen as the captain responds appropriately to his role as leader, and the other children respond appropriately to his leadership and assume their roles as the crew members.

■21. to *spontaneously participate* in activities *previously avoided* (without teacher structure). (Same as socialization objective S-27.)

Example:

Child has previously avoided taking part in group activity involving making up a story and talking into a tape recorder. Child spontaneously offers to take part in the activity.

■22. to *implement* appropriate alternative behavior toward others (minimal interpersonal interaction needed).

Examples:

a. *When one child is verbally or physically annoying another child, the child with mastery of this objective will be able to select and implement an appropriate behavior, such as informing the teacher, asking the other child to leave him alone, or removing himself from the situation.*

b. *Child is able to select and implement a positive approach to interaction with others. A child wishes to join an ongoing activity and is able to verbally request or otherwise signal his desire to be included in the activity, rather than resort to inappropriate behavior, such as withdrawing or causing a disruption.*

■23. to *verbally express cause and effect* relationship *between feelings and behavior*, between group members, and between individuals (group problem solving). (Same as communication objective C-29.)

Example:

Group is engaged in a project, such as painting the club house, and one member of the group is not participating. Child is able to express his own feelings and those of the group that result from the other child's failure to help in the activity by stating, "I'm mad, and we're all mad because he won't help us paint." Group is then able to arrive at a solution to the problem and continue with the activity.

■24. to respond to *provocation* with verbal and body control (with verbal support from teacher).

Examples:

a. *A child is being verbally and/or physically provoked by another child and is given verbal support by the teacher, such as, "Tom is just trying to make you mad." Child is then able to maintain control.*

b. *During work time, a child is called "stupid" because he is having difficulty with his work. The teacher says, "Everybody has different kinds of work, and some children are better at some things than others." Child who was provoked continues with his work.*

■25. to respond to suggestions of a *new, real-life* experience, or change with appropriate verbal and body control (can come either from teacher or another child).

Examples:

a. *The teacher suggests to child that he join the Boys' Club and helps him to do so. Child attends and participates in Boys' Club activities.*

b. *Public school teacher suggests that child begin taking physical education class at school instead of another class; child complies.*

c. *Child conforms to rule established by parents (cleaning his room once weekly; being at home at a certain hour for dinner daily).*

d. *Child has begun to refrain from teasing with peers at Center. He exhibits the same restraint toward siblings at home upon suggestion of teacher.*

e. *During conference between child and teacher, it is suggested that child's time spent at Center be reduced from three to two days. Decision is jointly reached, and child is able to maintain appropriate behavior at school, functioning with reduced support from Center.*

STAGE V:
Applying Individual/Group Skills in New Situations

STAGE V BEHAVIOR GOAL: *TO RESPOND TO CRITICAL LIFE EXPERIENCES WITH ADAPTIVE AND CONSTRUCTIVE BEHAVIOR*

■26. to *respond* to a critical interpersonal or situational experience *with constructive suggestions* for change, as with constructive problem-solving behavior.

Communication Objectives

STAGE I:
Responding to the Environment with Pleasure

STAGE I COMMUNICATION GOAL: *TO USE WORDS TO GAIN NEEDS*

- 0. to *produce sounds* (child must master c. below to master objective).
  Examples:
  a. *Child makes undifferentiated sounds*
  b. *Child vocalizes combinations of consonants and vowels*
  c. *Child repeats his own pattern of vocalizing for social or adaptive expression (several patterns desirable)*
     1) *eee, nnnn, ahhh*
     2) *ba ba, da da da, du gu du*
- 1. to *attend* to person speaking. (Child moves or looks toward adult when adult initiates verbal stimulus. Eye contact not necessary.)
  Example:
     Teacher greets children as they arrive. "Here is Johnny." Johnny directs his body or eyes toward teacher, or he may smile without looking directly at teacher.
- 2. to *respond* to verbal stimulus with a *motor behavior* (object present; teacher does not use gestures).
  Examples:
  a. *Teacher says, "Ball." Child shows recognition by looking, touching, or body movement toward ball.*
  b. *Teacher says, "Bye-bye." Child waves.*
- 3. to *respond* to verbal stimulus and single object with a *recognizable approximation of the appropriate verbal response.* (Child gives verbal approximation to indicate use or correct answer to question, "What is this?" [object present; function or name acceptable].)
  Examples:
  a. *Teacher says, "Ball." Child attempts a "b" sound.*
  b. *Teacher says, "What is this?" (milk). Child says, "Mi."*
     (Teacher may have to repeat the word for the child before the child makes the approximation.)
  c. *Teacher says, "What do you want?" (scissors). Child says, "Cuh-cuh."*
- 4. to *voluntarily* use *recognizable single word approximations* in several activities to describe or label a situation, object, or event. (Child produces recognizable approximation spontaneously, e.g., "wa-wa" for water.) (Same as academic objective A-9.)
  Examples:
  a. *Teacher puts milk on the table, and child spontaneously says, "Mi, mi."*
  b. *Teacher blows bubbles, saying, "I have bubbles, bubbles." As teacher begins blowing bubbles again, child excitedly attempts to say, "Bu, bu."*
  c. *Child sees car going down street. Child says, "Ca."*
  d. *Teacher is hopping, encouraging children to model. She is saying, "Hop-hop-hop-hop." Suddenly child says, "Op, op."*
- 5. to produce a *recognizable single word* in several activities to obtain a *desired response from adult* or to label object for adult (e.g., "water" instead of "wa-wa" for water). (Verbal cues may be used.)
  Examples:
  a. *Teacher puts milk on the table, and child says, "Milk."*
  b. *At art time, teacher is holding art materials. Teacher says, "I have paper. Do you want paper?" Child says, "Paper! Paper!" Teacher gives child paper.*
  c. *Child takes music box out of toy cabinet and holds it up to the teacher, saying, "Box."*
- 6. to produce *recognizable single words* in several activities to obtain a *desired response from another child* or to label for child. (Verbal cues may be used.)
  Examples:
  a. *At play time, child sees another child with his favorite truck. He walks up and says, "Truck."*
  b. *Child A tries to sit in child B's chair. B begins to get upset. Teacher says, "Tell him to move." B says, "Move."*
- 7. to produce a *meaningful*, recognizable *sequence of words* in several activities (without a model) to obtain a desired response from others or to label. (Gestures or verbal cues may be used.)
  Examples:
  a. *Child says, "I want a cookie."*
  b. *Child starts to take toy away from another child. Teacher says, "Ask him for it." Child says, "Give me that truck!"*
  c. *Child says to teacher, "Go away."*
  d. *Child sings a simple song.*
  e. *Child says, "Me big fire truck."*

STAGE II:
Responding to the Environment with Success

STAGE II COMMUNICATION GOAL: *TO USE WORDS TO AFFECT OTHERS IN CONSTRUCTIVE WAYS*

■ 8. to *answer* a child's or an adult's *questions* or *requests* with *recognizable*, meaningful, relevant *word(s)*. (Response does not have to be accurate or constructive.)

Examples:

    a. Child A says, "Give me that truck." Child B says, "This is my truck."

    b. Teacher says, "Would you like another cookie?" Child says, "I don't want your old cookie!"

    c. Teacher says, "What is this?" Child says, "Ball."

■ 9. to exhibit a *receptive vocabulary* no more than two years behind chronological age expectations (as indicated by the PPVT or other means).

Example:

    The child comprehends what others are saying even if he does not talk (gesture or words acceptable).

■10. to *label simple feelings* in pictures, dramatic play, art, or music: *sad, happy, angry, afraid* (by gesture or word).

Examples:

    a. Teacher shows picture of child crying and asks, "Is he sad or happy?" Child says, "Sad."

    b. Teacher shows two pictures and asks, "Which is sad?" Child points to correct choice.

    c. Child paints picture and says, "This is a mean picture."

■11. to use simple word *sequences* to command or request of another child or adult in ways *acceptable to classroom procedures*. (Bizarre language content or socially inappropriate word sequences are not acceptable; behavior is not a consideration.)

Example:

    Child can say to teacher or another child, "I want your red color." Or, "Give me milk." If child uses loud or whiney voice, teacher can repeat more appropriately, and child will say it again modeling teacher.

■12. to *use* words to *exchange minimal information with an adult*. (Child initiates conversation; requests or questions not applicable.)

Examples:

    a. During milk and cookie time, child says, "My Mommie makes cookies."

    b. Child says to teacher, "This is a red crayon."

    c. Child says, "I want to go home."

■13. to *use* words spontaneously to *exchange minimal information with another child*. (Minimal verbal spontaneity with information content; requests or questions are not applicable.)

Self explanatory

STAGE III:
Learning Skills for Successful Group Participation

STAGE III COMMUNICATION GOAL: *TO USE WORDS TO EXPRESS ONESELF IN THE GROUP*

■14. to *accept praise* or *success* without inappropriate behavior or loss of control.
   Examples:
   a. *Child accepts a pat on the back as praise. (A child does well on a task; teacher touches shoulder or pats back to reinforce, and the child does not pull back or act inappropriately.)*
   b. *Teacher says, "John, you did a good job on your work today." The child accepts the praise.*
   c. *After telling a story in class, the child looks to the teacher for support. The teacher smiles at the child, and this reinforcement is accepted positively.*

■15. to verbally *recall group rules* and procedure. (Same as behavior objective B-13.)

■16. to use words spontaneously to *describe own* ideas, activity, work, or self to another adult or child.
   Examples:
   a. *When asked by the teacher to walk on stilts the child says, "I can't walk on stilts. I am too short."*
   b. *When questioned about a watercoloring, a child explains what it represents and why he painted it. He says, "This is the house that I used to live in, and I am making all the trees the same way they used to be."*
   c. *When discussing a role playing activity, a child might say, "I had to walk around a lot and check everybody to make sure that they were being good."*

■17. to contribute to *making group expectations* of conduct and procedure. (Same as behavior objective B-14.)

■18. to *verbalize consequences* if group's expectations are not reached. (Same as behavior objective B-15.)

■19. to use words or nonverbal gestures to *show pride* in own work, activity, or to make positive statements about self.
   Examples:
   a. *During work time a child says, "Hey, look at my work. I'm all finished."*
   b. *During recreation a child says, "Boy, today I kicked the ball really well, farther than anyone else!"*
   c. *During art a child may simply hold up his picture, without any comment, to show someone.*

■20. to use *appropriate words* or gestures to *show feeling responses* to environment, materials, people, or animals. (Teacher uses classroom activity to elicit response.)
   Examples:
   a. *A child may suggest that they (the group) hang some pictures on the wall because the wall looks so blank.*
   b. *A child reports to the teacher or class, "Last night the thunder storm was really loud, and I could not sleep."*
   c. *A small puppy is brought into the classroom, and the child is aware that one must handle the animal gently. He displays this behavior both physically and verbally, or is able to express his feelings and say, "I am afraid of dogs."*

■21. to give *simple reasons* for group expectations. (Verbal cues from teacher may be used.) (Same as behavior objective B-16.)

STAGE IV:
Investing in Group Processes

STAGE IV COMMUNICATION GOAL: *TO USE WORDS TO EXPRESS AWARENESS OF RELATIONSHIP BETWEEN FEELINGS AND BEHAVIOR IN SELF AND OTHERS*

■22. to *verbally recognize* feelings in others: sad, happy, angry, afraid (either spontaneously or in response to questions).
Examples:
    a. *Child enters the room and slams the door. Another child comments, "Johnny must be really mad."*
    b. *Teacher asks, "How did that make Tom feel?" Child responds, "I guess he didn't like it."*

■23. to *recognize* and *acknowledge* feelings *in self:* sad, happy, angry, afraid.
Example:
    Child enters the classroom smiling and states that he made an A on his spelling test at school. The teacher, or another child, replies that he must be happy about doing so well on his test. The child is able to nonverbally shake his head to affirm; smiles; verbally responds to acknowledge that he is happy; or does not deny the statement.

■24. to use words *to praise* or personally support *others.*
Examples:
    a. *Child praises another child for a good catch in softball.*
    b. *Child supports another child by providing assistance on a math worksheet.*
    c. *Child stands up for a child being criticized by others.*

■25. to *express experiences and feelings* through art, music, dance, or drama. (Child does not need to give verbal explanation.)
Examples:
    a. *Child has been on a fishing trip with his family over the weekend. At art time, he draws a picture of himself and members of his family in a boat fishing.*
    b. *For music, each child contributes his interpretation of a thunder storm using various percussion instruments.*
    c. *After a difficult time completing his work at work time, a child aggressively pounds clay on the table.*

■26. to *use words* to express *own feelings* spontaneously and appropriately.
Examples:
    a. *During game time, child verbally expresses happiness over having hit a home run in softball.*
    b. *Child says, "When I use red paint, it makes me feel bad."*
    c. *Child tells another child, "I don't like you to say that."*

■27. to *use words* appropriately to express awareness of feelings *in others* (peers, adults).
Examples:
    a. *Child is able to express awareness of another child's feelings by stating, "Johnny really feels bad about losing his new watch."*
    b. *Child is able to determine teacher's feelings and verbally comments, "Mr. Jones thinks that Joe is acting silly."*

■28. to relate *real-life* experiences and feelings through stories, art, drama, or music with accompanying verbal expressions.
Examples:
    a. *During the planning of a child drama about a circus, a child expresses the fear he experienced when he first encountered a lion at the circus (with accompanying facial expression).*
    b. *Following a story read by the teacher about a runaway child, a child responded, "Oh well, I ran away from home once, but when it started to get dark I was afraid and ran home."*
    c. *During art, a child says, "I'm going to make a clay boat just like the one we used for fishing at summer camp. Boy, you should have seen the fish I caught! It was this big." (Child uses hands in expressing the size of the fish.)*

■29. to *verbally express cause and effect* relationship *between feelings and behavior,* between group members, and between individuals (group problem solving). (Same as behavior objective B-23.)
Example:
    Group is engaged in a project, such as painting the club house. One member of the group is not participating. Child is able to express his own feelings and those of the group that resulted from the other child's failure to help in the activity by stating, "I'm mad, and we're all mad because he won't help us paint." Group is then able to arrive at a solution to the problem and continue with the activity.

STAGE V:
Applying Individual/Group Skills in New Situations

STAGE V COMMUNICATION GOAL: *TO USE WORDS TO ESTABLISH AND ENRICH RELATIONSHIPS*

■30. to use words to initiate and maintain *positive relationships* (peer and adult).

Socialization Objectives

STAGE I:
Responding to the Environment with Pleasure

STAGE I SOCIALIZATION GOAL: *TO TRUST AN ADULT SUFFICIENTLY TO RESPOND TO HIM*

■ 1. to be *aware* of others (child looks at adult or another child when adult or another child speaks directly to child or touches him).
Examples:
    a. Child is sitting at the table staring at the wall. Teacher calls child by name and touches child on the back. Then child turns head toward adult. (Child may not be responding to his name as much as to the physical contact from the teacher.)
    b. Child is aimlessly wandering around the room. Teacher puts her arm around the child and says child's name. Child turns head away from adult. (Child is obviously aware of the contact from the adult but resists looking at the adult.)
    c. Child shows awareness of others by body language or averted gaze but not necessarily by eye contact.
    d. Child shows some interest in baby games such as peek-a-boo.

■ 2. to *attend* to other's behavior. (Child looks at another when attention is not on child directly.)
Example:
    Teacher is giving help to child. Second child watches the teacher and child together.

■ 3. to *respond* to adult when child's name is called. (Child looks at adult or away; appropriate or inappropriate response acceptable.)
Example:
    Teacher calls child's name. Child looks up or around to teacher. (In this objective, child does not need to be physically aroused, as in socialization objective S-1. Child differentiates his own name from other children's names. He may look away, instead of toward teacher, when name is called.)

■ 4. Child *interacts nonverbally* with *adult* to meet needs.
Examples:
    a. Child moves adult's hand to get cookie.
    b. Child points to desired object.
    c. Teacher turns on toy radio. Radio winds down. Child comes to adult to turn it on again.
    d. Child tries to bite teacher's arm after a frustrating experience.

■ 5. to engage in *organized solitary play* (with direction from teacher if necessary; age-appropriate play not necessary).
Examples:
    a. Child purposefully piles blocks together, knocks them down, repeats, or builds a house. Teacher may initiate activity by stacking blocks as example and saying, "Let's stack the blocks."
    b. Child climbs up and down the slide.
    c. Child puts toys in box, then dumps them out.
    d. Patterned play.

■ 6. to respond to adult's verbal and nonverbal *requests to come* to him. (Child moves next to adult and looks at him, and child accepts adult's touch.)
Examples:
    a. Teacher says, "Come over here by me." Child moves next to teacher and allows teacher to put arm around him.
    b. During story time on floor, teacher holds arm out to child to get him to move next to her. Child moves over by teacher and looks at her.

■ 7. to demonstrate *understanding* of *single verbal requests* or directions given directly to child. (Teacher does not use gestures.)
Example:
    Teacher says, "Sit down." Child sits down. Teacher says, "Hang up your coat." Child hangs up coat without physical intervention.
    "Put the ball in the cabinet."
    "Pick up the truck." } *Child complies.*
    "Give me the box."

■ 8. to produce a *recognizable single word* or sign in several activities to obtain a *desired response from adult* or to label for adult (e.g., "water" instead of "wa-wa" for water; verbal cues may be used.)

■ 9. to produce *recognizable single words or signs* in several activities to obtain a *desired response from another child* or to label for child. (Verbal cues may be used.)
Examples:
    a. At play time, child sees another child with his favorite truck. He walks up and says or signs, "Truck."
    b. Child A tries to sit in child B's chair. B begins to get upset. Teacher says, "Tell him to move." B says or signs, "Move."

■10. to produce a *meaningful*, recognizable *sequence of words or signs* in several activities (without a model) to obtain a desired response from *others* or to label for others. (Gestures or verbal cues may be used.)
Examples:
    a. Child says (or signs), "Go away."
    b. Child says (or signs), "Big fire truck."

■11. to exhibit a *beginning* emergence *of self* (indicated by any of these: age-approximate human figure drawing; gesturing pleasure at one's work; use of personal pronoun (I, me, my); or looking at self in mirror).
   Examples:
   a. *Child looks at self in mirror; child does not avoid it.*
   b. *Child uses personal pronoun but may not be gramatically correct ("Me going" or "Me toy").*
   c. *Child takes his drawing up to teacher with smile and conveys pride in work.*
■12. to *seek* contact with adult *spontaneously*. (Child moves next to adult or touches him.)
   Examples:
   a. *Child walks into room at beginning of class and comes to teacher for a hug.*
   b. *During play time, child moves next to teacher and strokes her hair.*

STAGE II:
Responding to the Environment with Success

STAGE II SOCIALIZATION GOAL: *TO PARTICIPATE IN ACTIVITIES WITH OTHERS*

■13. to *participate spontaneously* in specific parallel activities with another child using similar materials but not interacting.
Example:
> *Child plays with toy truck while another child is using a car. They are organized individually, i.e., each runs on his own highway, and "traffic" of other child serves as no impetus for interaction.*

■14. *to wait* without physical intervention by teachers. (Verbal support or touch may be used.) (Same as behavior objective B-9.)
Examples:
   a. *Child races up to roll on the mats but is out of turn. Teacher says, "Wow, you are really happy about having mat time! I can't wait to see how well you do your cartwheel after Ricky finishes." Child goes in turn.*
   b. *Mike wants the cookies, and he wants them NOW. Teacher says, "You can have a cookie after John." Mike is able to wait.*
   c. *Child wants his turn first at kickball. Teacher says, "I remember that fly ball you caught yesterday. You were standing right here." Or, "Everyone gets a chance to kick and catch. It's your turn to catch now." Child moves to field.*
   d. *Child runs out of the room ahead of the group. Teacher says, "Wait at the door." Child waits.*

■15. to *initiate* appropriate minimal movement toward another child within the classroom routine. (Child, through gesture and action, begins minimal appropriate social interaction with another child.)
Examples:
   a. *Child remembers that another child missed his turn.*
   b. *Child wants to sit by a certain child.*
   c. *Child goes over to join another child already engaged in play.*

■16. to *participate* in a verbally directed sharing activity. (Child passes materials or gives toy to another.)
Examples:
   a. *Child passes cookies within the classroom structure.*
   b. *Child gives toy to another. (Verbal cues may be used.)*
   c. *Child can use same paint, water, or box of crayons that another child is using.*

■17. to *participate* in cooperative activities or projects with another child during play time, indoor or outdoor. (Child is involved actively with another child; verbal support or touch may be used.)
Examples:
> *(Involvement in a free-play situation or organized game where a child is able to organize his play and allow for successful interaction with another child in the group.)*
   a. *Child attends a "tea party" with other children.*
   b. *Child puts out "fire" at another child's "home."*
   c. *Child stays in circle and plays "drop the hankie" following structure of group's game.*

■18. to *participate* in cooperative activities or projects with another child during organized class activities. (Child is involved actively with others; verbal support or touch may be used.)
Examples:
> *(The child engages in activities which the teacher directs by determining the procedure that will guide the children toward desired outcomes, products, etc.)*
   a. *Child has a defined place on a large piece of paper for a group mural on which each child has a specific area to complete.*
   b. *Child role plays a story book character as other children serve as audience.*
   c. *Child makes cold drink mix with another child.*

STAGE III:
Learning Skills for Successful Group Participation

STAGE III SOCIALIZATION GOAL: *TO FIND SATISFACTION IN GROUP ACTIVITIES*

■19. to *take turns* without verbal reminders from teacher.
  Examples:
  a. *During game time, a child waits in his chair until time for him to take his turn.*
  b. *During recreation, a child plays his correct position while waiting for his turn to bat.*
  c. *Child accepts the appointment of another child as leader after teacher explains that he will have a turn at being leader.*

■20. to *share* materials, activities (minimal verbal reminders from teacher).
  Examples:
  a. *During a group discussion about where materials should be placed in the room, a child is able to offer his ideas or feeling about the way that it should be done. "Let's keep all work materials on that shelf and keep our art stuff on this one."*
  b. *A child may have all the red paint during art time, but when another child asks for some of the red paint, he does share.*

■21. to *suggest* activities or preference for play materials to the teacher for group activity.
  Examples:
  a. *A child says to the teacher, "We have played kick ball a lot, so let's play softball today."*
  b. *A child says, "I like to play with the stilts, so during game time today, can we use them?"*
  c. *Child says, "Let us play with the instruments today instead of singing."*

■22. to participate *without inappropriate response* to activity suggested by *another child.*
  Example:
  When a suggestion is made, such as in socialization objective S-21, and the teacher decides to follow the suggestion, a child is able to participate in these activities without inappropriate response such as, getting mad, running away, disrupting the activity, or using abusive language.

■23. to indicate *developing friendship* by preference for a particular child or children.
  Examples:
  a. *A child puts his arm around another child or asks him to be on his side during a recreational activity.*
  b. *A child makes a peanut butter sandwich at snack time for another child and passes it to him spontaneously.*
  c. *A child helps another child appropriately, and usually spontaneously, with his work.*

■24. to *recognize* and describe characteristics of others.
  Examples:
  a. *A black child notices a white child's hair is different and talks about the differences.*
  b. *A child might say, "John is really fat, so he cannot run very fast."*
  c. *"John is taller than me, so he can reach higher."*
  d. *"I do not like John; he talks all the time and always gets the rest of us in trouble."*

STAGE IV:
Investing in Group Processes

STAGE IV SOCIALIZATION GOAL: *TO PARTICIPATE SPONTANEOUSLY AND SUCCESSFULLY AS A GROUP MEMBER*

■25. to *suggest* appropriate group activity directly to peer group (without teacher participation).
Examples:
    a. Child suggests to group, "Let's ask Mr. Jones if we can play football today at recreation."
    b. Child suggests to group, "Let's make a TV show for the teachers and the other kids."

■26. to respond appropriately to choices for *leadership* in the group (either not being selected or being selected leader). (Same as behavior objective B-20.)

■27. to *spontaneously participate* in activities *previously avoided* (without teacher structure). (Same as behavior objective B-21.)

■28. to verbally indicate preferences among members of the group by *differentiating personal characteristics*.
Examples:
    a. Child states that he wants to go sit next to Tom because Tom is good in math and has offered to help him with his work.
    b. Child states that he wants Johnny to be on his team in softball because Johnny is a good player and never strikes out.

■29. to *physically* or *verbally assist* another child in difficult situation; to come to support of another.
Examples:
    a. One child has become upset during art time because he didn't get the model car that he wanted. Another child is able to assist him by offering to trade models with him.
    b. One child is having difficulty learning to walk on stilts. Another child supports him verbally by stating, "You stayed up longer that time. You'll get it."

■30. to participate in *group planning* and constructive problem solving (with or without minimal teacher participation).
Examples:
    a. A field trip is being discussed in the group, and several different suggestions are made as to where the group should go. The teacher says to the group, "Now, how can we decide where we are going to go?" A child in the group suggests taking a vote in order to decide.
    b. Child is faced with a group activity, such as softball, where he doesn't feel that he can be successful. Teacher asks group, "How can we assign positions so that everyone will be successful?" Group discusses alternatives and concludes that child will be a good catcher.

STAGE V:
Applying Individual/Group Skills in New Situations

STAGE V SOCIALIZATION GOAL: *TO INITIATE AND MAINTAIN EFFECTIVE PEER GROUP RELATIONSHIPS INDEPENDENTLY*

■31. to *initiate* and *maintain* effective interpersonal and group relationships.

Academic Objectives

STAGE I:
Responding to the Environment with Pleasure

STAGE I ACADEMIC GOAL: *TO RESPOND TO THE ENVIRONMENT WITH PROCESSES OF CLASSIFICATION, DISCRIMINATION, BASIC RECEPTIVE LANGUAGE, AND BODY COORDINATION*

■ 1. to *react* to sensory stimulus by *attending* toward source of stimulus by body response or by looking (in situations using tactile, motor, visual, auditory, taste, and smell stimuli). (Same as behavior objective B-1.) Child must have two out of six modalities.
Examples:
   a. *After teacher blows bubbles, child attends briefly by looking or responding with body language (visual stimulus).*
   b. *When teacher starts to play guitar, child attends briefly by turning head to source of sound, looking at guitar or teacher, or smiling (auditory stimulus).*
   c. *When teacher places child's hand in water, child indicates awareness by splashing or clapping hands together, withdrawing hands, or looking briefly at water (tactile stimulus).*

■ 2. to *respond* to stimulus by *sustained attending* to source of stimulus (continued looking at object or person after initial stimulus-response has occurred). (Same as behavior objective B-2.)
Examples:
   a. *After initial stimulus, child continues to watch teacher strum guitar during a song or continues to smile or move body to music.*
   b. *Child continues to look at or play in water.*

■ 3. to *respond* spontaneously to *single* environmental *stimulus* with a motor behavior: object, person, sound, (Same as behavior objective B-3.)
Examples:
   a. *Child sees block, picks it up, and throws it.*
   b. *Teacher holds out guitar. Child explores it.*
   c. *Teacher turns on music box (out of child's view). Child comes to see.*

■ 4. to respond with motor and body responses to *complex* environmental and verbal *stimuli* (through imitation "Do this"; through completion of verbal direction; minimal participation in the routine; *given physical intervention and verbal cues*). (Same as behavior objective B-4.)
Examples:
   a. *Teacher says, "It's time to play in the water." Teacher puts her hands in the water and splashes (to show child what to do). Then child puts hands in the water and splashes.*
   b. *Teacher says, "This is a boat. Let's push it." Teacher pushes boat as example. Child does not respond, so teacher places child's hand on boat. Then child begins to play with boat. Teacher says, "Good, you're playing with the boat" and pats child on the back.*
   c. *Teacher announces, "It's play time." Child gets up but is not sure in which direction to move. Teacher steers child (with hand on back) to play area. Child sits down in play area but doesn't initiate play, so teacher hands child a toy. Child takes toy.*

■ 5. to respond with rudimentary *fine* and *gross motor skills* to simple manipulative tasks associated with *24-month* age level. Child must have mastered two skills in each area in order to master this objective.
Fine Motor Examples:
   a. *Child can build tower of six to seven blocks.*
   b. *Child can align two or more blocks together to make a train.*
   c. *Child imitates circular stroke and vertical stroke.*
   d. *Child can maintain spoon in upright position.*
   e. *Child can pull on or take off a simple garmet (shoes, socks, or panties).*
   f. *Child turns knob (door knob or jar lid).*
Gross Motor Examples:
   a. *Child can walk unassisted.*
   b. *Child can run.*
   c. *Child can climb.*
   d. *Child can kick a ball.*

■ 6. to *imitate* simple, familiar *actions* of *adult.*
Examples:
   a. *Teacher says, "Bye-bye" and waves. Child waves.*
   b. *Teacher bounces ball then gives ball to child. Child attempts to bounce ball.*
   c. *Teacher stacks up blocks and knocks them down. Teacher pushes blocks to child. Child imitates.*

■ 7. to respond by *simple discrimination* of objects. (Child gives correct motor or verbal response to a command such as, "Give me ____." Or, "Touch the ____." (Two different objects presented.)
Example:

> Teacher puts crayons and scissors on table and says to child, "Give me the crayons." Child can discriminate between the two objects and hands the correct item to teacher.

■ 8. to *respond* to question by naming single object with a *recognizable approximation* of the *appropriate verbal response.* (Child gives approximation, by word or sign, to question, "What is this?" [object present; function or name acceptable].)

■ 9. to *voluntarily* use *recognizable single word approximations* in several activities to describe or label a situation, object, or event. (Child produces recognizable approximation spontaneously, e.g., "wa-wa" for water.) (Same as communication objective C-4.)
Examples:

> a. Teacher puts milk on the table, and child spontaneously says, "Mi, mi."
> b. Teacher blows bubbles, saying, "I have bubbles, bubbles." As teacher begins blowing bubbles again, child excitedly attempts to say, "Bu, bu."
> c. Child sees car going down street. Child says, "Ca."
> d. Teacher is hopping, encouraging children to model. She is saying, "Hop-hop-hop." Suddenly child says, "Op, op."

■10. to demonstrate short-term *memory* for sound patterns, objects, or people.
Examples:

> a. For sounds, by repeating simple sound patterns.
> b. For objects, by searching for hidden objects.
> c. For people, by indicating awareness of their absence.

■11. to match *similar objects* with *different attributes.* Visual matching of concrete objects having same attributes. Teacher should provide a verbal direction while presenting this task: "Find one that's the same." Or, "Let's put all the trucks here." Child does not need to understand verbal direction.
Examples:

> a. Child fits geometric blocks into puzzle box opening without using trial-and-error method.
> b. Child can do simple (single pieces) puzzle, fitting shapes into matching spaces.
> c. Child is presented with red and blue beads. Teacher demonstrates putting red beads in one box and blue in another. Child continues task.
> d. At play time, child gets several different trucks and puts them in one place together.

■12. to produce *recognizable single words* to *label* simple pictures or objects (spontaneously or elicited). No models given.

■13. to perform *body coordination* activities at the three/four-year level. Child must master at least two skills in order to master objective.
Examples:

> a. Child can ride a tricycle.
> b. Child can alternate feet when going up stairs.
> c. Child can stand balanced on one foot.
> d. Child can catch bounced ball.
> e. Child can throw ball, two hands overhead.
> f. Child can jump forward.

■14. to *match identical pictures* when presented with both identical and different pictures. (Teacher should provide a verbal direction while presenting the task, "Find one that's the same," or comparable statement. Child must understand verbal direction.)

■15. to recognize several *body parts* (*eye, hand, foot, nose, leg, arm, knee*) (any correct response acceptable: gesture, word, etc.).

■16. to perform *fine motor* coordination activities at the *three/four-year* level. Child must master at least two skills in order to master objective.
Examples:

> a. Child builds a bridge from cubes.
> b. Child copies a circle.
> c. Child draws man with two parts.
> d. Child buttons and unbuttons.
> e. Child strings beads.
> f. Child snips with scissors.

■17. to recognize several *colors* (any correct response acceptable: gesture, word, etc.).

STAGE II:
Responding to the Environment with Success

STAGE II ACADEMIC GOAL: *TO PARTICIPATE IN CLASSROOM ACTIVITIES WITH LANGUAGE CONCEPTS OF SIMILARITIES AND DIFFERENCES, LABELS, USE, COLOR; NUMERICAL PROCESSES OF ORDERING AND CLASSIFYING; AND BODY COORDINATION*

■18. to recognize *uses* of several objects or toys.
   Examples:
   a. *Teacher has object or picture of object, like a shovel. Child knows what it is used for and can tell or act it out.*
   b. *Teacher hands ball and says, "What can you do with this?" Child says or acts it out by throwing, kicking, bouncing, or rolling it.*

■19. to recognize *detail in pictures* by gesture or word.
   Example:
   Teacher says, "Where's the girl in the picture?" "Where's her nose?" Child points or describes correctly.

■20. to recognize *one different object* in a set of three objects. Teacher should provide a verbal direction while presenting this task: "Find the one that's different." Or, "Which one doesn't belong." Child must understand verbal direction.
   Examples:
   a. *Teacher presents box with two identical trucks and one doll. Teacher says, "Find one that doesn't belong."*
   b. *Teacher presents two spoons and one fork. Teacher says, "Which one is different?"*

■21. to *count* with *one-to-one* correspondence to *five*.
   Example:
   Child can count five objects.

■22. to recognize *pictures* that are the same and ones that are different. Child must understand teacher's directions: "Find the one that's the same." "Find the one that's different," or comparable statement.
   Example:
   Child is presented with three pictures. Two are identical; one is different. Teacher says, "Show me the one that's different." After child identifies picture that is different, teacher removes the two identical pictures and adds another picture making the different picture one of two now the same. A third, different, picture is added. Teacher says, "Now, find the ones that are the same." (Teacher needs two different sets of identical pairs and one different card for this task.)

■23. to *count* with *one-to-one* correspondence to *ten*.
   Example:
   Child can count ten objects.

■24. to perform *eye-hand coordination* activities at the *five-year level*.
   Examples:
   a. *Child draws a recognizable person with body.*
   b. *Child copies triangle, rectangle.*
   c. *Child prints a few letters from memory.*
   d. *Child copies first name from model.*
   e. *Child draws simple house representation.*
   f. *Child cuts with scissors along lines.*

■25. to recognize symbols, numerals, and written words that are the *same* and ones that are *different*. (All forms must be mastered; child need not know how to read words in order to recognize differences among them but must understand verbal directions.)
   Example:
   Teacher shows child a card with several words, two identical and one different. Teacher asks, "Which one is different?" "Now, which ones are the same?"

■26. to *categorize* simple *pictures* that are *different but have* generally *similar characteristics* or associations.
   Examples:
   a. *Teacher gives child a stack of picture cards and says, "Put all the people in this pile and put all the animals in this pile."*
   b. *Teacher prepares worksheet for child and says, "Draw a line to the pictures that belong together." (Sheet contains pictures of chicken and egg, dog and bone, pencil and paper, paint and brush.)*

■27. to *write* a *recognizable approximation* of *first name*, without assistance. (Adult may initiate request; no model used.)
   Self explanatory

■28. to *discriminate* concepts of *differences* in *up, down; under, over; big, little; tall, small; hot, cold; first, last*.
   Self explanatory

■29. to perform *body coordination* activities at the *five-year level*.

Examples:
    a. *Child skips, using alternate feet.*
    b. *Child walks on walking board.*
■30. to *recognize groups* of objects to *five* ("How many?").
Example:
    Teacher holds up card with dots for brief viewing. Child identifies number without counting.
■31. to *listen* to story telling.
Example:
    Child can direct and maintain attention to the story being told or read by the teacher. (Verbal support or touch may be used.)

STAGE III:
Learning Skills for Successful Group Participation

STAGE III ACADEMIC GOAL: *TO PARTICIPATE IN THE GROUP WITH BASIC EXPRESSIVE LANGUAGE CONCEPTS; SYMBOLIC REPRESENTATION OF EXPERIENCES AND CONCEPTS; FUNCTIONAL, SEMICONCRETE CONCEPTS OF CONSERVATION; AND BODY COORDINATION*

■32. to recognize *groups* of objects *to ten.*
   Examples:
       a. Teacher holds up card with dots for brief viewing. Child identifies number in groups without counting.
       b. When playing with dominoes, child recognizes number groups without counting.
■33. to demonstrate *left to right orientation* for visual motor tasks.
   Examples:
       a. Child looks at left page before right page of picture book.
       b. Child puts sequence pictures together so that story is shown as happening from left to right.
       c. Child completes work sheet with left to right movement.
■34. to recognize *written names* for *color words* (red, blue, yellow). (Child selects appropriate color word.)
   Self explanatory
■35. to recognize *written labels* (own name, chair, table, part of written schedules).
   Self explanatory
■36. to *recognize* and *write numerals* to represent groupings (1 to 10). (For mastering this objective, child must be able to accomplish both activities, recognizing numerals and writing numerals to represent groups from 1 to 10.)
   Examples:
       a. Child can recognize numeral (e.g., 1 = "one") and can show teacher corresponding numbers of objects.
       b. Child can look at a group of objects and write the correct numeral.
■37. to *write first* and *last name* and date with written *example to copy.*
   Self explanatory
■38. to perform *eye-hand coordination* activities at the *six-year level.*
   Examples:
       a. Drawing a person with arms, legs, clothes, etc.
       b. Writing first name legibly from memory.
       c. Tying shoes.
■39. to perform *body coordination* activities at the *six-year level.*
   Examples:
       a. Throwing and catching a ball with control.
       b. Recognizing right and left.
       c. Walking backwards.
       d. Clapping in rhythm.
       e. Roller skating.
■40. to *recognize* and *write numerals* to represent groupings (11 to 20).
   Examples:
       a. Child recognizes numeral 15 ("fifteen") and shows teacher corresponding number of objects (one-to-one counting not used).
       b. Child looks at group of objects drawn on work sheet and can write correct numeral without one-to-one counting.
■41. to *write alphabet* or simple words (with or without model).
   Self explanatory
■42. to *do* numerical operations of *addition* and *subtraction* through ten.
   Example:
       For mastering of this objective, child should be able to write the correct answer to all numerical operations of addition and subtraction through 10 with 90-percent accuracy.
■43. to use *ordinal concepts* verbally (first, fifth, last).
   Examples:
       a. A child is able to find the fourth drawer in a treasure hunt.
       b. Child says, "I do not want to be second; I want to be first."
       c. "I was the first (second, last) to get to class today."

■44. to *listen to a story and respond* with appropriate answers to questions; by comments or gestures.
Examples:
    a. *Teacher reads a story; child laughs at appropriate incidents.*
    b. *Teacher begins to tell a story; child contributes what comes next.*

■45. to *read* basic primary vocabulary words *spontaneously* in sentences.
Example:
    To master this objective child should have 90% reading accuracy for 100 first grade reading words.

■46. to *do* simple numerical operations of *addition* and *subtraction* above 10.
Example:
    To master this objective child should be able to add and subtract with 90-percent accuracy (no regrouping—borrowing or carrying).

■47. to *write* basic words *from memory* or dictation.
Example:
    To master this objective child should be able to write 30 basic words from memory or dictation with 90-percent accuracy.

■48. to *participate* in group activity for *writing experience story*, dictating to teacher, or working on murals.
Examples:
    a. *After an experience story, a child is able to work with other children doing a group watercolor about the story on a large single piece of paper.*
    b. *While dictating a group story for the teacher to write, the child can verbally give ideas or information that contributes to the story.*

STAGE IV:
Investing in Group Processes

STAGE IV ACADEMIC GOAL: *TO SUCCESSFULLY USE SIGNS AND SYMBOLS IN FORMALIZED SCHOOL WORK AND IN GROUP EXPERIENCES*

■49. to *write* full name, address, date, *from memory*.
  Self explanatory

■50. to *read* and *write* basic vocabulary spontaneously *in complete sentences*.
  Self explanatory

■51. to *read* and *write* quantitative words for measurement of distance, time, money, fractions.
  Self explanatory

■52. to *contribute* to *group projects* requiring expressive skills.
  Examples:
   a. *The group is using the tape recorder to record a story that they are making up for special time. Child is able to take his turn and contribute to the group story.*
   b. *Child is able to work with other members of the group in writing a script for a play.*
   c. *Child is able to role play a situation developed by the group.*

■53. to *write* individual *experience stories*. (Child writes own experience story with teacher assistance on difficult words.)
  Example:
   Child is able to write an individual story based on a topic, such as, my class's field trip, my favorite sport, etc.

STAGE V:
Applying Individual/Group Skills in New Situations

STAGE V ACADEMIC GOAL: *TO SUCCESSFULLY USE SIGNS AND SYMBOLS FOR FORMALIZED SCHOOL EXPERIENCES AND PERSONAL ENRICHMENT*

■54. to *write for communication* of information to others.
Self explanatory
■55. to *read for pleasure* and for personal information.
Self explanatory
■56. to *write of feelings* and attitudes in prose or poetry.
Self explanatory
■57. to *read to obtain information* on the feelings and behaviors of others.
Self explanatory

Developmental Therapy Objectives Rating Form

DTORF
Developmental Therapy Objectives Rating Form (Revised)

Child's Name _____ Class Stage _____ Raters: _____

Date _____ Type Rating (Check one)–Baseline _____, 5th week _____, 10th week _____

	Behavior	Communication	Socialization	(Pre)academics

STAGE I	___ 0. indicate awareness
	___ tactile
	___ auditory
	___ motor
	___ taste
	___ visual
	___ smell
	___ 1. react by attending
	___ 2. respond by sust. attend.
	___ 3. simp. stim/motor behav.
	___ 4. complex stim./imit.
	___ 5. assist in self help
	___ 6. respond indep./play mat.
	___ 7. indicate recall of routine
		___ 0. produce sounds
		___ 1. attend speaker
		___ 2. resp. verb.
		    stim./mot. beh.
		___ 3. resp./verbal approx.
		___ 4. wrd. approx./descr./
		    label/volunt.
		___ 5. recog. word/to adult
		___ 6. recog. word/to child
		___ 7. word sequence
			___ 1. aware/others
			___ 2. attend/others beh.
			___ 3. resp. to name
			___ 4. interact/adult nonverb.
			___ 5. solit. play
			___ 6. resp. request/come
			___ 7. dem. under./sing. req.
			___ 8. recog. wd./sign adult
			___ 9. recog. wd./sign child
			___ 10. word seqs/others
			___ 11. begin. emerg./self
			___ 12. contact/adult spont.
				___ 1. same as B-1
				___ 2. same as B-2
				___ 3. same as B-3
				___ 4. same as B-4
				___ 5. fine/gross mot./24 mo.
				___ 6. imitate acts of
				    adults
				___ 7. discrim. of obj.
				___ 8. approx. naming object
				___ 9. same as C-4
				___ 10. short-term memory/sound,
				    obj. & people.
				___ 11. match simil.
				    obj. w/diff. attri.
				___ 12. wrd./label pic., obj.
				___ 13. body coord./3-4 yr.
				    level
				___ 14. match identical pic.
				___ 15. recog. body parts
				___ 16. fine motor coord./3-4 yr.
				___ 17. recog. colors

STAGE II	___ 8. use play mat. appro.
	___ 9. to wait/no interven.
	___ 10. particip./sitting
	    no interven.
	___ 11. particip./movement
	    no interven.
	___ 12. spon. particip./rout.
		___ 8. answer/recog. word
		___ 9. recept. vocab./2
		___ 10. label feel./pict.
		___ 11. command, request/
		    simple wrd. seq.
		___ 12. use words ex. min.
		    info./adult
		___ 13. use words ex. min.
		    info./child
			___ 13. parallel activ.
			___ 14. same as B-9
			___ 15. init. min. move./child
			___ 16. sharing activ.
			___ 17. coop. act./child
			    at play
			___ 18. coop. act./child
			    in organ. activ.
				___ 18. recog. use of obj.
				___ 19. recog. detail in pictures
				___ 20. recog. diff. obj.
				___ 21. count to 5 (1 to 1)
				___ 22. recog. same/diff. pictures
				___ 23. count to 10 (1 to 1)
				___ 24. eye-hand coord./5-yr. level
				___ 25. recog./shapes, symbols,
				    numerals, words/same/diff.
				___ 26. categorize diff. pictures/
				    similar charac.
				___ 27. write recog. approx. of
				    first name w/o asst.
				___ 28. discrim. differences
				    (up-down, etc.)
				___ 29. body coord./5-yr. lev.
				___ 30. recog. grps. to 5
				___ 31. listen to story telling

STAGE III	___ 13. vb. recall rules/proced.
	___ 14. contrib. to grp. expect.
	___ 15. vb. conseq./expect.
	___ 16. vb. reasons/expect.
	___ 17. vb. other ways beh./
	    indiv.
	___ 18. refrain when others
	___ 19. main. control & comply
		___ 14. accept praise
		___ 15. same as B-13
		___ 16. spon. describe work
		___ 17. same as B-14
		___ 18. same as B-15
		___ 19. pride/words/gestures
		___ 20. vb./feeling/resp.
		___ 21. same as B-16
			___ 19. turns w/o remind.
			___ 20. share/min. remind.
			___ 21. sug. to teacher
			___ 22. partic./act. suggest
			    child
			___ 23. pref./child
			___ 24. desc. charac. of
			    others
				___ 32. recog. grps. to 10
				___ 33. left-right visual orien.
				___ 34. recog. writ. names for
				    color words
				___ 35. recog. written labels
				___ 36. recog. & write numerals for
				    groups/1-10
				___ 37. write first/last name/date
				    with sample
				___ 38. eye-hand coord./6-yr. level
				___ 39. body-coord./6-yr. level
				___ 40. recog. & write numerals for
				    grps./11-20
				___ 41. write alpha./simple words

(continued)

	Behavior	Communication	Socialization	(Pre)academics
STAGE III				___ 42. do add-subtract thru 10 ___ 43. use ordinal/concepts verbally ___ 44. lstn. to story & resp. appro. ___ 45. read prim. vocab./sentences ___ 46. add-subtract above 10 ___ 47. write basic words/memory or dictation ___ 48. partic. grp. act./write, tell, mural
STAGE IV	___ 20. resp. appro./leader choice ___ 21. spon. partic./activ. prev. avoid ___ 22. implem. alter. beh. ___ 23. vb. express cause & ef. ___ 24. resp./provocation/ control ___ 25. resp. appro./ new suggest.	___ 22. vb. recog. feel/others ___ 23. vb. recog. feel/self ___ 24. verb. praise/others ___ 25. non vb./express./ feel./art, music ___ 26. spon. express. own feel./words ___ 27. express others feel. ___ 28. vb. express. exper./ feel./art, music ___ 29. same as B-23	___ 25. suggest. act./grp. ___ 26. same as B-20 ___ 27. same as B-21 ___ 28. diff. charac./others ___ 29. phys./vb. support/ others ___ 30. partic. grp. plng. & pb. solv.	___ 49. write name, ad., date/memory ___ 50. read, write/sentences ___ 51. read, write quant. words ___ 52. contribute grp. project/ expressive skills ___ 53. write indiv. exper. stories
STAGE V	___ 26. construc. suggest.	___ 30. maintain posit. relats. verb.	___ 31. init. & main./ interp. & grp. rel.	___ 54. write for commun. ___ 55. read/pleas. & info. ___ 56. write of feel. & attit. ___ 57. read/info. feel. & beh. of others

Progress Notes

Bibliography

Adler, J. 1973. Looking for Me. University of California Press, Berkeley.

Alkema, C. J. 1971. Art for the Exceptional. Pruett Publishing Co., Boulder, Col.

Anthony, E. J. 1956. The significance of Jean Piaget for child psychiatry. Br. J. Med. Psych. 29:20–34.

Anthony, E. J. 1967. Psychoneurotic disorders. In: A. M. Freedman and H. I. Kaplan (eds.), Comprehensive Textbook of Psychiatry. Williams & Wilkins, Baltimore.

Bobroff, A. 1960. The stages of maturation in socialized thinking and in the ego development of two groups of children. Child Dev. 31:321–338.

Cane, F. 1951. The Artist in Each of Us. Pantheon Books, New York.

Carter, J. L., and Miller, P. K. 1975. Creative art for minimally brain-injured children. Academic Ther. 6: 245–252.

Castillo, G. A. 1974. Left-Handed Teaching. Praeger Publishers, New York.

Champernowne, H. I. 1971. Art and therapy: an uneasy partnership. Am. J. Art Ther. 10:131–143.

Combs, C. 1975. Developmental therapy curriculum objectives. In: M. M. Wood (ed.), Developmental Therapy, pp. 17–35. University Park Press, Baltimore.

Crosscup, R. 1966. Children and Dramatics. Charles Scribner's Sons, New York.

Denny, J. M. 1972. Techniques for individual and group. J. Art Ther. 11:117–134.

DiLeo, J. H. 1970. Young Children and Their Drawings. Brunner-Mazel Publishers, New York.

Ekstein, R., and Caruth, E. 1976. On the structure of inner and outer spielraum—the play space of the schizophrenic child. In: E. Schopler and R. J. Reichler (eds.), Psychopathology and Child Development, pp. 311–318. Plenum Press, New York.

Elkind, D. 1976. Cognitive development and pscyhopathology: observations on egocentrism and ego defense. In: E. Schopler and R. J. Reichler (eds.), Psychopathology and Child Development, pp. 167–183. Plenum Press, New York.

Erikson, E. 1963. Childhood and Society. 2nd Ed. W. W. Norton and Co., New York.

Erikson, E. 1973. Growth and crisis of the healthy personality. In: S. G. Sapir and A. C. Nitzburg (eds.), Children with Learning Problems, pp. 37–79. Brunner/Mazel, New York.

Fenichel, C. 1976. Socializing the severely disturbed child. In: E. Schopler and R. J. Reichler (eds.), Psychopathology and Child Development, pp. 219–227. Plenum Press, New York.

Flavell, J. H. 1963. The Developmental Psychology of Jean Piaget. D. Van Nostrand Co., New York.

Freud, A. 1973. The concept of developmental lines. In: S. G. Sapir and A. C. Nitzburg (eds.), Children with Learning Problems, pp. 19–36. Brunner/Mazel, New York.

Gonick-Barris, S. E. 1976. Art for children with minimal brain dysfunction. Am. J. Art Ther. 15:67–73.

Henry, W. 1956. An Analysis of Fantasy. John Wiley and Sons, New York.

Hermelin, B., and Frith, U. 1971. Psychological studies of childhood autism: can autistic children make sense of what they see and hear? J. Spec. Educ. 5:107–117.

Hewett, F. M. 1968. The Emotionally Disturbed Child in the Classroom. Allyn Bacon Co., Boston.

Hutchison, M. A. 1974. Promoting Growth with Creative Expression. 1973. Workshop Proceedings, 249 12th Street, S.E., Washington, D.C.

Jung, C. G. 1964. Man and His Symbols. Aldus Books Limited, London.

Kaufman, B. N. 1975. Reaching the "unreachable" child. New York Magazine 8:43–49, February 3.

Kaufman, B. N. 1976. Son Rise. Harper and Row, New York.

Kawasaki, T. 1971. Niji no eshi Yotchan. Tachibona Shyobou, Tokyo, Japan.

Kohlberg, L. 1970. Moral Development. Holt, Rinehart, and Winston, New York.

Kohlberg, L., and Turiel, E. 1971. Research in Moral Development: The Cognitive-Developmental Approach. Holt, Rinehart, and Winston, New York.

Kramer, E. 1958. Art Therapy in a Children's Community. Charles C Thomas, Springfield, Ill.

Kramer, E. 1971. Art as Therapy with Children. Schocken Books, New York.

Kramer, E. 1972. The Practice of Art Therapy with Children. Am. J. Art Ther. 11:89–110.

Langer, S. K. 1967. Mind: An Essay on Human Feeling. Vol. 1. Johns Hopkins Press, Baltimore.

Lindsay, Z. 1972. Art and the Handicapped Child. Van Nostrand Reinhold Co., New York.

Lindstrom, M. 1957. Children's Art. University of California Press, Los Angeles.

Loevinger, J. 1976. Ego Development. Jossey-Bass Publishers, San Francisco.

Lowenfeld, V., and Brittain, W. L. 1970. Creative and Mental Growth. 5th Ed. The Macmillan Company, New York.

Mahler, M. S. 1952. On childhood psychoses and schizophrenia: Autistic and symbiotic infantile psychoses. Psychoan. Study Child. 7:286–305.

Maslow, A. H. 1971. The Farther Reaches of Human Nature. The Viking Press, New York.

McKay, D. 1975. Group reports: instruction and curriculum, group B. Art Educ. December:15–17.

Moore, P. 1976. Art and the autistic child. Arts and Activities 79:28–30.

Morishima, A. 1975. The training methodologies and educators' role of three successful art talents in Japan. A paper prepared for the 53rd Annual International Convention of the Council for Exceptional Children, Los Angeles, California.

Moustakas, C. 1959. Psychotherapy with Children. Ballatine Books, New York.

Mussen, P. H., Conger, J. J., and Kagan, J. 1969. Child Development and Personality. 3rd Ed. Harper & Row, New York.

Naumberg, M. 1973. An Introduction to Art Therapy. Teachers College Press, Columbia University, New York.

Piaget, J. 1932. The Moral Judgment of the Child. Routledge and Kegan Paul, London.

Piaget, J. 1936. The Origins of Intelligence in Children. 2nd Ed. International Universities Press, New York.

Piaget, J. 1951. Play, Dreams and Imitation in Childhood. W. W. Norton and Co., New York.

Piaget, J. 1954. The Construction of Reality in the Child. Basic Books, New York.

Piaget, J. 1959. Judgment and Reasoning in the Child. Littlefield, Adams, and Co., New Jersey.

Pine, S. 1975. Fostering growth through art education, art therapy and art in psychotherapy. In: E. Ulman and P. Dachinger (eds.), Art Therapy in Theory and Practice, pp. 60–95. Schocken Books, New York.

Purvis, J., and Samet, S. (eds.). 1976. Music in Developmental Therapy. University Park Press, Baltimore.

Rappaport, D. 1960. Psychoanalysis as a developmental psychology. In: B. Kaplan and S. Wapner (eds.), Perspectives in Psychological Theory: Essays in Honor of Heinz Werner, pp. 209–255. International Universities Press, New York.

Rhyne, J. 1973. The Gestalt approach to experience, art, and art therapy. Am. J. Art Ther. 12:237–248.

Robbins, A. 1973. A psychoanalytic prospective towards the inter-relationship of the creative process and the functions of an art therapist. Art Psychotherapy 1:7–12.

Rogers, C. R. 1961. On Becoming a Person. Houghton Mifflin, Co., Boston.

Rubin, J. A. 1975. Art is for all human beings especially the handicapped. Art Educ. December:5–10.

Ruttenberg, B., and Wolf, E. G. 1967. Evaluating the communication of the autistic child. J. Speech and Hear. 32:314–324.

Rutter, M. 1970. The description and classification of infantile autism. Proceedings of the Indiana University Colloquium on Infantile Autism. Charles C Thomas, Springfield, Ill.

Schwartz, F. 1974. Art for the exceptional. Art Educ. October:15–18.

Taylor, F. D., Artuso, A. A., and Hewett, F. M. 1970. Creative Art Tasks for Children. Love Publishing Co., Denver, Col.

Torrance, E. P. 1970. Encouraging Creativity in the Classroom. Wm. C. Brown Co., Dubuque, Iowa.

Treffert, D. A. 1970. Epidemiology of infantile autism. Arch. Gen. Psych. 22:431–438.

Ulman, E. 1975. Art therapy: problems of definition. In: E. Ulman and P. Dachinger (eds.), Art Therapy in Theory and Practice, pp. 3–13. Schocken Books, New York.

Williams, A. R. 1975. The stage one class: a place for responding and trusting. In: M. M. Wood (ed.), Developmental Therapy, pp. 157–174. University Park Press, Baltimore.

Wolff, P. H. 1960. The developmental psychologies of Jean Piaget and psychoanalysis. Psych. Issues 2:40–181.

Wolff, P. H. 1975. What Piaget did not intent. In: G. I. Lumbin et al. (eds.), Piagetian Theory and the Helping Professions, pp. 3–14. University of Southern California Publications Department, Los Angeles.

Wood, M. M. 1975. Developmental Therapy. University Park Press, Baltimore.

Index